Labour Law in Slovakia

Labour Law in Slovakia

Viktor Križan

This book was originally published as a monograph in the International Encyclopaedia of Laws/Labour Law and Industrial Relations.

Founding Editor: Roger Blanpain
General Editor: Frank Hendrickx
Volume Editor: Frank Hendrickx

Wolters Kluwer

Published by:
Kluwer Law International B.V.
PO Box 316
2400 AH Alphen aan den Rijn
The Netherlands
E-mail: lrs-sales@wolterskluwer.com
Website: www.wolterskluwer.com/en/solutions/kluwerlawinternational

Sold and distributed by:
Wolters Kluwer Legal & Regulatory U.S.
920 Links Avenue
Landisville, PA 17538
United States of America
E-mail: customer.service@wolterskluwer.com

ISBN 978-94-035-0999-0

e-Book: ISBN 978-94-035-1009-5
web-PDF: ISBN 978-94-035-1019-4

This title is available on www.kluwerlawonline.com

2024 update

The labour law of the Slovak Republic is governed primarily by the comprehensive Labour Code, which regulates the creation, change and termination of labour relations as well as the general regulation of working hours and rest periods, holidays, remuneration, safety and health protection, obstacles at work, the employer's social policy and liability for damage ensuring protection for employees while establishing clear guidelines for employers. The Labour Code regulates the rights and obligations of subjects of individual labour relations and collective labour law. The issue of collective bargaining and the resolution of disputes regarding the conclusion of a collective agreement and the fulfilment of obligations from a collective agreement are regulated by the Act on Collective Bargaining.

One prominent element of Slovak labour law is the existence of agreements on work performed outside the employment relationship. These agreements provide flexibility at the expense of social protection for short-term, seasonal or casual work, thus allowing employers to quickly respond to changes in the workforce and secure employees without the need to conclude classic employment contracts.

Slovak labour law also applies to state employees and employees performing work in the public interest. The Act on the Civil Service contains special provisions regarding job security, the rights and obligations of civil servants, and ethical behaviour, thereby ensuring efficient and transparent state administration. The Act on the Performance of Work in the Public Interest, together with the Act on Remuneration of Certain Employees in the Public Interest, in turn, regulate specific conditions for employees performing work in the public interest, including rules regarding working conditions, remuneration and work order, thereby ensuring stability and fairness in the public sector.

The aforementioned legal regulations guarantee thorough regulation of labour relations in private and public sectors, thereby supporting a flexible and dynamic labour market in the Slovak Republic.

The Author

doc. JUDr. Viktor Križan, PhD., born in 1982, studied law at the Faculty of Law of the University of Trnava in Trnava, Slovakia. He works as an associate professor at the Department of Labor Law and Social Security Law, Faculty of Law of the University of Trnava in Trnava, and vice-dean of the Faculty for Science, Research and Legislation.

In his practice, he focuses on labour law and social security law. Since 2016, he has been listed as a mediator and arbitrator of collective bargaining in the Ministry of Labour, Social Affairs and Family of the Slovak Republic. As part of his rich professional activity, he was a co-researcher of several projects and their responsible researcher. He actively publishes monographs and scientific and professional articles in the field of labour law and is also the co-author of two commentaries on the Slovak Labour Code.

The Author

Table of Contents

Table of Contents

List of Abbreviations

Act on Civil Service	Act no. 55/2017 Coll. on Civil Service and on amendments to certain laws as amended
Act on Collective Bargaining	Act no. 2/1991 Coll. on Collective Bargaining as amended
Act on Employment Services	Act no. 5/2004 Coll. on Employment Services and amendments to certain laws, as amended
Act on the Performance of Work in the Public Interest	Act no. 552/2003 Coll. on the Performance of Work in the Public Interest, as amended
Antidiscrimination Act	Act no. 265/2004 Coll. on Equal Treatment in Certain Areas and Protection Against Discrimination and the amendment of certain laws (anti-discrimination act) as amended
Civil Code	Act no. 40/1964 Coll. Civil Code as amended
Code of Contentious Civil Procedure	Act no. 160/2015 Coll. Code of Contentious Civil Procedure as amended
Coll.	Collection of Laws – the legal rules of the Slovak Republic are published in the official collection
Commercial Code	Act no. 513/1991 Coll. Commercial Code as amended
Constitution	Constitutional Act no. 460/1992 Coll. Constitution of the Slovak Republic, as amended
EU	European Union
ILO	International Labour Organization
Labour Code	Act no. 311/2001 Coll. Labour Code, as amended
Labour Office	Labour, Social Affairs and Family Office

List of Abbreviations

Preface

From the point of view of its essence, labour law has always been the legal branch with an essential social significance and protective mission because its primary task is to optimize the relationship between the production factors of labour and capital so that this relationship corresponds to the needs of capital and at the same time does not conflict with the human dignity of employees. As a separate branch of the legal order of the Slovak Republic, it regulates the mutual relations of subjects that arise during the performance of dependent work. The Slovak Republic has codified labour law; the first Labour Code was adopted in 1965 under no. 65. After political changes in 1989, the Labour Code was substantially amended in 1991, and new labour law regulations in collective bargaining and employment were adopted. 2001 was a turning point when civil service and public service laws were adopted together with the new Labour Code. The need for recodification resulted from the implementation of European Union (EU) law, which was created when the Slovak Republic joined the family of members on 1 May 2004. Since the accession of Slovakia to the EU, labour law has undergone several adjustments related to political changes in the country, which represent a kind of sinusoid between the liberal regulation of labour relations and social protection. Just as the amendment from July 2003 substantially revised the Labour Code and brought relatively extensive liberalization of labour relations, the amendment to the Labour Code, effective from 1 September 2007, returned the development of labour law in the Slovak Republic to a social essence – another significant amendment, effective from 1 September 2011 was aimed at employers to strengthen employee protection again from 1 January 2013. It can be stated that labour law in Slovakia has achieved a relatively high degree of harmonization with European law, even if shortcomings can still be identified, especially when it comes to adapting the jurisprudence of the Court of Justice of the EU.

This book's author presents the Slovak Republic's labour law contained in the Labour Code and other labour law regulations, especially in the Act on Collective Bargaining, which is the primary source of collective labour law in the Slovak Republic.

General Introduction

§1. General Background

I. Geography, Location, Size & Boundaries

1. The Slovak Republic is a country in Central Europe created by the former Czechoslovakia division on 1 January 1993. It is a Member State of the European Union (EU) and NATO. Regarding area and population, Slovakia is one of the smaller countries. Approximately 5,449,270 inhabitants live in the territory with an area of more than 49,036 km^2 (of which 49% are men and 51% are women). The Slovak Republic shares its borders with the Czech Republic to the northwest, Poland to the north, Ukraine to the east, Hungary to the south, and Austria to the southwest. The country is predominantly characterized by mountainous terrain, with a significant portion of its surface area comprising highlands. In the north, the Carpathian Mountains form a substantial arc extending into the region, while the Pannonian Basin stretches south. The capital and largest city is Bratislava, and the official language is Slovak.

2. In January 2009, Slovakia became the sixteenth member of the Eurozone, and its official currency is the euro (EUR).

II. The Political System

3. The Slovak Republic is a pluralist parliamentary democracy functioning as a parliamentary republic. It exhibits characteristics of a hybrid parliamentary-presidential system, incorporating elements of a presidential republic, such as an independent judiciary, the direct election of the president, and presidential veto power. The country is a unitary state. Its fundamental law is the Constitution of the Slovak Republic, which comprises a preamble, nine chapters, and 156 articles. The Constitution establishes the structure and relationships of state bodies, defining their powers and competencies. The second chapter of the Constitution delineates fundamental human rights and freedoms. The Constitution was adopted on 1 September 1992 and enacted on 1 January 1993. State power is divided into three branches: legislative (legislature), executive (executive), and judicial (judiciary).

4. The legislative power is represented by the National Council of the Slovak Republic, a unicameral parliament of 150 deputies elected for four years. The

National Council is the only legislative body of the Slovak Republic. Its deputies are elected every four years in direct, secret and general elections.

5. The government of the Slovak Republic is accountable to the National Council of the Slovak Republic. It comprises ministers from the political parties that form the majority coalition, which holds more than seventy-five deputies in the National Council. The government is led by the Prime Minister, who does not have a ministerial portfolio. The government's functions include drafting laws, issuing regulations, and establishing programmatic statements. A supermajority is required to approve laws, and a three-fifths majority is necessary to amend the Constitution.

6. The President of the Slovak Republic, the Prime Minister, and the Speaker of the Parliament are the highest constitutional officials in the country. As the head of state, the President holds a special status and is elected through direct elections for five years. The President's role is mainly representative, with powers that include authorizing the prospective Prime Minister to form a government, which the President subsequently appoints. Additionally, the President possesses the power to return legislation to the National Council for reconsideration, a process known as a 'small veto'. The President also serves as the commander-in-chief of the armed forces, signs international treaties, appoints constitutional judges, dissolves the parliament, calls referenda, and grants amnesty.

7. The judiciary oversees the legislative and executive branches, interpreting the Constitution and resolving conflicts. The judicial power in the Slovak Republic comprises the Constitutional Court of the Slovak Republic and a system of courts, including the Supreme Court of the Slovak Republic, as well as regional and district courts. The Constitutional Court, consisting of thirteen judges appointed by the President for a twelve-year term, holds the highest authority. It ensures that laws and government decisions comply with the Constitution and monitors the parliament and executive authorities' adherence to constitutional principles.

8. Since 1996, Slovakia has been divided into eight regions and seventy-nine districts. Regional and district offices represent regional and local state administration. Additionally, local self-government bodies operate at the regional level, with regions designated self-governing since 2002.

III. Vital Statistics

9. Slovakia has a population of over 5.4 million inhabitants. In the last years, there has been a decrease in the number of inhabitants, mainly due to the low birth rate. The most significant population decreases are observed in Bratislava, Myjava, Košice, Medzilaborce, and Sobrance districts. Conversely, the most notable population increases are in the Spiš, Orava, Ábov, and Zemplín regions.

10. The population distribution in Slovakia is uneven, primarily due to natural conditions. Population concentration is highest in the densely populated cities of the lowlands in western Slovakia, particularly in Bratislava, Trenčín, and Trnava. The mountainous areas are much less populated.

11. Demographic development in Slovakia is significantly influenced by migration. Historically, substantial migration waves have occurred abroad, especially in the USA, the Czech Republic, and other countries. Currently, of the total number of permanent residents in Slovakia, approximately a quarter of a million reside abroad. Internal migration is characterized by movements from the eastern to the western parts of the country and short-distance relocations between cities and their hinterlands, primarily for work. A negative aspect of this migration is the ongoing outflow of skilled labour, though it is less pronounced today.

12. The age structure of Slovakia's population is generally favourable. The largest demographic group consists of individuals of productive age (women aged 15–59 and men aged 15–61). Conversely, the pre-productive age group (residents aged 0–14) is the least numerous, which is concerning for long-term demographic trends. The post-productive population (women over 60 and men over 62) continues to grow, increasing the average age of the population, which currently stands at 38.7 years. The average life expectancy in 2021 was 71.3 years for men and 78.3 years for women.

A. *Employment*

13. The Slovak Republic operates a market economy comprising services and industry, with agriculture contributing 4% to the GDP. The country is considered economically developed. Following its accession to the EU, Slovakia implemented economic reforms and attracted foreign investments, leading to the highest growth rates in the region. However, in recent years, Slovakia's economic standing has declined within the regional rankings.

14. A significant long-term challenge for Slovakia is the pronounced economic disparity between regions and the overly concentrated focus on the automotive industry. The principal economic hubs are located in the metropolitan areas of Bratislava and Košice-Prešov, the Považie region from Trenčín to Liptovský Mikuláš, the Pohronie region (Banská Bystrica-Zvolen), and the Podunajská nížina region (Trnava-Nitra). Despite the availability of jobs, wages in Slovakia remain low, with the minimum wage set at EUR 750 for 2024.

15. As of March 2024, the registered unemployment rate is 5.07%, with the highest rates in the Prešov (8.47%), Košice (7.20%), and Banská Bystrica (7.13%) regions. The lowest unemployment rates are found in the Trnava (3.43%), Trenčín (3.41%), and Bratislava (2.88%) regions.

1. Agriculture

16. Slovakia has a developed agricultural sector, utilizing 19,350 km^2 of agricultural land, constituting 39.5% of the country's surface area. At the beginning of the twentieth century, agriculture employed 60% of the population. Today, agriculture, hunting, and related industries employ approximately 4.9% of the economically active population, equivalent to about 100,050 employees. The country's fertile soils are conducive to plant production, with the most extensive acreage dedicated to cereals, particularly wheat, corn, and barley, which occupy more than half of the cultivated land. The areas sown with vegetables, legumes, and oilseeds such as sunflower and rapeseed are expanding. In higher basins, crops like potatoes, rye, and various annual fodder crops are cultivated. Slovakia has a long-standing tradition in fruit growing and viticulture, with products that are well-known internationally.

2. Industry

17. Industry is the primary sector of the Slovak economy. At the beginning of the twenty-first century, low labour costs and tax reforms attracted foreign investors, particularly in the automotive industry, which holds a prominent position in Slovakia's economy. Slovakia produces the highest number of cars per capita in the world. Essential automotive plants include Volkswagen facilities in Bratislava, Stupava, and Martin; Stellantis Peugeot-Citroën in Trnava; Jaguar Land Rover in Nitra; and Kia in Žilina. Additionally, a Volvo car plant near Košice is currently under construction, with serial production expected to commence in 2026.

18. The second most significant industry is electrical engineering. Machine production in the middle and upper Považie regions is notable. Major engineering companies are located in Bratislava (automobiles), Galanta (televisions and household appliances), Poprad (cars, washing machines), and Tlmače (machinery for the energy industry). The largest chemical plants are in Bratislava, Šala, and Nováky, producing plastics, synthetic fibres, pharmaceuticals, and rubber products.

19. The food industry is the most evenly distributed in Slovakia. Wood processing, including sawmills, woodworking plants, and furniture manufacturing, as well as pulp and paper production in Ružomberok, Žilina, Štúrovo, and Harmanec, are vital components of the Slovak economy. A significant amount of raw, unprocessed wood is exported.

20. The textile and clothing industry, with plants in Trenčín and Púchov, has experienced a significant slowdown due to the import of cheaper products, mainly from Asian countries. However, companies focusing on producing textiles and sewing covers for the automotive industry are gaining prominence. Additionally, the footwear and glass industries are also present in Slovakia.

3. Services

21. The services sector, including banking and finance, is crucial to Slovakia's economy. The country is also well-positioned for tourism, boasting beautiful mountains, caves, lakes, historic towns, spas, castles, and chateaux that attract visitors. Slovakia's cultural and natural heritage includes seven sites on the UNESCO World Heritage List, comprising two natural and five cultural sites. However, the quality of services in some regions still falls short of European standards, limiting tourism potential. Significant tourism growth depends on enhancing the overall quality of services, including improvements in transport infrastructure.

B. Other Vital Areas

22. Western culture mainly influenced the historical development of the Slovak Republic's territory. However, the Slavic orientation regarding the Slavic peoples and cultures also played a role. The roots of Slovak culture go back to the Great Moravian Empire of the ninth century. Great Moravia, which also occupied the territory of today's Slovak Republic, belonged to Christian culture as early as the ninth century AD. During historical development, the Old Church Slavonic language used in Great Moravia was transformed into today's Slovak. The literature of the time was quite extensive, and the language and literature put the population living in this territory on the level of other contemporary nations as early as the ninth century.

23. This cultural heritage also positively impacted the development of Slovak national cultural standards. Culture in Slovakia developed in parallel with European trends, styles and eras of European art, even though Slovakia lost the opportunity to use its national language in the tenth century and became part of Austria-Hungary.

24. Separation from the Kingdom of Hungary and the period of the first Czechoslovak Republic in 1918 brought Slovak progress in all spheres of life – economy, education, culture, and the presentation of Slovakia abroad. Between 1918 and 1938, Czechoslovakia was the only Central European country that maintained a parliamentary democracy.

25. In connection with developments after Hitler's rise to power and the Munich Conference in 1938, the Slovak State was established in 1939. In August 1944, an uprising broke out in Slovakia, and in 1945, Czechoslovakia was restored. After the Second World War, Slovakia's territory and the restored Czechoslovak Republic gradually became part of the Soviet bloc. After the coup in February 1948, a communist dictatorship was established. In January 1969, Czechoslovakia became a federal state.

26. A massive people's movement led by a citizen's initiative removed the communist dictatorship in November 1989. The Czechoslovak parliament approved the agreement on the peaceful division of the republic in 1992.

27. The Slovak Republic is generally considered a Christian country. Currently, eighteen churches are registered; 84% of the population of the Slovak Republic are religious, and 23% are not. Almost 68% of the population professed Christianity (approx. 55.8% Roman Catholic, 5.3% Evangelical and 4% Greek Catholic), which began to spread in the territory of today's Slovak Republic already in the eighth century. In the ninth century, the Christian organization was relatively strong. Our ancestors integrated into the Central European social and cultural environment by accepting Christianity. The founding of its church organization in the ninth century was also of great political importance for the existence of Great Moravia.

28. At present, the population in the territory of Slovakia is ethnically almost uniform; up to 80% of the total population are ethnic Slovaks. They are most prominently represented in the north of Slovakia. After Slovak, the most represented are the inhabitants of Hungarian nationality, who live mainly in the south near the border with Hungary. The second largest minority are the Roma, who mainly live in the regions of eastern Slovakia (Spiš, Šariš and Gemer). The share of the Roma population is gradually increasing. Part of the population in the west of Slovakia claims to be of Czech, Moravian and Silesian nationality.

§2. Definitions and Notions

I. Distinction Between Labour Law and Other Branches of Law

29. In the legal order of the Slovak Republic, labour law is a separate legal branch that plays a vital role in the formation and development of social security for citizens. Labour law is a hybrid law branch containing private and public law elements. Labour law mainly regulates the social form of dependent work, in which the employee makes his workforce available to the employer for a reward and obeys his instructions while at the same time entering into relations with other employees. Not every work performance for another falls within the scope of labour law regulation. Only the performance of dependent work for another on a contractual basis falls under the labour regulation. Labour law is based not only on the physical definition of work but also on the economic one, according to which work is the production of physical needs and covers a person's needs and mental development. When performing dependent work, the employer organizes, leads and manages the work process, bearing the production and economic risk of the work performed. The labour law is mainly a mandatory law (ius cogens) which does not permit the parties to labour law relations any broader application of contractual freedom. In personal scope, labour law applies to almost all labour categories, including state and public administration employees.

30. The subject of regulation of labour law primarily includes relations arising between:

(a) employers and employees (individual employment relations);
(b) employers and employee representatives (collective labour relations); and
(c) relations arising in the implementation of citizens' right to work.

31. Individual labour law involves relations between the employee and the employer arising during dependent work. Individual labour law forms the focal part of labour law, which regulates individual ties between employer and employee in the performance of dependent work. Individual labour law is contained mainly in the Labour Code. There is a close relationship between individual labour law and civil law, which also expresses the subsidiary scope of the general provisions of the Civil Code to the first part of the Labour Code. It is described in section 1(4) of the Labour Code.

32. Relations between the employer and the collective of employees represented by employee representatives (trade union body, works council or employee confidant) are also part of labour law. These relations are called collective labour relations. Collective labour relations present a protective mechanism alongside individual labour law. This area also regulates collective agreements between these parties. The Labour Code governs substantive legal aspects of collective labour relations, while Act no. 2/1991 Coll. on Collective Bargaining primarily deals with procedural and legal aspects of collective labour relations. The Labour Code has subsidiary authority concerning the Act on Collective Bargaining. The correlation between labour law and civil law is relevant solely to individual labour law, as collective labour law emerged independently from civil law influences.

33. The subject of labour law also includes legal relations related to implementing citizens' right to work and access to employment work under Article 36 of the Constitution. These relationships arise while providing employment services between the relevant labour, social affairs, family offices, employers, and job seekers. The legal framework of employment services represents the Act on Employment Services. Similarly, as in collective labour relations, the domain of employment services within labour law is categorized as a public law aspect, distinct from civil law connections.

34. Although labour law is a separate legal branch of the legal order of the Slovak Republic, we must not forget that it is a matter of relative independence. Relative independence consists of the fact that all legal branches are closely related to each other, condition each other, follow each other, and form a unified and comprehensive system. Labour law is, to a greater or lesser extent, connected with most other branches of law.

35. There is a very close relationship between labour law and social security law because social security law regulates relations in the provision of employees, for example, in the event of incapacity for work due to illness, injury, or disability. It also governs tax obligations for employers and employees. Social security covers primarily the ways and means (institutions) applied by society to guarantee and provide material security to individual citizens who:

– cannot work for the reason recognized by society or;
– are in a situation in which they cannot cover the increased living costs by the income earned from their work.

36. The relatively extensive system of social security law is divided into three subsystems:

(1) social insurance;
(2) social support; and
(3) social assistance.

37. Labour law and civil law show a thin connection, which lies in the subsidiary scope of the Civil Code on labour relations. Some provisions of the Civil Code have a broader meaning and can also be applied to institutes of labour law. For example, the Labour Code does not regulate the concept of 'legal act' or grounds for the invalidity of legal acts, apart from specific grounds for invalidity specific to labour law. These are regulated in section 17 of the Labour Code. Similarly, the Labour Code does not restrict representation or the technique of forming contracts in labour law; the provisions of the Civil Code govern these issues. The scientific discussion focuses on labour law's status and further development, especially on the relationship to private law. Due to its general characteristics, labour law cannot be fully integrated into private or public law, even if private law elements prevail.

38. The legal norms of state law have a significant meaning for labour law. The Constitution enshrines general principles and principles that determine the direction of labour law. The legal norms of labour law subsequently elaborate and specify these general principles.

39. Criminal law is also essential for labour law. Its norms enshrine the legal definition of fault as one of the prerequisites for deriving subjective responsibility for damage, which is valid for all legal branches. Equally, the regulation of the facts of criminal offences is of immense importance, which can be fulfilled both by the employer when organizing the work process and by the employee when performing dependent work.

II. Personal and Material Applicability of Labour Law

40. When assessing the scope definition, it is necessary to distinguish between the scope of labour law and the scope of the Labour Code.

41. The material scope of labour law can be defined as the range of social relations to which the legal regulations of labour law apply. Substantial scope (meritorious) answers what labour law norms regulate legal relationships. Regarding labour law theory, work is the main subject of labour law research. It is about work as a human activity. The subject of labour law is not 'any work' but only 'dependent work'. The labour law regulates work that meets the characteristics of dependent work. The concept of 'dependent work' is based on the more general idea of 'work as a human activity', which must show signs of usefulness, permission and compliance with good morals. Work as a legally valid subject of an employment relationship must meet the characteristics of the work that the employee performs for the employer based on an employment contract or agreement. According to section 1(2) of the Labour Code, dependent work is work performed in the relationship of the superior of the employer and the subordination of the employee, personally by the employee for the employer, according to the instructions of the employer, on his behalf, during the working time determined by the employer.

42. We define the following defining features of dependent work:

– the superiority of the employer and the subordination of the employee;
– irreplaceability (personal performance of work by the employee for the employer);
– dependence and lack of independence (work management or work performed according to the employer's instructions);
– work performed for another (work in the name of the employer, under the name of the employer, not in one's name);
– work during the working time specified by the employer (time determination of work).

43. In addition to the positive definition of dependent work, dependent work is, according to section 1(3) of the Labour Code, defined negatively – dependent work can be performed exclusively in an employment relationship, in a similar employment relationship or exceptionally under the conditions established in this law and another employment relationship. According to special regulations, dependent work cannot be performed in a contractual civil or business law relationship.

44. A positive definition of dependent work is the right choice for contract form. The primary determinant of such a choice is the nature of the work performed. If the work performed meets the characteristics of dependent work, the natural person must have the legal status of an employee who performs work based on an employment contract. Suppose work performance does not fulfil the characteristics of dependent work. In that case, such work becomes the subject of relevant contract types from civil and commercial law environments.

45. The personal scope of labour law defines the range of legal entities (natural persons and legal entities) to which labour law norms apply. The personal scope specifies and co-determines the material jurisdiction of labour law. It is necessary to differentiate whether the labour regulation applies to all or only to Slovak Republic citizens or foreigners. Labour law relations between employees performing work on the territory of the Slovak Republic and a foreign employer, as well as between foreigners and stateless persons working on the territory of the Slovak Republic and employers based on the territory of the Slovak Republic, are governed by Slovak law unless the legal regulations on private international law provide otherwise. The employment relations of employees sent to perform work in the provision of services by a guest employer from the territory of another Member State of the EU or a state that is a contracting party to the Agreement on the European Economic Area to the territory of the Slovak Republic are governed by Slovak Labour Code, special regulations or the relevant collective agreement, which regulate:

(a) length of working time and rest;
(b) length of leave;
(c) minimum wage, minimum wage requirements, wage concession for overtime work, wage concession for work on a holiday, wage concession for work on Saturday, wage concession for work on Sunday, wage concession for night work, wage compensation for complex work performance, other mandatory wage components and holiday pay;
(d) safety and health protection at work;
(e) working conditions of pregnant women, mothers up to the end of the ninth month after giving birth, breastfeeding women and young employees;
(f) equal treatment of men and women and prohibition of discrimination;
(g) conditions under which an employee can be temporarily assigned, working conditions, including wage conditions and conditions of employment of a temporarily assigned employee if it is a temporary assignment to a user employer if an employment relationship exists between the posting employer and the employee during the posting period;
(h) accommodation conditions that the employer provides to employees;
(i) reimbursement of travel expenses, accommodation and meals during a business trip or when travelling to the usual place of work in the territory of the Slovak Republic.

46. When comparing individual types of the scope of labour law and the Labour Code, a significant differentiation is manifested in the material scope. The material scope of the Labuor Code is generally and relatively broadly regulated by its section 1, according to which labour relations are established between employers and employees, and that first from concluding an employment contract or one of the work agreements performed outside the employment relationship (agreement on work activities, agreement on the execution of work, or agreement on part-time work of students).

47. The scope of the Labour Code is divided into:

– direct;
– subsidiary; and
– delegated.

48. By direct limited applicability of the Labour Code, we mean that the Labour Code applies directly to certain labour relations but to a limited extent. The Labour Code excludes the application of some of its provisions or determines the specific requirements that will be applied to a given employment relationship. The Labour

Code excludes the application of some of its provisions for domestic work and telework; if the employer and the employee agree that the employee will schedule his working time, the employment relationship will be governed by the Labour Code with the following exceptions:

- the provisions on the schedule of designated weekly working time, continuous daily rest and continuous rest during the week do not apply;
- provisions on downtime do not apply, except for downtime for which the employer is responsible;
- the employee is not entitled to wage compensation in the event of important personal obstacles, except wage compensation in the event of the death of a family member;
- the employee is not entitled to wages for overtime, wage concessions for work on holidays, wage concessions for work on Saturdays, wage concessions for work on Sundays, wage concessions for night work and wage compensation for complex work performance.

49. The Labour Code also explicitly determines its specific provisions that will be applied to a given employment relationship, namely in the case of employment relationships based on work agreements performed outside of the employment relationship.

50. Delegated Labour Code applicability means that it may apply to certain categories of employees only when provided by a specific regulation or the Labour Code itself (section 2 of the Labour Code).

51. Delegated Labour Code applicability concerns civil servants not under an employment contract (Act no. 55/2017 Coll. on Civil Service as amended), persons exercising a public function and professional athletes when performing sports based on a contract on the professional performance of sports and sports experts when performing activities based on a contract on the performance of the activities of a sports expert. Specific laws and the Labour Code regulate the legal relations of all the above categories, which apply if these specific laws provide them.

52. The subsidiary applicability of the Labour Code means that the Labour Code may be applied to labour relations only when the specific regulations concerning the labour relations of some categories of employees do not provide differently. Subsidiarity applies primarily to employees performing work in the public interest (Act no. 552/2003 Coll. on the Performance of Work in the Public Interest as amended), employees who are obliged to ensure compliance according to a special regulation, and employees working in operation, maintenance and development of the gas transmission network, who are under the direct management authority of the statutory body of the operator of the gas transmission network, employees in transport, employees performing medical professions, teachers, professional surrogate parents, employees who are theatre artists or musical artists, crew members of ships sailing under the national flag of the Slovak Republic, employees of private security services, employees of churches and religious societies who perform clerical activities, employees working in the production and processing of explosives, explosive compounds, black powder, ammunition, explosives, explosive objects and explosive pyrotechnic compounds, and labour relations between the cooperative and its members (sections 3 and 4 of the Labour Code).

III. Definitions

53. There is no legal definition of labour law in the Slovak Republic. At present, labour law substantially regulates the legal relations arising from the performance of dependent work.

A. The Employer

54. An employer can demand work performance from an employee based on an employment contract. According to section 7(1) of the Labour Code, an employer is a legal entity or a natural person who employs at least one natural person in an employment relationship and, if stipulated by a particular regulation, also in similar employment relationships.

55. The employer acts in labour relations on his behalf and under his responsibility. In labour relations, the employer, who is a legal entity, performs legal acts by a statutory body or by a member of a statutory body. The employer, who is a natural person, acts personally. Employees authorized by them can also perform legal actions instead of them.

56. Other employer employees, such as the head of its organizational departments, are authorized to act on behalf of the employer resulting from their functions determined by the employer's organizational regulations. The employer may approve other employees in writing to perform certain legal acts in employment relations on his behalf. However, the scope of the authorized employee's authorization must be specified in the written authorization.

57. According to the Labour Code, executive employees are employees who, at individual levels of the employer's management, are authorized to determine and impose work tasks on the employer's subordinate employees, organize, manage and control their work and give them binding instructions for that purpose.

58. The ability of a natural person to have rights and obligations in employment relations as an employer arises from birth. A conceived child also has this capacity if it is born alive. The ability of a natural person to acquire rights and take on obligations in labour relations as an employer by his legal acts arises upon reaching the age of majority; until then, a legal representative acts for such person.

B. The Employee

59. According to section 11(1) of the Labour Code, an employee is a natural person performing dependent work for an employer in a labour law relationship unless otherwise stated in a particular regulation or a similar labour relationship. So, in the broadest sense of the word, employees also include natural persons who work based on agreements on work performed outside the employment relationship and persons who work in a state-employee relationship.

60. The ability to be an employee, i.e., to have the rights and obligations as an employee in employment relations and the ability to acquire these rights and take on these obligations through one's legal acts, unless otherwise stipulated, arises when a natural person reaches 15 years of age. However, starting a job cannot be agreed upon before completing compulsory schooling. The employee can agree on material responsibility on the day he turns 18. The work of a natural person under the age of 15 or older than 15 until the end of compulsory schooling is prohibited. However, these natural persons can perform light work, which by its nature and scope does not threaten their health, safety, further development or school attendance only when conducting or participating in cultural performances and artistic performances, sports events, advertising activities, or if it is a natural person who is older than 15 years until the end of compulsory schooling and other activities. The performance of light work is permitted at the employer's request by the relevant labour inspectorate in agreement with the appropriate state administration body in the public health sector.

§3. Historical Background

61. Until the second half of the twentieth century, labour legislation showed relative fragmentation and disparity in the legal regulation of labour relations. The labour shortage in the post-war period in less developed regions was solved by deploying graduates based on three-year placements. That meant the inclusion of graduates in the labour process regardless of their will.

62. The fragmentation of labour legislation has prompted considerations about the need to unify labour relations and create a new comprehensive legal regulation of these relations. An important landmark in the development of labour law was 1965 when Act no. 65/1965 Coll. Labour Code. With the adoption of the legal regulation in question, the process of codifying labour law was completed, and thanks to this, the legal regulation of all work categories was unified. The Labour Code became the primary source of labour law in the Czechoslovak Socialist Republic. The socialist order ensured citizens the right to work; work performance was an obligation in a socialist society. Citizens were obliged to work for the benefit of the entire socialist society, and this obligation was enshrined in Article 3 of the Constitution of the Czechoslovak Socialist Republic. Socialist work discipline showed elements of a strong ideology – it was created as part of the socialist work ethic based on diligent educational work carried out by the Communist Party, trade unions, youth organizations and the state. Labour Code expressed the will of the working people to adjust socialist labour relations to the interests of society and, thus, each individual. His task was to strengthen them and gradually develop their transition to communist ties. The socialist establishment was seen as the last stage of development before communism, where the principle 'from each according to his abilities, to each according to his needs' should apply.

63. Another important landmark in the development of labour law was the revolutionary changes in 1989. These relevant facts were the impetus for the start of the first reform of labour law, namely the adoption of three labour law regulations: Act no. 1/1991 Coll. on Employment, Act no. 2/1991 Coll. on Collective Bargaining and Act no. 3/1991 Coll., amending the Labour Code. The economic and social policy of the Czech and Slovak Federal Republic aimed to achieve full, productive and freely chosen employment. It means that work performance should not be a legal obligation for the state's citizens. Act no. 2/1991 Coll. on Collective Bargaining regulated the collective bargaining process between the relevant trade union bodies of trade union organizations and employers with the possible cooperation of the state, the aim of which is to conclude a collective agreement. Act no. 3/1991 Coll., which amends and supplements the Labour Code was an extensive amendment of the Labour Code. At the same time, the scope of mandatory, coercive provisions of the Labour Code was significantly reduced. This legislation aimed to create essential prerequisites for transitioning from a centrally planned economy to a market economy. At the same time, space was created for the exercise of contractual freedom in labour relations. Finally, because a single and uniform concept of labour relations became unsustainable in the new economic, economic and political conditions, a society-wide discussion on the return of the right to civil service was opened.

64. The second significant reform of labour law was implemented in 2001. The need for the recodification of labour law was conditioned on the one hand by the requirements of practice because, despite the fundamental amendment of the Labour Code, the Labour Code still did not respond sufficiently to the needs of the market economy and did not create the necessary prerequisites not only for the exercise of contractual freedom of participants in individual labour relations but also to exercise the contractual freedom of the parties to the collective agreement. At the same time, international aspects connected with integrating the Slovak Republic into global economic and social structures determined the need for the recodification of labour law. It created the essential prerequisites for the entry of the Slovak Republic into the EU. The second labour law reform was completed by adopting the Labour Code, Act no. 312/2001 Coll. on Civil Service, and Act no. 313/2001 Coll. on Public Service. With the adoption of the three mentioned legal regulations, there was a fundamental differentiation of labour relations depending on the work categories of employees. At the same time, there was a division in the labour law regulation of labour relations between the business and non-business spheres. Civil service and public service have separated themselves from the legislation of the Labour Code, not in an absolute way, but with some aspects of interdependence in the form of delegated or subsidiary scope of the Labour Code. In 2003, Act no. 313/2001 Coll. on

Public Service was abolished and replaced by Act no. 552/2003 Coll. on the Performance of Work in the Public Interest, Act no. 553/2003 Coll. on the Remuneration of Certain Employees when Performing Work in the Public Interest, as well as Act no. 514/2003 Coll. on Liability for Damage Caused in the Exercise of Public Authority. In 2009, Act no. 312/2001 Coll. on Civil Service, which was built on a career system (legally guaranteed service and salary progression), was abolished by Act no. 400/2009 Coll. on Civil Service, which introduced more extraordinary politicization of the civil service and reduced transparency. Only as part of the reform of efficient and open state administration was the given legal regulation replaced by another Act no. 55/2017 Coll. on Civil Service.

§4. Role of Government Institutions in the Shaping and Administration of Labour and Industrial Relations Policy

65. Intervention by the government and other central bodies of state administration, especially the Ministry of Labour, Social Affairs, and Family of the Slovak Republic, in labour relations remains notably pronounced. Considering the nature of this intervention, the scope of central bodies of state administration can be categorized into:

- legislative functions;
- administrative tasks; and
- inspection activities.

I. The Competence of the Government

66. The Government of the Slovak Republic is the supreme authority of the executive power. The Government of the Slovak Republic is authorized to issue orders for implementing Acts within its limits, which are generally binding. General authorization from the Constitution is usually concretised in legislative practice by the government's special authorization in the individual Acts, empowering it to regulate some issues in greater detail by its order. The government also decides on draft acts and fundamental measures to ensure the economic and social policy of the Slovak Republic.

II. The Competence of the Ministry of Labour, Social Affairs and Family

67. The Ministry of Labour, Social Affairs and Family of the Slovak Republic is the central body of the state administration for labour relations and legal relations of elected officials of local self-government bodies, safety and health protection at work, labour inspection, employment strategy, coordination of its creation and labour market policy, social insurance, old-age pension savings and supplementary pension savings, state social benefits, social services, support for the social integration of a physical person with a severe disability into society and assistance in material need, social protection of children, social guardianship and coordination of state family policy, gender equality and equal opportunities, and coordination of state policy in the given area, and social economy and family businesses.

68. The task of the Ministry of Labour, Social Affairs and Family of the Slovak Republic is to constantly modernize legislation in the field of labour to increase employment. As part of the effort to create a balanced labour market, it also pays attention to the protection of employees and the requirements of employers. Like other ministries, the Ministry of Labour, Social Affairs and Family of the Slovak Republic prepares draft laws and other generally binding regulations and supervises compliance with legality within its scope. In the field of labour law, the Ministry further manages the performance of state administration carried out by the Central Office of Labour, Social Affairs and Family (hereinafter 'the Central Labour Office') and the Offices of Labour, Social Affairs and Family (hereinafter 'the Labour Office'), approves the internal organizational structure of the Central Labour Office, adopts the proposals of the Central Labour Office for the establishment and abolition of the workplace of the Central Labour Office, controls the performance of state administration in the field of social affairs and employment services, carries out state administration in the second instance in matters in which the Central Labour Office, decides in the first instance administrative proceedings, determines to the Central Labour Office, tasks in the field of labour market policy resulting from the employment strategy, determines, in cooperation with the Statistical Office of the Slovak Republic, departmental statistical surveys and administrative resources in the field of social affairs and labour market policy ensures the creation of analyses and forecasts of developments in the labour market and publishes them on its website, determines the minimum content, scope and periodicity of collection and processing of data in the field of social affairs and employment services, is responsible for creating a concept of development in the field of social affairs and employment services, directs the employment of third country with a place of work on the territory of the Slovak Republic and the employment of citizens of the Slovak Republic abroad.

69. In collective labour law relations, its competence is concerned mainly with depositing higher-order collective agreements and information on their deposition in the Collection of Laws, provision of copies of higher-order collective agreements, appointment of mediators and arbitrators in case of collective disputes and keeping lists of mediators and arbitrators.

III. The Competence of the Central Office of Labour, Social Affairs and Family

70. In the field of labour law, the Central Labour Office carries out state administration in the field of social affairs and employment services and performs tasks according to special regulations in the areas of employment services, employment of nationals of a third country with a place of work in the territory of the Slovak Republic and employment of citizens of the Slovak Republic abroad, preparation and implementation of projects and programmes financed from the state budget, from the funds of the EU and co-financed from the state budget or other sources. The Central Labour Office directs, controls, coordinates and methodically directs the performance of the state administration in the field of social affairs and employment services carried out by the labour offices, performs state administration in the second instance in matters in which the labour office decides in the administrative procedure in the first instance, determines the territorial districts in which extraordinary measures in the field of employment services will be implemented in the relevant calendar year, approves the internal organizational structure of the labour offices, processes statistical reports and submits them to the ministry, cooperates with self-governing regions in the creation of regional development concepts in the field of social affairs and employment services, implements obligations arising for the Slovak Republic from concluded international agreements in the field of social affairs and employment, in the performance of state administration in the field of social affairs, and fulfils the tasks of the liaison body according to Regulation no. 883/2004 and Regulation no. 987/2009.

IV. The Competence of Labour, Social Affairs and Family Offices

71. In the field of labour law, the Labour Office carries out state administration in the field of social affairs and employment services and performs tasks in the areas of employment services, employment of nationals of a third country with a place of work in the territory of the Slovak Republic and employment of citizens of the Slovak Republic abroad, as well as preparation and implementation projects and programmes financed from the state budget, from the funds of the EU and co-financed from the state budget or other sources. Furthermore, in the performance of state administration in the field of social affairs, the Labour Office fulfils the tasks of the relevant institution according to the coordination regulations of the EU, obtains documents and assesses them to provide subsidies within the purview of the Ministry, keeps records of natural persons and legal entities to give subsidies within the ambit of the Ministry, performs other tasks, if so established by a special regulation.

72. The labour offices are also responsible for providing suitable employment for job seekers and those interested in employment, keeping records of job applicants, job vacancies, and employers in their territorial district. Labour offices provide information and advisory services, professional advisory services, apply active measures on the labour market in their territorial district, implement projects aimed at improving the situation on the labour market in their territorial district financed from the resources of the European Social Fund, ensure tasks connected with mass redundancies according to of the Labour Code, accept requests from citizens for employment mediation in the Member States of the EU and submit them to the Central Labour Office, carry out employment mediation for job seekers, job seekers and citizens, provide them with information about employment opportunities abroad and information about living and working conditions in the Member States of the EU, as well as provide information to citizens about employment opportunities abroad.

V. Labour Inspection

73. Labour inspection is regulated through Act no. 125/2006 Coll. on Labour Inspection as amended. Labour inspection is a system of state bodies that enforce compliance with regulations governing labour relations and working conditions. The labour inspection acts as a control body, an advisory body, and a repressive one. Labour inspection is the inference of responsibility for violations of labour law regulations and for breaches of obligations arising from collective agreements, as well as providing free advice to employers, natural persons who are entrepreneurs and who are not employers, and employees within the scope of basic professional information and advice on ways to comply with labour law regulations most effectively.

74. The National Labour Inspectorate is a state administration body that provides tasks in the field of labour inspection with nationwide scope, manages and controls labour inspectorates, and unifies and rationalizes the working methods of labour inspectorates. It is also the appeal body in matters decided by the labour inspectorate.

75. Labour inspectorates are state administration bodies that ensure the performance of labour inspections of employers and natural persons who are entrepreneurs and are not employers. Labour inspectorates supervise compliance with labour regulations, legal regulations governing civil servant relations, rules to ensure safety and health protection at work, laws governing the prohibition of illegal work and illegal employment, obligations arising from collective agreements and by observing the employer's responsibility to conclude an employer contract and pay contributions to supplementary pension savings for employees performing risky jobs. They carry out inspections at all workplaces of employers and natural persons who are entrepreneurs and are not employers, including at their workplaces located on private land and in the residences of natural persons, in all areas where a domestic employee (section 52 of the Labour Code) performs an agreed work, in all premises in which the employee performs work according to the agreement on work performed outside the employment relationship (section 223 of the Labour Code).

VI. Economic Social Council

76. The Economic Social Council of the Slovak Republic, the so-called tripartite, is a primary tool of social dialogue between three social partners – employers, employees and the government. In Slovakia, this tripartite body is established by Act no. 103/2007 Coll. on Tripartite Consultations at the National Level. This act deals with the trilateral consultations between the state and its social partners who, through their representatives, negotiate and discuss substantial economic and social development and employment issues to achieve consensus. The Economic and Social Council of the Slovak Republic is a consultative and negotiating body of the government and social partners at the national level. It is a democratic means of solving economic and social problems, ensuring employment development and social harmony. The tripartite social dialogue has an important social and political function. It has resulted in joint decisions on fundamental economic and social measures, particularly on preparing drafts of new laws.

77. Its outputs are not binding, but they still fulfil the vital function of supporting dialogue between social partners and the government. Each side of the social dialogue has seven seats in the tripartite, so twenty-one representatives meet. There are always seven employee representatives, seven employer representatives and seven government representatives at trilateral negotiations. However, the specific persons may differ at each meeting, depending on the topics discussed, so there are many more nominees in the tripartite.

78. The current position of the tripartite in Slovakia is weak for several reasons, such as the low motivation of the social partners to find an agreement, non-respect of the agreement between the social partners by the government, the government's critical attitude towards the functioning of the tripartite until now, the effort of the social partners to gain influence on legislation and government measures other than through tripartite.

VII. Other Institutions

79. Inspection of adherence to labour law regulations can also be carried out by the trade union body and employee representatives for labour protection. If no trade union body is present in the enterprise, the works council and employee representatives for labour protection monitor the adherence to labour law and other regulations.

§5. Sources of Labour Law

80. Sources of law can be social, economic, moral and political circumstances affecting the applicable law and normative legal acts issued by law-making bodies. Based on this, the sources of law can be divided into material and formal. The material sources of law represent the natural, geographical, demographic, social, economic, moral and political, technological, ecological, international political and other conditions of life of a particular society, which influence the creation of law and from which the creation of law is based. Formal sources of law represent the proper forms of law in which the law is contained.

I. Relationship (Hierarchical Order) Between the Different Sources of Labour Law

81. The legal order of the Slovak Republic belongs to the continental type of legal culture, which is typical of the so-called written law. Its hierarchical structure consists of the fact that at the top are the Constitution and constitutional acts, followed by Acts that must follow the Constitution and constitutional Acts, and then implementing legislation, which must follow the previous sources. They are a particular category in terms of Article 7(5) of the Constitution, international treaties on human rights and fundamental freedoms, international treaties, the implementation of which does not require a law, and international treaties that directly establish the rights or obligations of natural persons or legal entities and which have been ratified and declared in the manner established by law, which has priority before the laws.

82. In addition to normative legal acts, the sources of labour law also include collective agreements, internal company normative acts, technical standards, good manners, international agreements and legally binding acts of the EU.

II. Constitution

83. The Constitution of the Slovak Republic, from the point of view of labour law, contains several provisions that relate to labour relations. They result in certain rights that the Constitution of the Slovak Republic grants to people in general, some to citizens and some only to employees.

84. The Constitution enshrines the prohibition of discrimination (Article 12(1)), the prohibition of forced labour and services (Article 18), the right of everyone to freely choose a profession and prepare for it, as well as the right to start a business and carry out other gainful activities, the right of citizens to work and the right to adequate material security for those who are not sins cannot exercise this right under the conditions established by law.

85. However, Article 36 of the Constitution is significant for the field of labour law, according to which employees have the right to fair and satisfactory working conditions. To the extent defined by law, citizens have the right to remuneration for the work performed sufficient to enable them to have a decent standard of living, protection against arbitrary dismissal from employment and discrimination in employment, protection of safety and health at work, the maximum permissible length of working time, adequate rest after work, the shortest permissible length of paid leave for recovery, the right to collective bargaining. Every employee has the right that his remuneration for the work performed is not lower than the minimum wage.

86. From the point of view of the labour relations system, everyone's right to freely associate with others to protect their economic and social interests, trade union freedom, and the right to strike must also be considered extremely important (Article 37). The Constitution also enshrines the right to special protection for women, juveniles, persons with disabilities (Article 38) and pregnant women, who are guaranteed special care, protection in working relationships and corresponding working conditions (Article 41(2)).

87. All the rights mentioned above have been written into the whole system of labour law relations, especially in the Labour Code. The general principle governs their application and interpretation that the application of Constitutional Acts, Acts and other generally binding regulations must conform to the Constitution (Article 152(4)).

III. Acts of the Legislature and the Executive

88. In its essence, labour law consists of many legal regulations. The primary labour regulation in the form of the Act is the Labour Code (Act no. 311/2001 Coll. as amended). Labour Code regulates individual labour relations concerning the employment of natural persons (employees) by legal entities or natural persons (employers) and collective labour relations.

89. To the acts governing labour relations can be assigned the Civil Service Act (Act no. 55/2017 Coll. as amended) regulates legal relations in civil service performance, and the Act on the Performance of Work in the Public Interest (Act no. 552/2003 Coll. as amended). The content of the performance of the state service is the rights and obligations of the state and the civil servant, resulting from the performance of the state service or related to the performance of the state service. The delegated scope of the Labour Code is applied to the performance of the state service. The Act on the Performance of Work in the Public Interest regulates the rights and obligations of employees and employers in the performance of work in the public interest (e.g., state bodies, municipalities, higher territorial units, legal entities in the field of public administration). The subsidiary scope of the Labour Code is applied to the performance of work in the public interest.

90. Sources of labour law also include other acts, namely:

- Act no. 2/1991 Coll. on collective bargaining as amended.
- Act no. 152/1994 Coll. on the social fund, as amended.
- Act no. 283/2002 Coll. on travel reimbursements as amended.
- Act no. 461/2003 Coll. on social insurance as amended.
- Act no. 462/2003 Coll. on income compensation in case of temporary incapacity for work of an employee, as amended.
- Act no. 553/2003 Coll. on the remuneration of certain employees when performing work in the public interest, as amended.
- Act no. 5/2004 Coll. on employment services as amended.
- Act no. 365/2004 Coll. on equal treatment in certain areas and protection against discrimination (anti-discrimination law), as amended.

- Act no. 650/2004 Coll. on supplementary pension savings as amended.
- Act no. 82/2005 Coll. on illegal work and illegal employment, as amended.
- Act no. 124/2006 Coll. on safety and health protection at work, as amended.
- Act no. 125/2006 Coll. on labour inspection, as amended.
- Act no. 103/2007 Coll. on tripartite consultations at the national level (Tripartite Act), as amended.
- Act no. 663/2007 Coll. on the minimum wage as amended.
- Act no. 54/2019 Coll. on protecting whistleblowers of anti-social activity, as amended.

91. From the point of view of subsidiarity, the Civil Code (Act no. 40/1964 Coll. as amended) is also considered an essential source of labour law, the use of which is assumed by the Labour Code in section 1(4) in the sense that, unless the Labour Code provides otherwise in its first part, the general provisions of the Civil Code apply to individual labour relations in connection with the performance of dependent work by natural persons for legal entities or natural persons and to collective labour relations.

92. The source of labour law is also implementing legislation. The legal basis of the implementing legislation can be found in the Constitution, which distinguishes between the following types:

- regulations (according to Article 120 of the Constitution, they are issued by the Government of the Slovak Republic for implementing the Acts and within its limits);
- decrees and measures (according to Article 123 of the Constitution, ministries and other state administration bodies can issue them based on Acts and within their limits if authorized by law).

93. As an example, we can mention:

- Government regulation no. 272/2004 Coll., establishing a list of jobs and workplaces that are prohibited for pregnant women, mothers up to the end of the ninth month after giving birth and breastfeeding women, a list of jobs and workplaces associated with a specific risk for pregnant women, mothers up to the end of the ninth month after childbirth and breastfeeding women and which establish certain obligations for employers when employing these women.
- Government regulation no. 286/2004 Coll., establishing a list of jobs and workplaces prohibited for minor employees and establishing certain obligations of employers when employing minor employees.
- Government regulation no. 387/2006 Coll. on requirements for ensuring safety and health marking at work.
- Government regulation no. 392/2006 Coll. on minimum safety and health requirements when using work equipment.
- Decree of the Ministry of Labour, Social Affairs and Family of the Slovak Republic no. 500/2006 Coll., establishing a sample record of a registered occupational accident.

– A Measure of the Ministry of Labour, Social Affairs and Family of the Slovak Republic no. 368/2023 Coll. about the amounts of food allowance.
– A measure of the Ministry of Finance of the Slovak Republic no. 401/2012 Coll., establishing the introductory meal allowance rates in euros or foreign currency for foreign business trips.

IV. Collective Agreements

94. Collective agreements are a specific and unique law source typical only for labour law. Next to normative legal acts, they are the second most important source of labour law, although they are essentially private law contracts. It is valid that, above all, in the collective agreement, working and wage conditions from labour relations can be adjusted beyond the scope of the provisions of legal regulations.

95. Collective agreements, which consist of a binding and normative part, regulate individual and collective relations between employers and employees, as well as the rights and obligations of the contracting parties. Collective agreements are not a source of law in their entire scope; they are only in their normative part.

96. The Labour Code (section 231(1)) is based on the principle of convenience for the employee. In a collective agreement, working conditions can be adjusted more favourably than those regulated by the Labour Code or another regulation of labour law unless the Labour Code prohibits it or it follows from the provision that cannot be deviated from it. Likewise, the employment contract is invalid because it regulates the employee's claims to a lesser extent than the collective agreement.

97. The claims that arise from the collective agreement by individual employees are applied and satisfied, like other claims of employees from the employment relationship.

V. Internal Normative Acts

98. Internal normative acts issued by the employer based on authorization by the Labour Code are also considered a source of labour law on the condition that they regulate or establish wage, salary or other rights of employees in labour relations or detail the provisions of the Labour Code or special legal regulations. These acts have a regulatory nature, but without the presumption of correctness – the invalidity of their provisions can, therefore, be considered the invalidity of legal acts. In terms of hierarchy, they have lower legal force than collective agreements. They must follow legal regulations or may not regulate rights to a lesser extent than the law guarantees. The primary condition for their binding is that employees are adequately familiarized with their content. As an example of internal normative acts, it is possible to mention the work order, which the employer can issue after the prior consent of the employee representatives; otherwise, it is invalid (section 84) or the rules on safety and health protection at work issued by employers in agreement with employee representatives (section 39 (2)).

VI. Technical Standards

99. According to section 39(1) of the Labour Code, technical standards are considered sources of labour law, provided that they regulate issues related to protecting life and health. The legal basis for their issuance is Act no. 55/2018 Coll. on providing information on technical regulations and obstacles to the free movement of goods and Act no. 56/2018 Coll. on product conformity assessment, making the specified product available on the market.

VII. Good Morals

100. The term 'good morals' is not defined in the Labour Code, but we encounter this correction directly within the framework of the basic principles in Article 2 of the Labour Code. The negative limit to exercising subjective rights and obligations arising from employment relationships is represented by the prohibition of abusing these rights to the detriment of the other participant in the employment relationship or co-employees. The concept of 'good manners' is closely related to the ideas of 'morality'. Good manners are among the principles of private law. They are used as a criterion limiting subjective rights in their content or, more often, limiting the exercise of subjective rights. The content of the term 'good manners' consists of generally applicable moral standards or standards of morality in which there is a general interest in respecting them. The basic meaning of the order to act by good morals is to exclude a gross violation of morality in the exercise of law, to ensure basic decency in the exercise of subjective rights, or to maintain a certain ethical minimum in the exercise of subjective rights. According to the provisions on the invalidity of legal acts, actions of the subject contrary to good morals and abuse of law are subject to absolute invalidity. The prohibition of abuse of rights represents a legal norm, the violation of which by an authorized entity is an illegal act. The peculiarity of such an unlawful act is that it does not arise due to a breach of a legal obligation but instead occurs during the exercise of a right in a manner prohibited by law. This peculiarity of an illegal act in the unlawful exercise of subjective rights distinguishes it from other illicit acts. An illegal act in the case of abuse of rights is committed by an authorized subject who violates a specific obligation established by law (prohibition of abuse), but only in the phase of realization of the subjective right. In a given case, abuse occurs if one party acts contrary to society's basic, generally recognized moral principles regarding relationships and actions between people. Good morals can be equated with generally socially recognized principles of conduct in legal relations (honesty, non-abuse of the exercise of rights, non-harassment of the exercise of law, and respect for the equality of participants in civil relations).

101. The Labour Code directly refers to good morals not only in the basic principles but also mentions them in normative provisions. Also, according to section 39 of the Civil Code, which can be applied in labour law thanks to the subsidiary scope of the Civil Code, a legal act is invalid if its content or purpose contradicts the law, circumvents it or goes against good morals.

§6. International Labour Law

102. International labour law is based on a system of international agreements, the adoption of which is the result of the action of international organizations founded by states as sovereign subjects of international law to protect human rights or to regulate the minimum level of working conditions with universal scope. A significant part of international labour law also consists of bilateral agreements concluded between individual states to provide a more favourable employment regime for citizens of the contracting states.

103. The standard-setting activities of the United Nations and the conventions and recommendations of the International Labour Organization (ILO) emerged over time among the primary sources of international labour law. Conventions of the ILO become binding for a Member State upon ratification of the convention by its competent authorities. The Slovak Republic is a Member State of both international organizations mentioned above and has acceded to many binding documents. In addition, according to Article 7(5) of the Constitution, international treaties on human rights and fundamental freedoms, international treaties for the execution of which no law is necessary, and international treaties that directly establish the rights or obligations of natural persons or legal entities and which have been ratified and declared in established by law, have priority over laws. This essential provision of the Constitution prioritizes international treaties on human rights and freedoms over national legislation. These include multilateral agreements, primarily conventions adopted within the ILO framework.

104. Concerning labour law in the Slovak Republic, sources of international law must include not only sources of law created by the United Nations and the ILO but also sources of international private labour law, sources of law by European regional organizations (Council of Europe, EU) and bilateral international treaties.

I. United Nations Sources

105. The number of international resources created by the United Nations mainly includes:

- Universal Declaration of Human Rights, adopted in 1948.
- International Covenant on Civil and Political Rights, adopted in 1966 (published in the Collection of Laws under no. 120/1976).

- International Covenant on Economic, Social and Cultural Rights, adopted in 1966 (published in the Collection of Laws under no. 120/1976).
- Convention on the Elimination of All Forms of Racial Discrimination, adopted by the General Assembly in 1965 (published in the Collection of Laws under no. 95/1974).
- Convention on the Elimination of All Forms of Discrimination against Women, adopted in 1979 (published in the Collection of Laws under no. 62/1987).

II. Sources of the International Labour Organization

106. Czechoslovakia was one of the founding members of the ILO in 1919. After the country's break-up in 1993, the Slovak Republic became an ILO Member State in the same year. Currently, the Slovak Republic is bound by seventy-six conventions. Out of seventy-six Conventions ratified by Slovakia, of which sixty-eight are in force, five have been denounced, two instruments abrogated, and none have been ratified in the past twelve months. Regarding the scope of the legislation, the Slovak Republic has ratified 10 out of 10 Fundamental Conventions, 4 out of 4 Governance Conventions (Priority), and 62 out of 177 Technical Conventions.

III. Sources of the Council of Europe

107. The Council of Europe is the oldest international political organization in Europe. Since its foundation in 1949, human rights have been the focus of its activities. Following on from this area, it considers the support of the economic and social development of the Member States to be one of its primary goals. It achieves its goal – to stimulate the development and improvement of the legislation of the Member States in the social field through the adoption of binding legal documents.

108. Since its inception, the Slovak Republic has been a Member State of the Council of Europe; therefore, the Council's sources of law have a special significance as sources of labour law. Of the many agreements adopted by the Council of Europe, the Convention on the Protection of Fundamental Human Rights and Freedoms, to which the Slovak Republic has been bound since its inception (published in the Collection of Laws under no. 209/1992), is of particular importance for labour law. The European Social Charter was ratified by the Slovak Republic in 1998 (published in the Collection of Laws under no. 329/1998), the European Social Charter (revised), and then in 2009 (published in the Collection of Laws under no. 273/2009).

109. The Slovak Republic is considered bound (under Article A paragraph 1 letter b), Article A paragraph 2 and Article B of the European Social Charter (revised)) by the following provisions of the European Social Charter (revised):

- Article 1 Right to work (paragraphs 1–4).
- Article 5 The right to organize.

– Article 6 Right to collective bargaining (paragraphs 1–4).
– Article 7 Right of children and juveniles to protection (paragraphs 1–10).
– Article 12 Right to social security (paragraphs 1–4).
– Article 13 Right to social and medical assistance (paragraphs 1–3).
– Article 16 The Right of the family to social, legal and economic protection.
– Article 19 The right of migrant workers and their families to protection and assistance [paragraph 1, paragraph 4 letter a) and b), paragraphs 5, 6, 7, 9 and 11].
– Article 20 The right to equal opportunities and to equal treatment in matters of employment and occupation without discrimination based on gender [letter a) to d)].

110. The Slovak Republic considers itself (under Article A paragraph 1 letter c), Article A paragraph 2 and Article B of the European Social Charter (revised)) also bound by the following additional provisions of the European Social Charter (revised):

– Article 2 Right to proper working conditions (paragraphs 1–7).
– Article 3 Right to safe and healthy working conditions (paragraphs 1–4).
– Article 4 Right to adequate remuneration (paragraphs 1–5).
– Article 8 Right of employed women to maternity protection (paragraphs 1–5).
– Article 9 Right to counselling when choosing a profession.
– Article 10 Right to vocational education and training (paragraphs 1–5).
– Article 11 Right to health protection (paragraphs 1–3).
– Article 14 Right to benefit from social services (paragraphs 1 and 2).
– Article 15 The right of persons with disabilities to independence, social integration and participation in the life of society (paragraphs 1 and 2).
– Article 17 The right of children and adolescents to social, legal and economic protection (paragraphs 1 and 2).
– Article 18 The right to perform gainful activity in the territory of the other contracting parties (paragraphs 1, 2, 4).
– Article 21 Right to information and consultation [letter a) and b)].
– Article 22 The right to participate in determining and improving working conditions and the working environment [letter a) to d)].
– Article 23 The right of older people to social protection [first indent letter a) and b), second indent letter a) and b) and third indent].
– Article 24 Right to protection in cases of termination of employment [letter a) and letter b)].
– Article 25 The right of workers to protect their claims in the event of the insolvency of their employer.
– Article 26 Right to dignity at work (paragraphs 1 and 2).
– Article 27 The right of workers with family responsibilities to equal opportunities and equal treatment (paragraphs 1, 2 and 3).
– Article 28 The right of workers' representatives to protection in the company and to facilitate the conditions for the performance of their activities, which are provided to them [letter a) and letter b)].
– Article 29 The right to information and consultation in collective redundancies procedures.

– Article 30 The right to protection against poverty and social exclusion [letter a) and letter b)].

IV. Sources of the European Union

111. The law of the EU is a unique legal system that differs from international law and the Member States' national law. The original European Communities, which transformed into today's EU, obtained from the Member States the authority to create legal norms binding not only for these states but also for the national subjects of these states, i.e., for natural and legal persons. Thus, they made their legal order a supranational legal norm applicable to all Member States.

112. European labour law can be characterized as a law enshrined in both primary and secondary law of the EU, regulating relations between employee and employer. Even though the EU's labour law and the regulation of labour relations have always been and, in essence, remain the domain of the national law of the Member States, the purpose of rulemaking was primarily to lead to a sure convergence of legislation in individual issues and problem areas. The effort of the EU is thus to ensure a certain minimum standard in all Member States. The Slovak Republic, as a Member State of the EU, is also bound by these regulations.

V. International Private Law

113. The application of international private law comes into consideration in employment relations where one party is a foreigner; this includes employment relations in which either the employee is a foreigner or the SR citizen is employed by an employer with the status of a foreigner.

114. According to Regulation (EC) no. 593/2008 of the European Parliament and of the Council of 17 June 2008 on the law applicable to contractual obligations (Rome I), the freedom of the parties to choose the applicable law should be one of the essential elements of the system of conflict of laws norms in the field of contractual obligations. According to Article 3 of the Rome I Regulation, the contract is governed by the legal order chosen by the contracting parties, whereby the choice must be made explicitly or demonstrated by the contract's provisions or the case's circumstances. The contracting parties can choose the legal system that will govern the entire contract or only a part of it.

115. The clash of different legal orders in contractual obligations in labour law matters is dealt with by Article 8 of the Rome I Regulation. According to this article, the individual employment contract is governed by the legal order chosen by the parties under Article 3. However, this choice of law must not deprive the employee of the protection provided to him by such provisions, which cannot be deviated from by agreement according to the law, which in the absence of choice would be decisive according to paragraphs 2, 3 and 4 of this article.

116. Unless the parties to the contract choose the applicable law for an individual employment contract, the contract will be governed by the law of the country in which the employee usually performs work under the contract or, if this is not the case, by the law of the country from which he performs such work. A change of the country of the usual place of work is not considered if the employee temporarily works in another country. When the applicable law cannot be determined according to the place of usual performance of work or the place of the country from which the employee performs work, the individual employment contract is governed by the regulations of the country of the place of business through which the employee was employed.

117. For labour relationships to which the Rome I Regulation cannot be applied, it is possible to apply Act no. 97/1963 Coll. on international private and procedural law. Provision section 16 of the cited regulation regulates the issue of labour law. The relations from the employment contract are governed unless the participants agree on something else by the law of the place where the worker performs the work. However, suppose a worker works in one state based on an employment relationship with an organization with its headquarters in another. In that case, the law of the organization's seat is decisive, except if it were a person who resides in the state where the work was performed. The working conditions of employees of transport companies are governed by the law of the company's registered office in railway and road transport, in river and air transport by the law of the place of registration, and in maritime transport by the law of the state under whose flag the transport is carried out.

118. If the parties to the employment relationship agree on the choice of another conflict criterion, section 36 of the previously cited regulation protects the weaker party to the employment relationship in the form of a public order reservation. The reservation of public order means that the legal regulation of a foreign state cannot be used if the effects of this use would contradict such principles of the social and state establishment of the Slovak Republic and its legal order, which must be insisted on without reservation.

119. Under the provisions of section 5 of the Labour Code, the labour law relations of employees performing work in the territory of the Slovak Republic and a foreign employer, as well as between foreigners and stateless persons working in the territory of the Slovak Republic and employers with a place of business in the territory of the Slovak Republic, are governed by the Labour Code, unless legal regulations on international private law provide otherwise.

Part I. The Individual Employment Relation

Chapter 1. Definition and Concepts

120. Individual labour law relations dominate labour law regulation; however, the Labour Code and no other regulation do not define this concept. By them, legal theory understands the legal relationship between the employee and the employer as individual participants in the employment relationship. All relationships arising in causal connection with the performance of non-independent (dependent) work by an employee for the employer must be considered individual labour relations, regardless of whether the performance of non-independent work for the employer continues or has already been terminated.

121. Individual labour relations can be further divided into primary and secondary.

122. We differentiate primary employment relations into:

- fundamental labour relations – this includes the employment relationship ('pracovný pomer') and labour relations established by agreements on work outside the employment relationship. These are employment relationships that are covered by the material direct full, material direct limited or subsidiary scope of the Labour Code;
- similar labour relations include state employee relations, service relations and other labour relations (e.g., relations arising in the performance of a public function relations of members of cooperatives, as long as the performance of work is part of them). These legal relationships are subject to the delegated scope of the Labour Code.

123. Secondary labour relations can be characterized as those derived from primary labour relations. As part of these relations, internal control is carried out, for example, through employee representatives or through various commissions, such as the Commission for Safety and Health at Work, which the employer creates. This also includes relationships resulting from breach of obligations or damage. Among the secondary labour relations, we include control, liability and sanctions.

§1. The Different Categories of Employees

124. As we have already mentioned in the section on historical development, in 2001, there was a fundamental differentiation of labour relations depending on the work categories of employees. At the same time, there was a division in the labour law regulation of labour relations between the business and non-business spheres. Civil service and public service have separated themselves from the legislation of the Labour Code, not in an absolute way, but with some aspects of interdependence in the form of delegated or subsidiary scope of the Labour Code. Before 2001, the Labour Code applied in full to all categories of employees (public employees and civil servants). Currently, the Labour Code fully applies to employees in the private sector.

125. The Labour Code applies subsidiarily to employees performing work in the public interest, employees who are required to ensure compliance according to a special regulation, and employees working in operation, maintenance and development of the gas transmission network who are under the direct management authority of the statutory body of the operator of the gas transmission network, employees in transport, employees performing a medical profession, teaching employees, professional surrogate parents, employees who are theatre artists or musical artists, crew members of ships sailing under the national flag of the Slovak Republic, employees of private security services and employees working in the production and processing of crackers, explosive compounds, black powder, ammunition, explosives, explosive objects and explosive pyrotechnic compounds. Labour relations of employees of churches and religious societies who perform clerical activities are governed by the Labour Code; if the Labour Code, a particular regulation, an international treaty to which the Slovak Republic is bound, a contract concluded between the Slovak Republic and churches and religious societies, or internal rules of churches and religious companies do not establish otherwise.

126. Employees performing civil service, public functions, judges and prosecutors, and professional athletes are subject to the Labour Code only to a limited extent based on delegated authority.

I. Categories of Employees

127. In the legal literature, various criteria divide employees into individual categories. From the broader range of criteria for dividing employees into individual categories, three essential criteria for dividing employees characterized by specific differences can be deduced. It is about:

- distribution of employees depending on whether employees perform physical work or mental work;
- distribution of employees according to individual occupations;
- division of employees into individual categories depending on the increased need for their special protection.

128. The criterion for dividing employees into blue-collar workers and white-collar workers depends on whether the employees perform physical, manual or mental work. This historically oldest division of employees into workers and clerks has already practically lost its meaning in the era of radical changes in the technical level of production, also under the influence of the development of EU Law.

129. One of the job categories of employees, depending on the profession, is employees performing work in the public interest. Unlike civil servants, employees performing work in the public interest are considered to be employees subject to labour regulations. The Labour Code applies subsidiarily to these categories of employees when performing work in the public interest.

130. The division of employees depending on special protection is one of the usual criteria in current labour regulations abroad. These are primarily those particular categories of employees who, from the point of view of their actual position in the employment relationship, deserve special protection and against whom positive discrimination is applied in labour legislation. This mainly concerns the work category of employees with disabilities, pregnant women – employees, women – employees on maternity leave, men – employees on paternity leave, and women or men – employees on parental leave.

II. Professional Athletes

131. Sports increase work characteristics if a professional athlete is included in a specific sports club, regularly receives a reward for his work performance, and is included in the collective of other colleague athletes. Such a professional activity of an athlete shows all the characteristic features of dependent activity, and the athlete himself shows all the distinguishing features of the term employee. As in the employment relationship of other human work activities, it is a personal, free performance of work in individual and economic subordination to whoever is its customer (respective sports club or organization). Such work is dependent, even if it is not a typical private law relationship.

132. According to the current legal status, professional athletes are subject to the delegated scope of the Labour Code. According to section 31 of Act no. 440/2015 Coll. on Sport, as amended, a sports contract is concluded between the athlete and the sports organization, establishing the professional athlete's working relationship with the relevant sports organization. In contrast to an employment contract, the subject of a sports contract is the remunerated practice of sports by an athlete for a sports organization, which, however, may not contain restrictions on sports activities after the end of the contractual relationship. The contract on professional sports practice establishes a complex legal obligation for the professional athlete. The sports organization undertakes to pay the athlete the agreed salary and to create suitable conditions for the performance of the sport in the contract on the performance of professional sports.

133. According to section 35 of the Act on Sport, a contract for the professional practice of sports contains several content elements similar to an employment contract, which include the type of sport but also the salary conditions of the athlete, the start date of the sport and the place of the sport, the amount of leave, the method of taking it and others, in particular, the length of the notice period and sanctions for breach of contractual obligations as well as the scope of confidentiality.

III. Top Managers

134. A specific category of natural persons is managers. The Labour Code does not define the term 'manager'; nevertheless, managers can be defined as 'managerial employees'. Although the principle of subordination and superiority still exists between managers and employers, the subordination principle is weakened.

135. In practice, we usually distinguish two basic categories of managers – managers who are simultaneously members of the statutory bodies of the company, so-called top managers, and managers with the status of managerial employees, so-called line managers.

136. The Labour Code does not expressly exclude that an employment relationship can bind members of statutory bodies of legal entities. According to the majority of the literature and jurisprudence, the performance of the function of a member of a statutory body should not be carried out in an employment relationship because the status of a member of a statutory body of legal entities does not correspond to all the legal characteristics of an employment relationship. Their legal status should be governed solely by commercial law regulations.

IV. Apprentices Within the Dual Education System

137. The legal status of apprentice pupils preparing for a profession is under Act no. 61/2015 Coll. on Vocational Education and Training and amendments to specific laws. Practical teaching is carried out by pupils at the workplaces of the employer or practical teaching workplaces. In the system of dual education, the pupil prepares for the performance of a profession according to the specific needs and requirements of the employer based on the conclusion of a contract on dual education between the employer and the secondary vocational school based on which the employer undertakes to provide pupils with practical training at their own expense and responsibility. Based on the dual education contract, the secondary vocational school organizes vocational education and training in the dual education system.

138. As part of dual education, the employer concludes a learning contract with the student, the object of which is the employer's commitment to prepare the student for the performance of a profession at a practical teaching workplace, and the student undertakes to participate in practical teaching directly with the employer according to his specific needs and requirements. In the dual education system, the employer is solely responsible for the organization, content, and quality of the student's practical training and, for this purpose, pays all the costs associated with financing the practical training. The learning contract must be in writing, and the relationship established by the learning contract most often ends on the day the student ceases to be a school student. The employer may terminate the learning contract for exhaustive reasons due to the loss of medical capacity to perform the profession he is preparing, or the student, if the employer repeatedly violates his obligations arising from the learning contract, may terminate the learning contract.

139. During practical classes, the student only performs practice and productive work corresponding to the profession he is preparing for. He is obliged to observe the internal rules of the workplace of practical teaching. During practical training in health and safety at work, the student has the rights and obligations of an employee. Suppose he causes damage during practical teaching and does not remove it by returning it to the previous state. In that case, the secondary vocational school or the employer can demand compensation from him up to four times the legal minimum wage.

140. The employer pays the student's meal costs during the practical lessons and may also cover the student's accommodation costs in the school dormitory and travel expenses.

141. The employer provides a reward for the productive work performed by the student in practical teaching. If the student's practical teaching takes place in the workshop of the secondary vocational school, the reward for productive work is provided by the secondary vocational school. For fields of study with insufficient graduates, the student can also receive an incentive scholarship amount, which depends on the student's performance.

V. Home Workers and Teleworkers

142. According to section 52 of the Labour Code, if the work that could be carried out at the employer's workplace is carried out regularly within the scope of the established weekly working time or part of it from the employee's household, it is home work, or telework, if the work is carried out using information technologies, in which it occurs regularly for the electronic transmission of data at a distance. The employer and the employee can agree that the employee will schedule his working time during the entire week for home work or telework or that the home work or telework will be performed during flexible working time. If an employee schedules his working time when working from home or teleworking, his employment relationship is governed by this law with the following deviations:

- the provisions on the schedule of specified weekly working time, continuous daily rest and continuous rest during the week do not apply;

- provisions on downtime do not apply, except for downtime for which the employer is responsible;
- the employee is not entitled to wage compensation in the event of important personal obstacles at work, except for wage compensation in the event of a leave of absence due to the death of a family member;
- the employee is not entitled to wages for overtime work, wage concessions for work on holidays, wage concessions for work on Saturdays, wage concessions for work on Sundays, wage concessions for night work and wage compensation for rugged work performance unless the employee and employer agree otherwise.

143. When home work or telework is provided, the employer is obliged to take appropriate measures, such as to ensure, instal and regularly maintain the technical equipment and software necessary for the performance of telework, except in cases where the employee performing telework uses his technical equipment and software in agreement with the employer; to ensure data protection, which is processed and used during telecommuting, especially about software equipment; to reimburse demonstrably increased expenses of the employee associated with the use of own tools, own equipment and own objects necessary for the performance of domestic work or telework; inform the employee about all restrictions on the use of technical equipment and software, as well as about the consequences in case of violation of these restrictions; prevent the isolation of an employee performing domestic work or telework from other employees and allow him to enter the employer's workplace, if possible, for meeting with other employees; or to allow an employee performing domestic work or telework access to deepening their qualifications in the same way as a comparable employee with a place of work at the employer's workplace.

VI. Employees Performing Work Based on Agreements on Work Performed Outside the Employment Relationship

144. Although the employment relationship based on agreements on work performed outside the employment relationship does not show the characteristics of an employment relationship, the natural person performing work in this employment relationship is called an employee. Compared to the employment relationship, this is qualitatively different, with only a supplementary character to the employment relationship. In addition to the first and sixth parts of the Labour Code, the provisions on working time with certain exceptions, as well as the provisions of section 119 of the Labour Code on the minimum wage, provisions of sections 129 to 132 on the maturity of remuneration, wage payments and deductions from remuneration, the provisions as mentioned above will be applied accordingly. In the case of work performed based on agreements on work performed outside the employment relationship, the provisions on the agreed remuneration increased by at least the amount of the minimum wage per hour for work on a holiday, and the provisions of section 122a, section 122b, section 123 and section 124 of the Labour Code on wage benefits for work shall also be applied on Saturday, about the salary discount for working on Sunday and the salary discount for performing night work.

145. Differences in the legal status of employees performing work based on agreements on work performed outside the employment relationship are mainly in providing wage compensation in the event of certain obstacles to work on the part of the employee that interfered with working time.

VII. 'Quasi' Employees (Economically Dependent Employees)

146. Due to the absence of personal subordination, these are natural persons who do not exhibit the characteristics of an employee and, therefore, the characteristics of dependent labour. Still, however, these are persons who do not exhibit all the legal characteristics of entrepreneurial activity, as defined by the Commercial Code or the Trade Act (e.g., labour sales representative position). It can also be persons who are not typical entrepreneurs because they do not perform gainful activity for profit or in their name. This category of persons is on the border between an employee's legal status and a self-employed person's legal status. It is a model of a hybrid 'quasi-employee', working for an employer but integrated or separated from the relevant corporate structure, economically dependent, and significantly less personally dependent. It does not correspond to all the characteristics of entrepreneurial activity (the natural person performing the work does not have his own company or capital) nor dependent activity in an employment relationship.

147. Since labour law regulates relations concerning the performance of dependent work, applying labour law relations to these persons is impossible if the characteristics of dependent work cannot be identified during the performance of an economically dependent activity.

§2. The Individual Labour Contracts

148. An employment contract is the sole and exclusive legal basis for establishing an employment relationship, even if, under certain circumstances, an employment relationship can also be established by law (section 58(7) of the Labour Code). It is generally understood as the unanimous expression of the will of the employer and the employee towards the establishment and creation of an employment relationship. The employment contract is a bilateral legal act through which the natural person and the employer jointly express their will to establish the employment relationship.

149. Although section 42(2) of the Labour Code also mentions election and appointment as a prerequisite for performing the function, its construction is such that it does not disturb the position of the employment contract as the only legal act by which an employment relationship can be established. However, before concluding a written employment contract, there must be an act of appointment or election (and the employment contract should follow and refer to it).

150. The parties may conclude a valid employment contract only if they have complied with all prerequisites for the validity of legal acts as defined by the provisions of sections 15 to 17 of the Labour Code and section 34(a) following applicable provisions of the Civil Code on the requisites of legal acts; as the Civil Code is subsidiarily applied to the general section of the Labour Code. The content of the employment contract as a legal act must not be so formulated as to make the employee renounce some of his/her rights in advance. The necessary prerequisites of a validly concluded employment contract comprise the requisites of the will, which must be accessible and severe. The requisites of manifesting the will must be definite and intelligible. It also must not be at variance with the law, must not circumvent the law, contradict its purpose, and must not be contrary to morality. For instance, the parties to the contract may not use their contractual freedom at variance with the mandatory provisions of labour legislation, in particular, the Labour Code. However, they may fully develop their contractual freedom in the formulation of the content of the employment contract based on dispositive (non-mandatory) provisions of labour legislation. If the employment contract as a legal act does not comply with the requisites of a subject, will, a manifestation of will and legal act as a whole, the law declares it null and void.

151. As a bilateral legal act, the employment contract must also comply with the requirements for legal acts under section 34 and following applicable provisions of the Civil Code and section 17 of the Labour Code to have the legal power to establish a valid employment relationship.

I. Different Categories of Labour Contracts

A. Labour Contract for a Definite Period and an Indefinite Period

152. An employment relationship for a defined period is an employment relationship with a limited duration. Section 48 of the Labour Code regulates some special rules to prevent abuse. An employment relationship for an indefinite period (and thus, it is not an employment relationship for a defined period) is: (a) if the duration of the employment relationship was not explicitly specified in the employment contract; (b) if the legal conditions for concluding an employment relationship for a certain period were not met in the employment contract or when it was changed; or (c) the employment relationship for a certain period was not agreed in writing. An employment relationship agreed in this way ends with a legal event or the expiry of the agreed working time without the employer applying any of the exhaustively stated grounds for termination, without any further restrictions (e.g., negotiations with the relevant trade union body or during the employee's temporary incapacity for work or pregnancy).

153. The Labour Code does not establish objective reasons for using an employment relationship for a defined period. Negotiating the length of the employment relationship is not an essential part of the employment contract, and failure to negotiate this length results in creating an employment relationship for an indefinite period. Thus, it will be an employment relationship, primarily in those cases where it is necessary to ensure that work is performed only for a certain period. The duration can be determined by a specific day of termination or even defined by some determinable event – for example, representing an employee on maternity leave, paternity and parental leave, when it is not always possible to estimate the specific day of termination of the employment relationship in advance that does not raise any doubt as to when the employment relationship should end.

154. The Labour Code (section 48(2)) establishes a limitation for the maximum duration of the employment relationship, namely two years. The Labour Code does not rule out that, in the case of an employment relationship for a defined period, it can be extended or renegotiated beyond two years if the conditions are met. Further extension or renegotiation of the employment relationship for a certain period of up to two years or more than two years is possible only due to: (a) surrogacy of the employee during maternity leave, paternity leave, parental leave, leave immediately following maternity leave, paternity leave or parental leave, temporary incapacity for work or an employee who has been released for a long-time period to perform a public function or a trade union function, (b) performing work in which it is necessary to substantially increase the number of employees for a temporary period not exceeding eight months in a calendar year, (c) performing work that is dependent on rotation seasons, they are repeated every year and do not exceed eight months in a calendar year (seasonal work), (d) performing work agreed in the collective agreement.

155. An employee in an employment relationship for a defined period cannot be favoured or restricted if it concerns working conditions and conditions of employment according to this law and working conditions related to safety and health protection at work according to a special regulation, compared to a comparable employee. The Labour Code establishes a special rule for chaining employment relationships with a university teacher or a creative employee of science, research and development, which is possible even if there is an objective reason for this arising from the nature of the activity of a university teacher or a creative employee of science, research and development established by a special regulation. Section 48(2–7) of the Labour Code does not apply to employment through temporary employment agencies (section 58).

B. Part-Time Work Contract

156. According to the scope of the employee's agreed weekly working time, employment relationships are divided into employment relationships within the scope of established weekly working time and employment relationships for shorter working time.

157. An employment relationship within the scope of established weekly working time is a legal relationship where the average scope of the employee's commitment (number of working time) to work for the employer within one week is the same as the established weekly working time according to section 85(8) of the Labour Code. An employee whose weekly working time does not reach the limit determined for the established weekly working time according to section 85(8) of the Labour Code is considered an employee in an employment relationship for a shorter weekly working time. If, for example, a specific employer has established a weekly working time of forty hours, and the scope of the employee's working time is lower than the established weekly working time, it is a part-time employment relationship. If the employer has established a weekly working time of thirty-eight hours, all lower working time of the employees in the week are employment contracts for shorter weekly working time.

158. The labour regulation of the Labour Code is based on the principle of equal treatment of employees working in an employment relationship for the established weekly working time and employees working in an employment relationship for shorter working time, including equal labour law protection against unilateral termination of the employment relationship by the employer. This fact is declared by the Labour Code in section 49(5), according to which an employee in an employment relationship for shorter working time may not be favoured or restricted compared to an employee employed by the employer for the established weekly working time. Equal treatment is necessary for employees working in an employment relationship for shorter weekly working time, regardless of the extent of the shorter weekly working time. Employees in an employment relationship for a shorter working time are entitled to a salary corresponding to the agreed shorter working time.

C. Trial Period

159. The probationary period is a particular period, agreed in the employment contract, that allows the employer and the employee to determine whether they are compatible. When the trial period expires, if the employment relationship is not terminated during the trial period, the employment relationship continues. The agreement regarding the probationary period is optional, and it is up to the contracting parties to decide whether they agree on a probationary period. Suppose the trial period is agreed upon for a period longer than the law allows. In that case, such an agreement is invalid only in the part where the trial period exceeds the maximum permissible limit. A trial period (section 45 of the Labour Code) cannot be validly negotiated after an employment relationship has already been established; therefore, it cannot be agreed retroactively, but at the latest on the day that was agreed upon as the day the employee starts work, i.e., on the day the employment relationship is established. Therefore, the beginning of the trial period is always the same as the beginning of the employment relationship.

160. The length of the trial period is a maximum of three months. The maximum length of the probationary period for senior employees directly subordinate to a statutory body or a member of a statutory body and senior employees under the direct management of these senior employees is a maximum of six months. However, the contracting parties can also agree on a shorter trial period. The statutory maximization of the probationary period's length is relatively mandatory; the Labour Code sets its length as the maximum and cannot be exceeded by the contracting parties. Agreeing on a more extended trial period would mean that the time exceeding the maximum duration of the trial period enshrined in the Labour Code would be an invalid agreement.

161. By law, the probationary period is extended by the time of obstacles to work on the part of the employee. Considering that the Labour Code only mentions the general connection between 'obstacles to work on the part of the employee' and the probationary period serves to test the employee, if the employee cannot perform work during this time, the purpose of the probationary period would not be fulfilled. From this point of view, it is all obstacles to work on the employee's part (i.e., the employee's temporary incapacity for work, maternity leave, parental leave, treatment, examination).

D. *Temporary Assignment Agreement*

162. A temporary assignment can be used to denote complex legal relationships between an employee, an employer and a third party (in section 40(10) of the Labour Code, it is referred to as a user employer), which is based on two bilateral legal acts – between the employee and the employer on the one hand, and the employer and the user employer on the other hand, based on which the employee temporarily performs dependent work according to the instructions and under the control and management of the user employer acting on behalf of the employer. With the temporary assignment of an employee to a host employer through a temporary employment agency (so-called agency work) or the employer himself deals section 58 of the Labour Code deals. The legal status of a temporary employment agency is governed by Act no. 5/2004 on Employment Services as amended.

163. When an employee is temporarily assigned to a host employer by a temporary employment agency, the agency is in an employer's legal position. A temporary employment agency concludes an employment contract with the employee, in which it undertakes to ensure the employee's temporary work performance for a host employer.

164. Agency employment differs from the standard form of employment by the particular content of the temporary employment agency's obligation as an employer towards the employee under the employment contract. The purpose of employing a temporary agency employee is his temporary assignment to the user employer, which also results from section 29(1) of the Act on Employment Services. Therefore, under section 58(4) of the Labour Code, the temporary employment agency is not obligated to assign work to the temporary agency employee in the employment contract. Instead, the temporary employment agency must ensure the employee works at the user's employer. This provision modifies the employer's obligation to assign work to the employee according to the employment contract according to section 47(1)(a) of the Labour Code.

165. In addition to the obligation of the temporary employment agency to ensure the temporary performance of work at the user's employer, an agreement on the terms of employment is another essential content of the employment contract of a temporary agency employee. The legislator does not specify the agreement's content on employment conditions or the term 'terms of employment' in more detail. It will not necessarily be the same term as 'working conditions and employment conditions' according to section 58(11) of the Labour Code, which is subject to the principle of equal treatment to a comparable employee of the user employer. The above can be deduced from the fact that the legislator uses a different wording of 'terms of employment' on the one hand and 'working conditions and employment conditions' on the other. The diction 'terms of employment' indicates that this defines the conditions under which employment with a temporary employment agency will occur and is not necessarily a determination of 'terms of employment'.

166. The written agreement on temporary assignment concluded between the employer and the employee must include, in particular, the name and registered office of the user employer, the day when the temporary assignment is established and the period for which the temporary assignment was agreed, the type of work and the place of work performance, wage conditions and conditions for unilateral termination of performance work before the expiration of the temporary assignment period. The requisites of the temporary assignment agreement are indicated in the relevant provision by the term 'in particular'; therefore, the Labour Code also allows other temporary assignment agreement requisites. The legal regulation does not preclude the employment contract of a temporary agency employee from being concluded for a certain period. In such a case, the Labour Code stipulates that the employment contract of a temporary agency employee for a certain period must also include the details of the agreement on a temporary assignment. The Labour Code does not explicitly prohibit the employment of a temporary agency employee from being extended for a certain period or renewed any number of times and for any short or long time. Temporary agency employees can thus be uncertain about the duration of their employment.

E. Employment Contract When Performing Work Outside the Territory of the Slovak Republic

167. If the place of work is agreed upon abroad, the Labour Code, in addition to general requirements, establishes other content requirements of the employment contract and the obligation to inform the employee about other requirements unless agreed upon with the employee in the employment contract. In the employment contract, the employer must also agree with the employee on the place of work in the state or states outside the territory of the Slovak Republic and the time of work in the state or states outside the territory of the Slovak Republic. Other requisites/information when performing work abroad are the currency in which the salary will be paid or part of it, information on other payments connected with the performance of work in the state or states outside the territory of the Slovak Republic in money or kind, information on whether it is ensured repatriation of the employee and what conditions apply to it. This does not affect the fact that special regulations may establish other mandatory parts of the employment contract for particular groups of employees.

168. When the place of work is outside the territory of the Slovak Republic, the employer is obliged to provide the employee with written information, at least to the extent of the following information, if they are not included in the employment contract: (a) the currency in which the salary will be paid or part of it, (b) information on other related services with the performance of work in the state or states outside the territory of the Slovak Republic in money or kind, (c) information on whether the employee's repatriation is ensured and what conditions apply to it.

F. Agreements on Work Performed Outside the Employment Relationship

169. Apart from a standard labour contract, which is the most frequent basis of the establishment of the employment relationship, the labour legislation of the Slovak Republic provides for a specific type of agreement – agreements on work performed outside the employment relationship – which are not known to the labour legislation of other countries (except the Czech Republic). These agreements establish a labour law relation but not an employment relationship. The labour law relation based thereon is looser than the employment relationship and represents only a supplementary form of labour engagement of citizens. Agreements are concluded in cases where the activity is usually small-scale or involves isolated work tasks. The employer can only conclude them exceptionally, e.g., for small-scale work or a one-off task. Agreements on work performed outside the employment relationship cannot be concluded for activities subject to protection under the Copyright Act.

170. Agreements are regulated in the ninth part of the Labour Code. Although the legal regulation of relations arising based on agreements on work performed outside the employment relationship is more liberal than in the case of an employment relationship, the provisions of the Labour Code, which are general, and further the provisions of the Labour Code, on which it expressly establishes. Regarding the ability to enter into agreements on work performed outside the employment relationship and the rights and obligations arising from these contracts, the employer and the employee require the same conditions as employment contracts.

171. To the employment relationship established by agreements on work performed outside the employment relationship, the general provisions of the Labour Code, selected provisions on working time and rest periods (section 85(1) and (2), section 90(10), sections 91 to 95, section 98 of the Labour Code), provisions on safety and health protection at work, enshrining the minimum wage and wage benefits for work on Saturdays, Sundays, for night work and rugged work performance (section 122a(1) to (3), section 122b(1) to (3), section 123(1) and (2), section 124 of the Labour Code) and provisions on substantial personal obstacles to work on the part of the employee (section 141 (1) and (2) letters a) to g) of the Labour Code), but without the provision of wage compensation applies. Sections 129 to 132 of the Labour Code shall apply appropriately to the due date of remuneration, payment of remuneration and deductions from remuneration.

172. If the average weekly working time exceeds three hours in four consecutive weeks, the provisions of the Labour Code also apply appropriately to the place of performance of work as an essential element of the agreement to the employment relationship established by agreements on work performed outside the employment relationship (section 43(1) letter b)), on written information from the employer when performing work outside the territory of the Slovak Republic (section 44a(2) to (5)), on information on working conditions and conditions of employment (section 47a(1) letters a) and d) and (2) to(5)) and about the change of working conditions and employment conditions due to posting for the performance of work in the provision of services to the territory of another Member State of the EU (section 54b (2) to (5)).

173. However, agreements on work performed outside the employment relationship are not covered by the provisions on on-call (sections 96 and 96a), overtime work (section 97), records of night work, on-call and overtime work (section 99), annual leave (sections 100 – 117), as well as other provisions of the Labour Code relating to the employment relationship.

174. The employer is obliged to provide the employee with written information about the days and periods in which the employee may be required to perform the work, the period in which the employee is to be informed about the work before its start, which must not be shorter than twenty-four hours. The employee is not obliged to perform the work if the employer requires the performance of the work contrary to the written information. When the employer cancels the work's performance within a period shorter than the period announced, the employee is entitled to compensation of the remuneration that he would have achieved if the work had been carried out, in the amount of at least 30% of the remuneration. This provision does not apply if the employer schedules the employee's working time, agrees with the employee that the employee schedules his working time, or the average weekly working time does not exceed three hours in four consecutive weeks.

175. On-call duty and overtime work cannot be ordered or negotiated with an employee performing work based on an agreement on work performed outside the employment relationship.

176. In the case of significant personal obstacles at work (except for an obstacle at work due to finding a new place before the end of the employment relationship), which intervened in the time for which the employer determined the performance of the work, the employer is obliged to justify this absence of the employee from work, but to the employee for this time does not include compensation.

177. Based on concluded agreements, employees are obliged:

- carry out work responsibly and adequately and comply with the conditions agreed in the agreement;
- perform work personally;
- comply with legal regulations relating to the work they perform, in particular legal regulations for ensuring safety and health protection at work, comply with other regulations on the work they perform, in particular, rules for ensuring safety and health protection at work, with which they have been adequately familiarized;
- properly manage entrusted funds and guard and protect the employer's property from damage, loss, destruction and abuse;
- notify the employer in writing without undue delay of all changes that concern his employment relationship and are related to his person, in particular a change in his name, surname, permanent residence or temporary residence, address for delivery of documents, and if, with the employee's consent, the payment is transferred to the account in a bank or branch of a foreign bank, as well as a change of bank connection.

178. Based on the concluded agreements, the employer is obliged to:

- create appropriate working conditions for employees, ensuring proper and safe work performance, in particular providing the necessary essential resources, materials, tools and personal protective work equipment;
- familiarize employees with legal regulations and other regulations relating to the work they perform, in particular with regulations for ensuring safety and health protection at work;
- provide employees with the agreed remuneration for the work performed and comply with other agreed conditions; the employee's claims or other benefits for his benefit cannot be negotiated more favourably for the employee than the claims and benefits resulting from the employment relationship;
- keep records of concluded agreements on work performed outside the employment relationship in the order in which they were concluded;
- keep records of the working time of employees who perform work based on an agreement on part-time student work and work activities.

179. The employee is liable to the employer, with whom he agreed, for damage caused by the culpable breach of duties during the performance of work or directly related to it, in the same way as an employee in an employment relationship. Compensation for damage caused by negligence may not exceed a third of the actual damage. It may not be higher than a third of the remuneration agreed for the performance of this work, except in cases of liability for deficiency and loss of objects. The employer is liable to the employee for the damage suffered during work performance following the concluded agreement or in direct connection with it, just as it is for employees in an employment relationship.

180. The legislation recognizes three types of agreements:

– work performance agreement;
– agreement on part-time work of students;
– agreement to perform work.

1. Work Performance Agreement

181. The employer can conclude a work performance agreement with a natural person if the expected scope of work (tasks) for which this agreement is concluded does not exceed 350 hours in a calendar year. The scope of work between the employee and the employer cannot exceed 350 hours in a calendar year, even if the work is performed based on several agreements on the performance of work for the same employer. The labour law relationship established by the agreement on the performance of work is mainly characterized by the fact that:

– the work commitment takes the form of a work assignment;
– it is a commitment defined individually, which must be defined by the result of the work;
– the employer does not control the course of his work process;
– the primary way of terminating the agreement is by fulfilling the work task.

182. The agreement on the execution of work is concluded in writing; otherwise, it is invalid. The written agreement on the performance of the work is concluded no later than the day before the day of the start of the work performance. The agreement on the execution of work must contain the following:

– work task;
– agreed on remuneration for its execution;
– the time in which the work task is to be performed;
– scope of work if its scope does not follow directly from the definition of the work task.

183. The work must be completed within the agreed time; otherwise, the employer may withdraw from the agreement. The employee may withdraw from the agreement if he cannot perform the work task because the employer did not create the agreed working conditions for him; the employer is obliged to compensate the employee for the damage caused.

184. The remuneration for the performance of the work task is payable after the completion and submission of the work. The employer can appropriately reduce the remuneration after negotiation with the employee if the work performed does not correspond to the agreed conditions.

185. If the employee dies before completing the work task and the employer can use its results, the right to a reward commensurate with the work performed and compensation for purposefully incurred costs does not expire and becomes part of the inheritance.

2. Agreement on Part-Time Work of Students

186. The employer can conclude an agreement on part-time work for students with a natural person who has the status of a high school student or a full-time higher education student according to a special regulation and who has not reached the age of 26. The subject of agreements on part-time work for students is regularly recurring work defined by type, just like in an employment relationship. Work based on an agreement on part-time work for students can be performed no later than the end of the calendar year when the natural person turns 26.

187. Based on an agreement on part-time work of students, students can work up to twenty hours per week on average; the average of the maximum permissible range of working time is assessed for the entire period for which the agreement was concluded, but the most extended period is twelve months.

188. The employer is obliged to agree in writing; otherwise, it is invalid. An integral part of the agreement is the confirmation of the student's status according to the said agreement. The agreement must state the agreed work, agreed remuneration for work performed, decided on the range of working time and the period for which the agreement is concluded. The agreement on part-time work for students is concluded for a certain period, no more than twelve months.

189. The employer must issue the employee one copy of the student part-time work agreement. Confirmation of student status is an integral part of the agreement. However, this confirmation is not required if the agreement is concluded between the end of the high school studies or the end of the summer semester at the university and no later than the end of October of the same calendar year.

190. In contrast to the employment contract, the agreement can also agree on the way of its termination. However, immediate termination of the agreement can only be agreed for cases in which the employment relationship can be terminated immediately. If the method of termination does not follow directly from the concluded agreement, it can be terminated:

- by agreement of the participants on the agreed date or;
- unilaterally only by termination without giving a reason with a fifteen-day notice period, which begins on the day the written termination was delivered.

3. Agreement to Perform Work

191. The agreement to perform work forms the basis of a labour law relationship that is not an employment relationship. The subject of the agreement, however, is defined generically, as a result of which it resembles an employment contract in this characteristic. Based on an agreement, work activities can be carried out for a maximum of ten hours per week or 520 hours in a calendar year if it concerns the performance of seasonal work according to Annex no. 1b of the Labour Code; for these purposes, the work activity agreement is referred to as the work activity agreement for the performance of seasonal work. In the case of an agreement on employment for the performance of seasonal work, (a) the scope of employment also includes employment performed by the employee for the same employer based on another agreement on employment for the performance of seasonal work, (b) the average weekly working time during the duration of the agreement, at most however, in four months, it may not exceed forty hours.

192. The employer must conclude the employment agreement in writing; otherwise, it is invalid. The agreement must contain the agreed work, the agreed remuneration for the work performed, the agreed range of working time, and the period for which the agreement is concluded, which must be stated in the employment agreement. The employer must issue one copy of the employment agreement to the employee. An employment agreement can be concluded for a maximum of twelve months, except for an employment agreement for the performance of seasonal work, which can be concluded for a maximum of eight months. The termination method can be agreed upon in the agreement. Immediate termination of the agreement can only be agreed upon in cases where the employment relationship can be terminated immediately. When the method of termination does not follow directly from the concluded agreement, it can be terminated by the agreement of the participants on the agreed date and unilaterally only by termination without giving a reason with a fifteen-day notice period, which begins on the day the written termination was delivered.

193. Remuneration for work performed is due and must be paid no later than the end of the calendar month following the month in which the work was performed.

G. Other Agreements

1. Managerial Contracts

194. The Labour Code did not establish managerial labour contracts, which would enable a looser labour law relationship with top managers. Although, at present, the Labour Code does not regulate this contract type for the labour law relations of top management of particularly business subjects, managerial contracts are used on an ever broader scale.

195. From the legal theory's point of view, according to their specific content, management contracts can be considered either employment contracts or contractual types of commercial law. If the management contract covers the performance of dependent work and contains the requirements according to section 43 of the Labour Code, it is an employment contract establishing an employment relationship. If the management contract does not correspond to the content requirements of the employment contract according to section 43 of the Code and the performance of the work in terms of its content corresponds more to an independent business activity, the management contract is an atypical contract according to section 269 of the Commercial Code.

196. Therefore, the contract referred to by the participants as a management contract is the legal basis of the employment relationship only if, in terms of its content, it corresponds to the content requirements of the employment contract according to section 43 of the Labour Code.

197. In addition to the content framework of the essential contents of the employment contract, the content of the management contract may also include other agreements of the participants that do not conflict with the mandatory provisions of the Labour Code and other labour law regulations. The mentioned procedure is under section 44(1) of the Labour Code, according to which additional conditions that the participants are interested in, especially other material benefits, can be agreed upon in the employment contract.

2. Employment Contract with a Student of a Secondary Vocational School or a Student of a Vocational School

198. An employer may conclude a future employment contract with a student of a secondary vocational school or a vocational school no earlier than on the day the student turns 15 years old, the subject of which will be the employer's commitment to accept the student into employment after taking the final exam, matriculation exam or graduation exam ratio, and the student's commitment to become an employee of the employer. In this case, the trial period cannot be concluded. The agreed type of work must correspond to the qualification that the student will obtain by completing the course or study field. The contract on the future employment contract is concluded with the legal representative's consent; otherwise, it is invalid. The employer may refuse to conclude an employment contract if he does not have a suitable job for the student because his tasks are changing due to the student's medical incapacity to perform work corresponding to the qualification that the student obtained by completing the course or study field, or if the student has not met the conditions of classification and assessment and these conditions were agreed in the future employment contract.

199. Part of the contract on the future employment contract is the commitment of the student of a secondary vocational school or vocational school that, after taking the final exam, matriculation exam or graduation exam, he will remain employed by the employer for a certain period, no more than three years, or the employer may demand payment of costs from him, which he spent on preparing him for a profession in the teaching field or in the field of study. The period of stay in the employment relationship does not include the time of extraordinary service during a crisis or alternative service during war and martial law, maternity leave, paternity leave and parental leave, absence from work due to serving an unconditional prison sentence and detention, if it occurred to a valid conviction.

200. If, during the time during which the employee undertakes to remain employed with the employer, an employment relationship or a similar employment relationship with another employer arises, the employee's obligation is transferred to the new employer, who is obliged to reimburse the previous employer for a proportionate part of the costs of preparing the student for a profession in the classroom department or the field of study unless otherwise agreed. The employee is obliged to stay with the new employer in an employment relationship for a period that corresponds to the costs paid; if the employee does not remain with the new employer in an employment relationship, he is obliged to pay him a proportional part of these costs. During the duration of the obligation to remain in the employment relationship with the employer, the employee is obliged to notify the employer with whom he has the responsibility to stay in the employment relationship with the employer, creating an employment relationship or a similar employment relationship with another employer.

201. The costs are covered for the entire time the student prepares for a profession in a secondary vocational school or a vocational school. The proportional part of the costs is the part that corresponds to the unfulfilled time of the obligation to remain in the employment relationship with the employer. The Code also lists reasons for which the employer's responsibility to pay costs does not arise.

3. Agreement on the Temporary Assignment of an Employee

202. The relationship between the employer (temporary employment agency) and the user employer based on an agreement on the temporary assignment of an employee according to section 58a of the Labour Code is generally considered in the literature to be a commercial relationship. However, the content of this legal relationship is primarily determined by the regulation specified in the Labour Code. The employer or temporary employment agency can agree with the user employer on the temporary assignment of an employee in an employment relationship to perform work. The employer may agree with the user employer on the temporary assignment of an employee in an employment relationship only if the employer has objective operational reasons, and the assignment should be done as soon as possible, three months from the date of the employment relationship.

203. The temporary assignment agreement concluded between the employer or temporary employment agency and the user employer must contain:

(a) name and surname, date and place of birth and place of permanent residence of the temporarily assigned employee;
(b) the type of work that the temporarily assigned employee will perform, including prerequisites for health fitness for work, mental fitness for work, or other prerequisites according to a particular law, if they are required for the performance of this type of work;
(c) the period for which the temporary assignment was agreed upon;
(d) place of performance of work;
(e) the day the temporarily assigned employee starts work at the user employer;
(f) working conditions, including wage conditions and employment conditions of the temporarily assigned employee, which must be at least as favourable as for a comparable employee of the user employer;
(g) the conditions under which the employee or the user employer can terminate the temporary assignment before the expiration of the temporary assignment period;
(h) number of the decision and date of issue of the decision by which the temporary employment agency was issued a permit to carry out the activities of the temporary employment agency.

204. The agreement between the employer or temporary employment agency and the user employer on the temporary assignment of employees must be concluded in writing; otherwise, it is invalid.

II. Form and Content

205. The Labour Code defines the requirements for the formal and content features of the employment contract. It also enables the parties to the employment relationship to agree on further details and working conditions within its dispositive (non-mandatory) provisions. The agreed working conditions must not contradict generally binding legal regulations and mandatory labour law standards. A substantial part of their legal obligations results from the employment contract and binding legal restrictions, the collective agreement, or the employer's work regulations, with which the employee must be familiar.

206. Under section 42(1) of the Labour Code, an employment relationship is established by a written employment contract between the employer and the employee, and the employer must provide the employee with a copy of the employment contract. It means that employment contracts must be concluded in writing. However, even if section 42(1) of the Labour Code requires that the employment contract be concluded in writing, according to section 17(2) of the Labour Code, an employment contract is also valid if it is concluded verbally or its conclusion can be implied. The omission of a written form of the employment contract does not invalidate the employment relationship (due to the protection of the employee), and therefore, oral or tacitly concluded employment contracts are also valid.

207. An employment relationship is established based on an employment contract concluded validly if the employee and employer agree on the 'significant essentials' specified under section 43(1) of the Labour Code, which include:

- employer and employee identification data;
- type of work and its brief characteristics;
- place of work performance (municipality, part of a village or other designated place) or places of work performance, if there are more, or the rule that the employee determines the place of work performance;
- commencing day of work;
- salary conditions.

208. It is invalid when the employment contract does not contain the above significant terms.

209. Regarding the employee's legal status, the type of work defined in the labour contract is also of substantial significance because, in principle, the employer must not change the type of work unilaterally beyond the defined framework. The Labour Code does not specify in detail how the type of work should be defined in the employment contract; in principle, it is valid that it can be a narrower but also a broader definition. It can also be cumulative or alternatively agreed types of work. The employer's discretion depends directly on the definition of the type of work and its characteristics, i.e., the scope of his rights towards the employee. The broader the definition of the type of work in the labour contract, the broader the employer's dispositive power. In addition to the employment contract, the extent of the employer's discretion is also completed by a number of the employer's internal organizational regulations or collective agreements. Besides defining the type of work, the Labour Code requires a brief description of the work in the employment contract. It should be a brief description of the working activities to be performed by the employee.

210. By stipulating the type of work in the employment contract, we must understand the definition of the work activities that the employee is to perform and the content of his work commitment. However, we also recognize the job description, which represents a more detailed description of the work (work activities) that the employee is required to perform within the agreed type of work. With reference to the job description, the employer cannot demand from the employee without further work outside of the agreed type of work.

211. A specific location can be agreed upon as the place of performance of work, such as the address of the employer's workplace, the employer's registered office, or, if the type of work allows it (the work is not performed in one place – taxi drivers, employees in delivery) and the boundaries of the municipal cadastre, parts of the village or another agreed place. The employer and the employee can also agree on several places of work performance as long as it realistically corresponds to the type of work and the employee's tasks. The place of performance of work agreed between the employer and employee can be in Slovakia or abroad, or a particular work performance method can be agreed upon, such as telework.

212. According to the applicable legislation, the employer is not entitled to change the place of work unilaterally agreed in the employment contract for any reason except by mutual agreement of the parties to the employment contract.

213. The day of commencement of work is of substantial significance for the commencement of the employment relationship. Under section 46 of the Labour Code, an employment relationship commences on the day agreed upon in the employment contract as the commencing day of work. The Labour Code does not contain any specific regulation on how to agree on the day of starting work. The day of commencing work can be determined by specifying a calendar day or in another explicit way that leaves no doubt. Based on the mentioned, employment is tied to the agreed day of starting work, not the day when the employee performs work for the first time. The employment relationship will be established even if the work is not performed on the agreed day – the employment relationship also commences when the employee does not start work on the agreed date if prevented from doing so by an obstacle to work of which, however, he is bound to notify the employer within a week; otherwise, the employer is entitled to withdraw from the labour contract.

214. As for the negotiation of wage conditions in the employment contract, the Labour Code does not specify this negotiation in more detail. Thus, the basic rule applies that the agreement must be under the general requirements for the validity of legal acts, such as sufficiently specific, understandable, made freely and without error, or an agreement by the law. However, concerning other provisions of the Labour Code, we can derive the basic rules for negotiating wage conditions in the employment contract, such as the wage must not be negotiated below the minimum wage level or minimum wage entitlement, the salary must always be agreed in money, or the salary must not be agreed below the level of information about the salary published in the job advertisement. If the wage conditions are agreed upon in a collective agreement, it is sufficient to refer to the relevant provisions of the collective agreement in the employment contract; otherwise, it is enough to refer to the relevant provisions of the Labour Code or a special regulation. When the wage conditions are not agreed upon in the employment contract, and the collective agreement provisions referred to in the contract have expired. In that case, the wage conditions agreed in the collective agreement are considered the conditions agreed in the employment contract until new wage conditions are agreed in the collective agreement or the employment contract, but no more than twelve months.

215. The provisions of the employment contract or other agreement between the employer and the employee, by which the employee undertakes to maintain confidentiality about his working conditions, including wage conditions and employment conditions, and which also prohibit the employee from performing other gainful activities outside the working time specified by the employer, are invalid;

this does not affect the limitation of other gainful activity after the end of employment based on the employee's agreement with the employer or according to special regulations.

216. Other than 'significant essentials' that the employer and employee are interested in, especially other material benefits (e.g., the conditions for the use of company vehicles, mobile phones or notebooks by the employee), can be agreed upon in the employment contract. An employment contract usually also includes an agreement on a trial period or an agreement on part-time work. Other possible parts of the employment contract are conditional and severance conditions. Under section 57 of the Labour Code, an employee can be sent for a business trip outside the municipality of his/her regular place of performance of work or permanent residence only for the necessary period and only with the employee's consent. Therefore, employment contracts often contain the employee's consent to being sent on business trips.

III. Ability to Conclude a Employment Contract

217. The principal prerequisite for the valid conclusion of an employment contract consists of the legal capacity of the potential employer and the potential employee.

218. The legal construction of a potential employee's capacity for legal acts in labour law is qualitatively different from civil law. For an employee's employment legal capacity, it is typical that all elements of employment legal capacity arise at the exact moment. The ability of a natural person to have rights and obligations as an employee in labour relations and acquire these rights and assume these obligations through his legal acts arises on the day when the natural person reaches 15 years of age. However, the following applies:

- the employer may not agree as the day of starting work a day that would precede the day when the natural person (employee) finishes compulsory school attendance;
- an employee can agree on material responsibility at the earliest on the day he turns 18;
- legal prohibitions for juvenile employees to perform specific jobs.

219. Even though the legal status of the legal representatives of minor employees cannot affect the validity of the employment relationship created in this way, the Labour Code imposes in several provisions on the employer the obligation to inform the legal representatives of minor employees not only about the creation of the employment relationship but mainly about its termination, especially in cases of its unilateral termination from by the employer.

220. The work of a natural person under the age of 15 or older than 15 until the end of compulsory schooling is prohibited. These natural persons can perform light work that by its nature and scope does not threaten their health, safety, further development or school attendance only when performing or participating in cultural performances and artistic performances, sports events, advertising activities, activities other than those listed, if applicable for a natural person older than 15 years until the end of compulsory schooling. The performance of light work is permitted at the employer's request by the relevant labour inspectorate in agreement with the relevant public health authority. The permit shall specify the number of hours and the conditions under which light work may be performed. The relevant labour inspectorate will withdraw the permit if the conditions of the permit are not respected.

221. An employer can conclude an employment contract with a minor only after a previous medical examination of the minor. In order to conclude an employment contract with a minor, the employer must request a statement from his legal representative.

222. The employer's legal capacity is codified differently depending on whether the employer is a legal entity or a natural person. A legal entity acquires employment legal capacity if its civil law grants it the status of a legal entity and if it employs at least one employee. The employer – a natural person acquires the capacity for legal acts by birth and the capacity for legal acts by reaching the age of majority.

223. The freedom of choice of the employer for the conclusion of an employment contract in the present state de lege lata is partly restricted by the legislator by the quota system. Under Act no. 5/2004 Coll. on Employment Services, every employer employing more than twenty employees is obliged to use at least 3.2% of disabled citizens if disabled employees are registered with the relevant Labour Office (section 63 of the Act on Employment Services) or the employer is obliged to place an order to fulfil the mandatory share of employment of citizens with disabilities (section 64 of the Act on Services in Employment). If the employer does not satisfy this obligation, it is necessary to pay a charge for each disabled employee who is not employed (section 65 of the Act on Employment Services).

IV. Procedure to Conclude an Employment Contract

224. The employment contract as a legal act must fulfil all requirements laid down by the Civil Code for a valid legal act. The employment contract is concluded as soon as the contracting parties have agreed on its content. The content of the employment contract is formed based on the Labour Code and the contracting parties' will. The process of concluding an employment contract is primarily governed by the general rules of private law contained in the Civil Code. The Civil Code regulates almost the entire procedure for concluding an employment contract. These are individual stages – offer, acceptance, being bound by the offer, and revocation.

225. Under the provisions of section 41 of the Labour Code, the employer has certain information obligations towards the job applicant prior to the conclusion of the contract. The employer must acquaint the natural person with the rights and obligations resulting from the employment contract and the working conditions and wage conditions under which he is to perform the work. When a special legal regulation requires medical fitness for work, mental fitness for work or another prerequisite for the performance of work, the employer may conclude an employment contract only with a physical person who is medically fit or mentally fit for this work or with a natural person who meets another prerequisite. An employer may only require information related to the work to be performed from a natural person applying for a first job. The employer may require a person already employed to submit a work report and a certificate of employment. The employer may not demand from a natural person information about pregnancy, family relationships, or integrity except for work that requires integrity according to a particular regulation or if the requirement of integrity is required by the nature of the work that the natural person is to perform, about political affiliation, trade union affiliation and religious affiliation. If the employer violates the above obligations at the beginning of the employment relationship, the natural person has the right to an adequate monetary compensation.

226. A natural person is obliged to inform the employer about the facts that prevent work performance or that could cause harm to the employer and about the length of working time at another employer if it is minor.

227. Aiming for public transparency in the selection, legal regulation within the civil service, and senior employees in the case of the Act on the Performance of Work in the Public Interest has special rules.

V. Faults in the Content of the Employment Contract

228. It is invalid if an employment contract does not contain the 'significant essentials' ('essentialia negotii'). In practice, an employment contract is flawed if the terms agreed upon by the parties conflict with mandatory labour law provisions; the parties' contractual freedom can only be exercised within the framework of mandatory provisions. According to the Labour Code, such actions by the contracting parties are considered invalid – a case of absolute invalidity of the employment contract. If an employment contract is invalid, it has no legal authority to establish an employment relationship. A de facto employment relationship arises when an individual starts working for an employer based on such a contract. If the employment contract is not validly agreed upon, an employment relationship, as a set of mutually related rights and obligations, cannot arise. It is only a partial factual relationship (not sanctioned by law). Court decisions on de facto employment relationships indicate that such a relationship arises when the employer and employee have not agreed on the essential conditions of the employment contract.

229. If an employment contract has other defects, it is considered valid except for the part that is invalid due to the defects, provided it can be separated from the valid parts of the contract.

230. A common fault in employment contracts is an error on the part of one of the parties. According to labour law regulations, an employer or employee may withdraw from an employment contract if they acted under a mistaken belief about a circumstance without which the contract would not have been concluded, and the other party was aware of this mistake. Withdrawal from the employment contract is also possible through mutual agreement between the contracting parties. However, the employer can only withdraw from the employment contract before the employee starts work. After the employee begins work, the employer is no longer entitled to withdraw from the concluded employment contract. Such an employment contract can only be terminated by the legal methods established in section 59 of the Labour Code.

Chapter 2. Rights and Duties of the Parties During the Employment

231. The employment relationship is distinctive in that it encompasses obligations not only agreed upon in the employment contract but also those mandated by universally binding legal regulations, such as the Labour Code, workplace safety and health regulations, and the employer's internal policies. According to the Labour Code, which provides a comprehensive definition of labour obligations, the employer is required, from the inception of the employment relationship, to assign work to the employee in line with the employment contract, remunerate the employee for the work performed, establish the necessary conditions for the successful fulfilment of the employee's duties, and adhere to other working conditions stipulated by legal regulations, the collective agreement, or the employment contract. Concurrently, from the commencement of the employment relationship, the employee is obligated to perform the work personally, follow the employer's instructions, adhere to the employment contract, work within the designated hours, and maintain labour discipline.

§1. Duties of the Employee

232. The duties of the employee are enshrined in several provisions of the Labour Code; they are defined on the one hand in general (section 47 of the Labour Code), on the other hand as primary duties of employees (section 81 of the Labour Code), primary duties of senior employees (section 82 of the Labour Code) and other duties (e.g., the employee's obligation to take action against imminent damage). Differentiation does not affect the legal nature of the employee's obligations, as they are all legal. An employee's culpable breach of duty can affect the legal qualification of the intensity of a violation of labour discipline, such as a grave or less serious violation of labour discipline, to which the Labour Code attaches substantially different legal consequences. Regarding personal scope, the complex legal obligations apply to all employees.

I. Obligation to Perform Work

233. The employee is obliged to work appropriately and adequately. However, the employee's work obligation is a multidimensional legal obligation. The proper work performance can be considered the performance from which the employer is expected to benefit. The performance of an employee where the work is submitted after the deadline, where the qualitative or quantitative requirements of the work are not met, cannot be considered proper work performance. However, the employer cannot transfer business risk to the employee. The employee must work in adequate conditions for proper work performance. The employee is not obliged to perform work that could endanger his health, even if this work is agreed upon in the employment contract. If such a situation were to occur in practice, the employer would be obliged to transfer the employee to another job unilaterally. The employee is also not obliged to work if there is an obstacle in work, which the employer is obliged to accept and, in some cases, to compensate with wages in the amount of the employee's average earnings.

II. Obligation to Comply with Employer's Instructions

234. According to the Labour Code, the employee's obligation to comply with the instructions of superiors expressly applies only to the fulfilment of instructions of superiors that are under legal regulations. It follows from the above that fulfilling the instructions of superior employees, which conflict with legal regulations, does not constitute the content of work discipline. A typical employer instruction is the job description, which aims to specify the type of work agreed upon in the employment contract. Regardless of the differences in the legal nature of the instructions, each employer's instruction should be according to the legal regulations and not exceed the employee's workload.

235. Instructions must primarily be issued within the authorized person's competence limits. When the employer's instruction exceeds the content of the employer's disposition authorization, contrary to the agreed type of work in the employment contract, it falls into the sphere of illegality. It is not exercising the employer's right; therefore, the employee's legal obligation to fulfil it cannot be correlated. Violating this only apparent obligation by the employee is not a violation of work discipline. Therefore, the employee is not obliged to comply with the employer's instructions, which conflicts with the legal regulations. He cannot even be legally disabled for failing to comply with an illegal instruction.

III. The Obligation to Be at the Workplace at the Beginning of Working Time, to Use the Working Time for Work and to Leave It Only after the End of Working Time

236. The employee's primary obligation is also his obligation to be at the workplace at the beginning of the working time and to leave it only after the end of the working time. At the same time, he is obliged to use the working time to perform his work. The employer determines the working time. Regarding content, the employee's obligation to be available to the employer as an essential prerequisite for work performance is not only an obligation to show up at the workplace; the multidimensionality of the employee's duty also lies in the obligation to be present at the workplace in a state of ability and capability to perform work. A violation of work discipline would be, for example, an employee not coming to work due to personal indisposition after drinking alcohol.

237. The obligation of the employee enshrined in the provisions of the Labour Code applies not only to the full use of working time but also to the full use of production means for the performance of assigned work. By violating this essential duty, the employee simultaneously violates another of his primary duties: not acting contrary to the employer's legitimate interests.

IV. Obligation to Observe Legality

238. The content of the Labour Code diction reflects the necessity of observing legality in labour relations. It includes two areas of the employee's legal obligations.

239. The first range of obligations is related to compliance with generally binding legal regulations concerning the content of the work performed by the employee. The employer must not be familiar with these generally binding legal regulations. Properly performing the employee's work according to the employment contract inevitably requires knowledge of generally binding legal regulations. Ignorance of them would not allow for proper work performance. Therefore, concerning generally binding legal regulations relating to the content of the employee's work, ignorance of them cannot be excused.

240. However, the employee's job duties relating to his work do not only result from generally binding legal regulations but also from other regulations that are not generally binding. The Labour Code conditions the obligation to comply with them on the legal obligation of the employer to familiarize the employees with them.

V. Obligation to Adhere to Prescribed Treatment During Temporary Incapacity for Work

241. This legal obligation of the employee is specific in that the employee violates it not while performing work but during temporary incapacity for work, when he receives income compensation for temporary incapacity from work, by violating the treatment regimen determined by the attending physician. In order to detect a violation of this obligation, the employer must extend the legal obligations of senior employees in employment contracts or work regulations beyond their workplace, for example, limited by the office, but should legally oblige them to check the fulfilment of this legal obligation in the field as well.

242. The treatment regime is defined by the provision of section 2 paragraph 11 of Act no. 576/2004 Coll. on Health Care as a person's lifestyle to support treatment determined by the attending physician. This conceptual definition is part of the regulation of the provision of health care. However, it is not entirely sufficient to provide income compensation in the event of an employee's temporary incapacity for work and sick leave (or the duration of the entitlement to the payment of these benefits). In addition to the lifestyle prescribed by the doctor to support the treatment, these are all the instructions (e.g., rules related to rehabilitation) and the doctor's recommendations aimed at stabilizing or improving the state of health and ultimately leading to the restoration of work capacity (employee).

VI. Obligation to Handle the Employer's Resources Properly and Protect His Property; Obligation Not to Act Against the Employer's Justified Interests

243. Among the employer's legitimate interests, we can include, for example, compliance with work discipline by employees, efficient use of working time, quality work performance, and protection of the employer's property, including cost minimization or prevention of possible damages and leakage of information. Acting contrary to the employer's legitimate interests may have a criminal dimension for the employee in addition to labour law. The obligation not to act contrary to the employer's legitimate interests applies to rank-and-file employees and senior employees. Compared to the substantive scope of the Labour Code governing the performance of competitive activities, it allows the employer to penalize the employee also in the case of other activities that are not the employee's gainful activity or cannot be qualified as a gainful activity that could have a competitive nature concerning the employer's subject matter.

244. The employee is also obliged to properly manage the funds entrusted to him by the employer. This obligation applies not only to funds entrusted by an agreement on material responsibility or an agreement on responsibility for the loss of entrusted objects but also to funds entrusted by the employer without such a special agreement. Proper management can be considered the actions of an employee who uses the employer's resources to perform work as specified by the operating instructions and technological procedures to the extent that it is for the employer's benefit. The employee's obligation to protect the employer's property from loss, destruction and misuse is related to managed management. Therefore, as part of proper management, care and concern for protecting the employer's property is required from the employee's side, which may, among other things, consist of its careful and reasonable use.

VII. Obligation to Maintain Confidentiality about Facts that he Learned During the Performance of His Job and Which Cannot be Disclosed to Other Persons in the Interest of the Employer

245. The obligation to maintain confidentiality about facts that the employee learned during the job performance and that cannot be disclosed to other persons in the employer's interest protects the employer's interests.

246. The employee's duty of confidentiality regarding facts that he learned during the performance of his job and which cannot be disclosed to other persons in the employer's interest does not apply to such facts that are the subject of notification of corruption or other anti-social activity. For violation of secrets, Act no. 54/2019 Coll. on the Protection of Whistleblowers of an Anti-social Activity does not consider the notification of a protected employee (whistleblower) about anti-social activity.

247. The facts about which the obligation of confidentiality applies on the part of the employee are the facts that the employee learned during the job performance and which cannot be disclosed to other persons in the employer's interest. Thus, the content of the legal obligation of confidentiality does not consist of all the facts the employee learned during the job performance. The scope of the mentioned facts can be significantly broader than the content of a trade secret, according to section 17 of the Commercial Code. It will be primarily in the employer's interest to enshrine the scope of facts that the employee must keep confidential and that cannot be communicated to other persons in his internal regulations. The employer has a relatively broad legal scope for their substantive definition. However, the scope of these facts must not conflict with the Basic Principles of the Labour Code, especially with the principle of exercising rights and obligations following good morals. According to section 17 of the Commercial Code, in connection with a trade secret, it must be such facts of a commercial, production or technical nature related to the company, which have a real or at least potential or immaterial value, are not ordinarily available, should be kept secret according to the will of the entrepreneur, and the entrepreneur accordingly ensures their secrecy. Violating a trade secret is unfair competition and can result in an employment relationship. Protection against the violation of trade secrets belongs to the entrepreneur even after the end of the employment relationship, but it does not form the content of the employment relationship. However, if it is not a trade secret that the employee acquired from the employer-entrepreneur in the course of the employment relationship, the knowledge that the employee acquired from the employer during the duration of the employment relationship does not enjoy legal protection and the employee can also use it for his own business, even if he creates a competitive environment with the former employer. Because the existing legal status restricts the employee after the end of the employment relationship in business activities identical or similar to the object of activity of his former employer, it simultaneously allows for their contractual restriction.

VIII. Prohibition of Competitive Activities by the Employee

248. In order to protect the legitimate (economic) interests of the employer, section 83 of the Labour Code restricts the employee from performing competitive activities. Limiting the performance of another employee's activity is, in essence, a clarification or a continuation of the employee's primary obligation not to act contrary to the employer's legitimate interests. The primary obligation not to act contrary to the employer's legitimate interests is broadly defined. It applies not only to the competitive earning activity of the employee but to any action contrary to the employer's legitimate interests. Violation of the prohibition of competition also automatically results in a violation of the duty to refrain from acting to the disadvantage of the employer, but the reverse, logically, does not apply.

249. An employee may, in addition to his work carried out in an employment relationship, perform other gainful activities that are competitive with the subject of the employer's activity only with the prior written consent of the employer. This legal provision defines the scope of the prohibition. Based on the legal definition, the decisive legal terms defining the framework of competitive activity are the gainful activity of the employee and the subject of the employer's activity. The scope of the term gainful activity of an employee must be perceived as any active activity of the employee, regardless of its contractual basis, from which he can reasonably expect income. The legal basis of the employee's performance of another gainful activity is not decisive; it can be another employment relationship (especially for shorter working time), an agreement on work performed outside the employment relationship, or the performance of business activities. The prohibition of competition is linked to the subject of the employer's activity.

250. The employer's consent is not required to perform scientific, pedagogical, publishing, tutorial, lecturing, literary and artistic activities.

IX. Obligation to Enhance the Employee's Qualifications for the Performance of the Agreed Type of Work

251. According to section 153(3) of the Labour Code, the employee must deepen his qualifications to perform the work continuously agreed upon in the employment contract. The employer has the right to order employees to participate in deepening qualifications, which is considered work performance, and the employee is rewarded with a salary. The extent of the employee's legal obligation to improve professional qualifications is determined by the type of work agreed upon in the employment contract.

X. General Obligation Duty and Notification Duty of the Employee, Duty to Take Action Against Impending Damage

252. The employee is obliged to act in such a way that there is no threat to life, health, damage to property or its destruction, nor unjust enrichment. If there is a risk of damage, the employee is obliged to notify the senior employee. Employees must take action if an intervention is needed to avert the damage threatening the employer. An employee does not have this obligation if critical circumstances prevent him from doing so or if he would expose himself, other employees, or close persons to grave danger. If the employee discovers he does not have the necessary working conditions, he must notify the senior employee. Failing to fulfil the employee's preventive duty to notify or take action, provided that other liability conditions are met, the employee's liability can be established even though the damage was caused by other causes not attributable to the employee. The employer proves all liability assumptions.

XI. Essential Obligations of Senior Employees

253. Senior employees have, in addition to general primary duties, rights and obligations resulting from their position as a senior employee. Who is a senior employee is determined by section 9(3) of the Labour Code so that the senior employees of the employer are employees who, at individual levels of the employer's management, are authorized to determine and impose work tasks on the employer's subordinate employees, organize, manage and control their work and give them binding instructions for that purpose. In addition to the primary duties according to section 81 of the Labour Code, a senior employee is obliged to:

(a) manage and control the work of employees;
(b) create favourable working conditions and ensure safety and health protection at work;
(c) ensure remuneration of employees under generally binding legal regulations, collective agreements and employment contracts and observe the principle of providing equal pay for equal work or work of equal value according to section 119a;
(d) create favourable conditions for increasing the professional level of employees and for satisfying their social needs;
(e) ensure that there are no violations of work discipline;
(f) ensure timely and effective measures to protect the employer's property.

XII. Obligations of the Employee Resulting from Special Laws

254. A wide range of employees' legal obligations also result from special laws, especially Act no. 124/2006 Coll. on Safety and Health Protection at Work. Provision section 12 of this imposes, for example, on an employee:

- the obligation to cooperate with the employer and the employee representative for safety to the extent necessary to enable them to fulfil their obligations in ensuring safety and health protection at work and the tasks imposed by the relevant labour inspectorate or supervisory authority;
- use the assigned personal protective equipment in the designated manner;
- participate in other training provided by the employer in the interests of safety and health at work and submit to verification of his knowledge;
- undergo preventive medical examinations;
- report without undue delay deficiencies in the field of safety and health protection at work to a senior employee or, as necessary, a safety technician, employee representative for safety, the relevant labour inspectorate or the relevant supervisory body, which could endanger safety and health protection at work, incredibly immediate and severe threats to life and health, and the extent possible participate in their elimination;
- not to consume alcoholic beverages, narcotics and psychotropic substances at workplaces and on the premises of the employer and during working time and outside these workplaces; not to come to work under their influence;

- undergo an examination carried out by the employer or the relevant state administration body to determine whether the employee is under the influence of alcohol, narcotics or psychotropic substances;
- comply with the designated smoking ban at workplaces;
- participate in rehabilitation stays.

XIII. Obligations of the Employee When Performing Work in the Public Interest

255. The legal obligations also apply to employees performing work in the public interest. A significantly more expansive range of legal obligations applies to these employees compared to the labour regulation of the Labour Code. In particular, these are obligations:

- to act and make decisions impartially and refrain from doing anything that could jeopardize trust in the impartiality and objectivity of actions and decisions when performing work in the public interest;
- to maintain confidentiality about facts that he learned while performing work in the public interest and which cannot be communicated to other persons, even after the end of the employment relationship;
- not to misuse information acquired in connection with the performance of work in the public interest for one's benefit or the benefit of close persons or other natural or legal persons;
- refrain from actions that could lead to a conflict of interests;
- to refrain from actions resulting from unauthorized promises or obligations binding on the employer;
- notify a superior, senior employee, or a law enforcement agency of the loss or damage to property owned by the employer or under the employer's management;
- prohibition of business for a member of a statutory body, as well as the performance of other gainful activities and membership in management, control or supervisory bodies of legal entities that carry out business activities with the exceptions in the Act on the Performance of Work in the Public Interest.

256. In addition to these implicitly stated obligations, an employee working in the performance of work in the public interest has, if he has the status of a senior employee:

- file a property declaration;
- jobs of a defined category of senior employees can only be filled through a selection process, and the applicant's ranking is legally binding for the statutory representative.

257. Compared with the labour regulation of the Labour Code, the employee's duty of confidentiality applies not only to the manager but also to the rank-and-file employee for the duration of the employment relationship.

§2. Duties of the Employer

I. Basic Obligations

A. *Obligation to Assign Work to the Employee*

258. When assigning work to an employee, the employer is bound by the type of work defined in the employment contract since determining the type of work in the employment contract is an obligatory part. The employer is not authorized to assign another type of work to the employee unless he has expressly agreed on this with the employee, e.g., in the form of an agreement on changing working conditions (section 54 of the Labour Code). The employer is obliged to assign work in such a way that the employee has the opportunity to perform it during working time. Non-assignment of work is an obstacle for the employer (section 142 of the Labour Code), and conversely, assigning work beyond the established working time constitutes overtime work, where the Labour Code sets several restrictions.

259. The assignment of work must correspond to the agreed type of work. If the agreed type of work was cancelled, e.g., after dismissal from the position, the employer cannot unilaterally assign work that falls under the agreed type of work. In the absence of the type of work that the employee should perform (after dismissal from the position), the provisions of the Labour Code regulating the obligation of the employee to perform work personally according to the employment contract during the specified working time and to observe work discipline and to be at the workplace at the beginning of working time are inapplicable, use the working time for work and leave it only after the end of working time.

B. *Obligation to Pay the Employee a Salary*

260. Salary represents the reward of the employer – monetary payment or payment of monetary value paid to the employee for the work performed. The condition for entitlement to wages is the performance of work. The employer must pay the employee wages correctly and on time (sections 129 and 130 of the Labour Code). In contrast, delay in payment of wages may result in the employee's right to immediate termination of employment (section 69 of the Labour Code).

C. *Obligation to Create Conditions for the Performance of Employee Work Tasks*

261. A prerequisite for the employee's ability to perform work is to have created the conditions for performing work tasks. The creation of conditions for the fulfilment of work tasks by the employer is closely related to the protection of work and its safety. The catalogue of the employer's obligations follows the Labour Code and the special Act no. 124/2006 Coll. on Safety and Health Protection at Work and other generally binding legal regulations. Safety and health protection at work is a state of working conditions that exclude or minimize the impact of dangerous and harmful factors of the work process and work environment on employees' health. In other words, the employer must create such conditions for the performance of work tasks, in which the influence of dangerous and harmful factors of the work process on employees' health is at least minimized. The employer is obliged to provide the employees with a safe workplace, work tools, and equipment appropriate for the nature of the work that the employees perform. At the same time, the employer is obliged to provide employees with personal protective work equipment according to special regulations. The employer bears the costs associated with creating a safe working environment or providing personal protective work equipment; these costs must not be transferred to the employees.

262. Among the many obligations of the employer in the field of safety and health protection imposed by the Labour Code, it is necessary to mention the obligation not to consider it a violation of work discipline if an employee refuses to perform the work he is in charge of if he justifiably believes that he is endangering his life or health or the life or health of others.

D. *Obligation to Acquaint the Employee with the Work Regulations, the Collective Agreement and the Legal Regulations Applicable to the Work Performed by the Employee upon Starting Employment*

263. In addition to generally binding legal regulations, the employer must comply with those rights and obligations regarding working conditions that are agreed upon individually with the employees in the employment contract or collective agreement. The content can include various benefits and advantages provided to employees (e.g., an extra day of paid leave, a higher number of leave days, higher allowances for working overtime, at night or on holidays, transport allowance). When a higher-level collective agreement covers the employer, such an employer must guarantee its employees the scope of rights and obligations agreed upon in a higher-level collective agreement.

II. Information Obligations of the Employer

A. *Obligation to Inform Employees about Working Conditions and Employment Conditions*

264. Under section 47a of the Labour Code, the employer is obliged to provide the employee with written information about his working conditions and terms of employment, at least to the extent of the following data, if the employment contract does not contain them:

(a) the method of determining the place of performance of work or the determination of the principal place of performance of work if several places of performance of work are agreed upon in the employment contract;

(b) established weekly working time, information on the method and rules for scheduling working time, including the expected working days and compensation period, the extent and time of the provision of breaks at work, continuous daily rest and continuous rest during the week, rules for overtime work, including wage concessions for overtime work;
(c) amount of leave or method of determining it;
(d) salary maturity and salary payment, including payment dates;
(e) the rules for termination of employment, the length of the notice period or the method of determining it, if it is not known at the time of providing the information, the deadline for filing a lawsuit to determine the invalidity of the termination of employment;
(f) the right to professional training provided by the employer, if provided, and its scope.

265. The employer will provide the employee with information within seven days from the beginning of the employment relationship if it concerns data according to letters a), b) and d), or within four weeks from the beginning of the employment relationship if it concerns data according to letters c), e) and f).

266. The employer can provide information as a reference to the relevant provision of the Labour Code, a particular regulation, or the relevant provision of the collective agreement.

B. *The Obligation to Acquaint the Employee with the Work Regulations, the Collective Agreement and the Legal Regulations Applicable to the Work Performed by the Employee upon Starting Employment*

267. When an employee starts work, the employee has the right to be informed by the employer not only of the employer's internal documents, such as the work rules or collective agreement, but also has the right to be informed by the employer of the legal regulations applicable to the work performed by the employee. This right of the employee corresponds to the obligation of the employer to provide information, the fulfilment of which the employer must be able to prove if necessary. Under section 7 of Act no. 124/2006 Coll. on Safety and Health Protection at Work, the employer must regularly, comprehensibly and demonstrably familiarize each employee with the employer's internal and safety regulations. Although it may seem that the Labour Code does not prescribe the very form of fulfilling the obligation, the employer must be able to demonstrate not only proper and demonstrable familiarization of the employee with the regulations but also their knowledge on the part of the employee and the continuous requirement and control of compliance with safety and health protection work. Only in this case can he be released from liability for damage in the event of an occupational accident.

C. Obligation to Familiarize the Employee with the Legal Regulations and Other Regulations for Ensuring Safety and Health Protection at Work, Which the Employee Must Comply with During His Work

268. In addition to familiarizing the employee with the regulations relating to the work performed, the employer is also obliged to familiarize the employee with the regulations relating to ensuring safety and health protection at work, which the employee must comply with.

D. Obligation to Submit Reports on Agreed New Employment Relationships to Employee Representatives Within the Time Limits Agreed With Him

269. The employer has to submit reports on agreed new working conditions to employee representatives. This obligation, therefore, concerns those employers with employee representatives. The scope (by law, this obligation applies to new employment relationships), deadlines (quarterly, half-yearly, annually), and the method of submission (e.g., in writing within fifteen days from the end of the period) will be agreed upon by the employer directly with the employee representatives, Labour Code in more detail does not regulate these obligations.

III. Further Obligations of the Employer

270. Further obligations of employers include the obligation to take care of employees, which includes increasing the professional qualifications of employees, ensuring their safety and health at work, providing food for employees, and many others.

271. The employer's care for employees also includes regenerating their force to maintain their performance and achieve employee satisfaction. The employer entity's care is reflected in the employer's obligation to provide the employee with a recreation allowance (section 152a of the Labour Code) as long as all legal conditions from this provision are met. The employee's allowance for employee recreation can be used by a child and another person living with the employee in the same household who participates in recreation with the employee.

272. In addition, under the conditions set out in sections 152b and 152c of the Labour Code, the employer can also provide employees with an allowance for a child's sports activities and state-supported rental housing.

A. Caring for the Working Conditions and Living Conditions of Employees

273. To improve the work culture and working environment, the employer creates appropriate working conditions and takes care of the appearance and arrangement of workplaces, social facilities and personal hygiene facilities. The employer establishes, maintains and increases social facilities, personal hygiene facilities and, according to special regulations, medical facilities for employees.

274. In addition, the employer is obliged to ensure the safe storage, in particular, of outerwear and personal items that employees usually carry to work, as well as the usual means of transport if employees use them to travel to and from work, except for motor vehicles. In agreement with the employee representatives, the employer may define the conditions under which he will also be responsible for the safekeeping of motor vehicles. The employer is also obligated to all other persons if they are active with him at his workplace.

B. Obligation to Provide Catering for Employees

275. Providing catering for employees is a vital part of the employer's social policy. The employer is obliged to provide meals for all employees, which means that this obligation arises when employing at least one employee and if all the conditions for providing meals are met. The employer is obliged to provide meals, regardless of whether the work is performed during the day, at night, during rest days, or on holidays, whether it is home work, telework or work from home (home office). This obligation also applies to the employer and the temporary employment agency in the case of the temporary assignment of an employee to perform work. The time criterion for the emergence of entitlement to catering provision or a financial allowance for meals for an employee is the performance of work lasting more than four hours within a work shift. If the work shift lasts more than eleven hours, the employer can provide additional catering or an additional financial allowance for catering. The employer is not obliged to provide meals for employees sent on a business trip who have not worked more than four hours at their regular workplace, as well as for employees to whom the employer provides a purpose-linked financial contribution for meals, as well as employees who perform work in the public interest abroad.

276. Catering is realized in three forms: catering in one's catering facility, catering in another employer's catering facility, or providing meals through meal vouchers. Since employees eat during their work breaks, the availability of meals is also important from a time point of view. If employees do not eat directly at their workplaces, the employer must provide meals nearby. As part of the provision of meals, the employer can provide employees with a purpose-linked financial allowance for meals. The employer will provide this allowance payment if the work conditions at the workplace preclude catering, if the employer cannot provide catering in another form or if the employee cannot use any of the methods of meals provided by the employer. If the employer provides the employee with a financial allowance for meals, he is no longer obliged to provide meals for the employee.

277. The minimum and maximum percentage rates determine the amount the employer contributes to catering. The minimum is 55% of the price of the meal. The maximum applies to each meal, up to the amount of 55% of the meal provided during a business trip lasting five to twelve hours according to Act no. 283/2002 Coll. on Travel Allowances (specifically, the amount of food allowance is regulated by a measure of the Ministry of Labour, Social Affairs and Family of the Slovak Republic). In addition, the employer contributes to the social fund under Act no. 152/1994 Coll. on the Social Fund. According to this Act, the employer provides employees with a meal allowance from the fund above the scope established by the Labour Code. The contribution amount is not limited by a minimum or a maximum; i.e., it can be up to the total amount of the meal ticket. The amount of the allowance for meals from the social fund is agreed between the employer and the trade union body in the collective agreement. If the employer does not have a trade union organization, it will be regulated in the internal regulation.

C. Education of Employees

278. The education of employees within the framework of labour relations provided by the employer is implemented through the deepening and improvement of qualifications. Even though the Labour Code does not contain a legal definition of either of these forms of education, both are an immanent part of employment relations and are a form of further education for employees during their employment relationship. In connection with taking care of the education of employees as one of the employer's tasks, the employer is obliged, by the Labour Code, to discuss the issue of deepening and increasing qualifications with employee representatives if they work in the organization. In connection with the education of employees, the Labour Code distinguishes, in addition to deepening and increasing qualifications, other forms of care for the employee's qualifications – training, apprenticeship, and requalification. The period of initiation, training, and retraining is the work performance for which the employee is entitled to a salary. Training and apprenticeship are connected with the stage of starting the performance of the work agreed in the employment contract. The requalification process is related to the transition or the transfer of an employee within his ongoing employment relationship, and an employee who changes workplace, type of work, or work method must be requalified.

279. On the one hand, the employer takes care of deepening the qualifications; on the other hand, the employees must constantly deepen the qualifications needed to perform the work agreed upon in the employment contract. It is necessary to understand that the employee has a specific acquired qualification (level of qualification), which he deepens. Deepening an employee's qualification includes updating and supplementing knowledge, improving skills, and maintaining or renewing already acquired knowledge and skills. It must be deepening, which refers to the qualifications the employee needs to perform the work agreed upon in the employment contract. The employer's obligation to deepen qualification and the employee's obligation to deepen his qualification continuously is linked to the employer's right to order the employee to deepen his qualification.

280. In the case of the institutes improving and deepening qualifications, the legal regulation allows the employer and the employee to enter into a so-called qualification agreement (section 155 of the Labour Code). The conclusion of a qualification agreement is a right for the employer, not an obligation. When agreeing on qualification enhancement, the employer undertakes to enable the employee to upgrade qualifications by providing work leave, wage compensation, as well as payment of other costs incurred for studies, and vice versa; the employee undertakes to remain employed by the employer for a certain agreed period after completing his studies. As an alternative, in the event of his non-stay, the Labour Code imposes reimbursement on the employee or reimbursement of costs to the employer that he spent on the employee's studies.

Chapter 3. Changes in Employment Relationship

281. A change in employment relationship can be considered a change in which it continues, but some of its elements change. A change in employment relations can mainly consist of a change in the subject of the employment relationship or a change in the content of the employment relationship.

282. Changes in the content of labour relations most often occur based on an agreement, i.e., based on a bilateral legal act, which also follows the principle of contractual labour relations.

283. The employer can unilaterally change the content of the employment relationship only exceptionally. The mentioned cases are exhaustively enshrined in section 55 of the Labour Code. A change in the content of the employment relationship, in addition to a unilateral and bilateral legal act, can also occur based on a change in legislation (e.g., a legal extension of the leave will also change the content of the employment relationship in favour of the employee), or based on an official decision (e.g., based on a court decision on payroll deductions).

284. The individual subjective rights and obligations that make up the content of the employment relationship change in some cases provided for by law, along with the change in the employee's status as a participant in the employment relationship. The employment relationship has a different content (summary of rights and obligations) if the employee is a minor, and if he reaches the age of majority, the content of the employment relationship also changes, for example, due to the employee's pregnancy.

285. A change in the subject of the employment relationship consists of a change of employer, which also has significant legal consequences in transferring rights and obligations from employment relations to the new employer. Changing the employee as the subject of the employment relationship is out of the question because the employment relationship is connected exclusively with the person of the employee.

§1. Change of the Subject

286. The basis of the legal regulation of the transfer of rights and obligations from employment relations is the Council Directive 2001/23/EC of 12 March 2001 on the approximation of the laws of the Member States relating to the safeguarding of employees' rights in the event of transfers of undertakings, businesses or parts of undertakings or businesses, which was through sections 27 to 31 of the Labour Code also implemented in the Slovak legal order. The transfer of an economic unit is the basis of the transfer of a company in the sense of Directive 2001/23/EC and established jurisprudence of the Court of Justice of the EU. According to section 28(2) of the Labour Code, an economic unit is understood as a unit that maintains its conformity as an organized grouping of resources (tangible components, intangible components and personal), the purpose of which is to carry out an economic activity, regardless of whether it is a primary or additional activity. A company or plant transfer within Directive 2001/23/EC can occur based on a contractual transfer or merger. After the transfer, the acquirer becomes the employer of the company's employees transferred by the transferor.

287. In contrast to the regulation of the EU, the Labour Code and no other Slovak labour legislation do not regulate the methods of liquidation of an employer with legal succession. However, it is possible to talk about a merger, fusion, division, separation or a change in the legal form of the employer. During a merger, several employers are combined so that one remains in existence and others that merge with it disappear and enter it with their property and personal substrate. In the case of a merger of employers, two or more employers cease to exist. Their merger creates a new legal entity to which all rights and obligations from the labour relations of previous employers are transferred. In the case of division of the employer, the employer may liquidate, and its assets may pass to another company or companies (fission), or it may not liquidate, and part of its assets pass to another company or companies (secession). For the above situations, the rights and obligations from the employer's labour relations are transferred to his legal successors (i.e., taking over employers) according to the conversion project. The taking over employer has the same rights and obligations after the business transfer as the previous employer. This transition of rights and obligations from the employment relationship is a consequence of the change in the employer's entity and a legal expression of the employee's protection while maintaining the previous employment relationship.

288. If the economic unit, which is the employer or a part of the employer, is transferred, or if the role or activity of the employer is transferred to another employer, the rights and obligations from labour relations are transferred only to the transferred employees to the receiving employer. After the transfer, the acquirer becomes the employer of the company's employees transferred by the transferor. Under these circumstances, the employees of the transferred company have the rights and obligations resulting from their employment relationship. In contrast, their rights and obligations are preserved during the company's transfer. When there is a transfer of rights and obligations from labour relations, the employer must also comply with the collective agreement agreed upon by the previous employer until it expires. During the company's transfer, the rights and obligations of the employees are preserved, and the functions of the employees' representatives are preserved until the end of their term of function.

289. If the employee's working conditions are to be fundamentally changed by the transfer and the employee does not agree to their change, according to section 29a of the Labour Code, the employment relationship is considered terminated by agreement due to redundancy on the day of the transfer. At the same time, such an employee is entitled to severance pay. At the same time, the company transfer is not a reason for dismissal; however, dismissals may occur for subsequent economic, technical or organizational reasons.

290. Consultations with employee representatives must precede the adoption of measures concerning employees. Employees must be informed in writing of the terms of the transfer either directly or through their representatives. This information relates in particular to the established or proposed date of the transfer, the reason for the transfer, the legal, economic and social consequences for the employees and the anticipated measures against the employees. The employer must discuss these measures with employee representatives no later than one month before implementing measures relating to employees. The taking over employer must also inform and negotiate the transfer of rights and obligations.

§2. Change of Content

291. A change in the content of the employment relationship means a change in the rights and obligations arising from the employment relationship. A change in the content of the employment relationship may affect not only one of the content requirements agreed upon by the participants in the employment contract but may also affect the entire complex of the employee's working conditions.

I. Agreement of Parties

292. The working conditions agreed upon in the employment contract between the employer and the employee are binding for the duration of the employment relationship. The Labour Code is based on the contractual nature of labour relations, which manifests in establishing, changing, and terminating labour relations.

293. The agreed content of the employment contract can be changed if the employer and the employee agree to change it (section 54 of the Labour Code). The subject of a mutual agreement between the participants of the employment relationship can only be those rights and obligations established by the will of the participants (e.g., in the employment contract) or result from the dispositive provisions of the Labour Code. Even if the employer is obliged to amend the employment contract in writing, failure to comply with this obligation does not invalidate the agreement.

294. The agreement and mutual consent of the participants in the employment relationship are necessary not only to change the essential requirements of the employment contract but also to change all other requirements agreed upon.

295. A particular type of agreement on changing working conditions is an agreement on the temporary assignment of an employee concluded according to section 58 of the Labour Code. The temporary change concerns the place of work, often also the type of work, even if the original employment relationship remains.

II. One-Sided Transfer to Other Work

296. The employer can only demand work tasks that fall within the framework of the type of work agreed upon by the employee; if the employee refuses to perform other work tasks, it is not a violation of work discipline. An exception to the contractual principle is the case of one-sided transfer when the employer is obliged to transfer the employee to a different type of work than was agreed upon in the employment contract. The employee is obliged to perform work of a different type than that agreed in the employment contract only in exceptional cases, namely in the cases established in section 55(2) and (4) of the Labour Code.

297. A distinction is made between cases when the employer is obliged to transfer the employee to another job (mandatory transfer) and when the Labour Code gives him the right or the possibility to decide to transfer the employee (optional transfer). The transfer should only be temporary because of the reassignment being made.

298. Unilateral mandatory transfer of an employee to another job is a manifestation of the protection of the life and health of the employee (e.g., occupational disease, incapacity for night work, performing work prohibited for pregnant women) or the protection of third parties (quarantine measure, court decision). The employer is obliged to transfer the employee to another job in cases according to section 55(2) of the Labour Code if:

(a) due to his health condition, according to a medical opinion, the employee has long-term lost the ability to continue to perform his current work, or if he is not allowed to perform it due to an occupational disease or because of the threat of this disease, or if he has reached the highest permissible exposure at the workplace determined by the decision of the competent public health authority;
(b) a pregnant woman, a mother up to the end of the ninth month after giving birth and a breastfeeding woman performs work that these women may not be employed in or which, according to a medical opinion, endangers her pregnancy or motherhood;
(c) it is necessary, according to a medical opinion or a decision of a public health authority in order to protect the health of other persons from communicable diseases;
(d) it is necessary, according to a valid decision of a court or other competent authority;
(e) an employee working at night based on a medical opinion is recognized as unfit for night work;
(f) a pregnant woman, a mother up to the end of the ninth month after giving birth, and a nursing woman working at night will request to be transferred to day work.

299. As part of the mandatory reassignment, the employee may be transferred within the scope of the conditions agreed in the employment contract. The employee cannot resist such reassignment; he is obliged to accept it. If reassignment within the agreed type of work is not possible, an agreement with the employee on reassignment to another type of work is necessary. If the employee does not agree to such a change to the employment contract, the reason for termination is as follows, according to section 63(1)(c) of the Labour Code. The employer can only reassign an employee to a suitable job that corresponds to the employee's health capacity for work, is suitable for the employee given his abilities and at the same time corresponds to the employee's qualifications.

300. Within the scope of optional reassignment, according to section 55(4) of the Labour Code, the employer is entitled to reassign the employee for the necessary time to a different job than was agreed upon if this is necessary to avert an emergency or to mitigate its immediate consequences. In this case, it may not be a suitable job in the above sense.

301. The employer is always obliged to discuss with the employee the reason for reassignment to another job and the period during which the reassignment should last. If, during a reassignment due to the threat of an occupational disease quarantine measure, or when averting an emergency or mitigating its immediate consequences, the employee would earn a lower wage per hour than when performing work according to the employment contract, he is entitled to a supplement of at least the amount of his average earnings before reassignment. The supplement is provided during the entire period of reassignment, the longest during twelve consecutive months from the date of reassignment (section 125(1) of the Labour Code).

302. After the reasons for the one-sided employee transfer disappear, the employer must return the employee to the performance of work agreed upon in the employment contract.

III. Business Trip

303. The agreed workplace can be changed by arranging a business trip. When the employer wants to send an employee on a business trip outside the municipality of the employee's regular workplace or residence for a necessary period, he can do so only with his consent. He does not have this obligation if sending on a business trip results directly from the nature of the agreed type of work and the place of work performance or the possibility of being sent on a business trip is agreed upon in the employment contract. On a business trip, the employee performs work according to the instructions of the senior employee who sent him on the business trip.

304. Act no. 283/2002 Coll. on Travel Allowances regulates more detailed conditions for carrying out work trips. According to this Act, an employer who sends an employee on a business trip determines the place and time of the trip, the place of work during the trip, and the duration of the trip. The employer can also determine the method of transportation for the work trip, the end of the work trip and other conditions of the work trip.

IV. Temporary Assignment

305. A particular type of agreement on changing working conditions is an agreement on the temporary assignment of an employee concluded according to section 58 of the Labour Code. The temporary change concerns the place of work, often also the type of work, even if the original employment relationship remains.

306. The institute of temporary assignment represents a special tripartite legal relationship, a grouping of three bilateral relationships. Two of them (the legal relationship between employers and the employment relationship between the employer/agency and the employee) are covered by written agreements, and the third (the employment relationship between the temporarily assigned employee and the user employer) is a sui generis employment relationship without contractual adjustment. The particularity of the mentioned legal relationships is the fact that the legal relationship between employers is a civil law relationship or commercial law, even if the Labour Code regulates some of its contents. Temporary assignment is a legal institution that leads to the temporary transfer of certain rights of the employer (employer, temporary employment agency) to another employer entity (user employer) based on a set of two agreements:

- an agreement on a temporary assignment for the performance of work to the user's employer, which concludes the employer and the employee; and
- an agreement on the temporary assignment of an employee to perform work for the user's employer, which is concluded by the employer and the user's employer. The agreement is not concluded according to the Labour Code; it is usually a commercial contract containing labour law elements and economic aspects of temporary assignment (e.g., enumeration of wage components, reimbursement of wage costs, procedure for replacing temporarily assigned employees).

307. The conclusion of a particular contract between the user employer and the employee is not required, even if the user employer gives instructions to the employee during the temporary assignment, organizes and controls the work of the employee, ensures safety and health protection concerning the temporarily assigned employees as well as to its employees. A user employer is an employer from an economic point of view; this employer uses the workforce or the employee's work performance temporarily assigned to him. The Labour Code does not prescribe any prerequisites or conditions for the user employer to accept a temporarily assigned employee. The user employer cannot take legal actions on behalf of the employer against the temporarily assigned employee (e.g., agree on a change to the employment contract, give a warning about a violation of work discipline and the possibility of termination, give a warning about unsatisfactory performance of work tasks). The employer or the agency provides the employee salary, wage compensation, and travel allowances during the temporary assignment.

308. The legal condition for the temporary assignment of an employee is the existence of objective operational reasons on the part of the employer and the duration of the employment relationship of the temporarily assigned employee at the time of the start of the temporary assignment of at least three months. In the case of a temporary employment agency, the legal condition for temporary assignment is the existence of a relevant permit to perform the activities of a temporary employment agency. In this case, the employment relationship does not have a prescribed minimum duration, and the employee can be temporarily assigned from the day of starting work according to the employment contract concluded with the temporary employment agency.

309. The working conditions and wage conditions of the temporarily assigned employee must be at least as favourable as those of a comparable employee of the user employer. Employment through an agency should be economically less advantageous for the user employer (subject to the conditions of the same wage conditions) than employing regular employees of the user employer in the given position. The higher costs of the user employer are compensated by greater flexibility at the end of the temporary assignment compared to the end of the employment relationship with a regular employee of the user employer. When the employer (agency) did not provide the temporarily assigned employee with a wage at least as favourable, the user employer is obliged to provide the temporarily assigned employee with this wage or the wage difference within fifteen days from the pay date. For the user's employer to check whether he must pay wages or a wage difference, the employer or the temporary employment agency is obliged to provide him with all the necessary data at the request of the user's employer.

310. A temporary assignment can be agreed upon for a maximum of twenty-four months, while repeated temporary assignments and temporary assignments of the same employee to the same user employer from all employers or temporary employment agencies. Extend or renegotiate the temporary assignment within twenty-four months at most four times. Illegal exceeding the maximum period of temporary assignment results in the termination of the employee's employment relationship with the employer (agency) and creating an employment relationship for an indefinite period with the user employer. This should effectively ensure the employee's right to labour law protection against violation of the maximum period of temporary assignment. In practice, there is a circumvention of the Labour Code in the form of agreeing on the provision of services, which consists of the performance of work by the employee, which this employee has so far performed as a temporarily assigned employee. Such an agreement must be assessed as an invalid legal act due to the circumvention of the Labour Code, and the situation must be assessed following section 58(7) of the Labour Code and grant the employee protection in the form of an employment relationship with the user employee. The temporary assignment ends at the end of the agreed time. Before the expiration of this time, the temporary assignment ends with the participants' agreement regarding the employment relationship or with the unilateral termination of the participants based on the agreed conditions.

311. Special protection of employees is represented by section 58(2) of the Labour Code, according to which the law introduced a rebuttable presumption of the existence of a temporary assignment in the case of the performance of work by an employee in which:

- a person other than the employer imposes work tasks on the employee, organizes, manages and controls his work and gives him instructions for this purpose;
- this activity is carried out mainly on the premises of this person and mainly with his working means or mainly on the equipment of this person; and
- it is an activity that a person has as the subject of his activity registered in the relevant register.

312. The employer or temporary employment agency can prove otherwise. Based on the legal presumption, employees who work in the temporary assignment regime receive protection by limiting the duration of such temporary assignment and the right to an additional payment of the wage difference.

V. Posting of an Employee

313. The general definition of the term 'posting' of an employee is not regulated in Slovak labour law. Usually, the term 'posting' refers to the cross-border employment of an employee. The legal definition of the term 'posting an employee to perform work in the provision of services' is contained in section 5(6) of the Labour Code, and it means:

(a) cross-border posting of an employee under the direction and responsibility of the posting employer based on a contract between the posting employer as a cross-border service provider and the recipient of this service if an employment relationship exists between the posting employer and the employee during the posting period, i.e., posting to perform work in the narrower sense of the provision of services;
(b) cross-border posting between a controlling person and a controlled person or between controlled persons if an employment relationship exists between the posting employer and the employee during the posting period, i.e., corporate posting or;
(c) cross-border temporary assignment to the user employer if there is an employment relationship between the posting employer and the employee during the posting period, i.e., cross-border temporary assignment.

314. During the posting, the content of the employment relationship between the posting employer and the seconded employee is regulated by the state's legal order, according to which the employment relationship was governed before the posting and secondly by the legal order of the state to which the secondment takes place. The working conditions and conditions of employment of a domestic employee are governed by the law of the state to whose territory the domestic employee is posted. During the first twelve months of posting, the seconded employee is subject to the legal order of the receiving country only to the extent of the so-called hard core of working conditions, defined in Article 3 of Directive 96/71/EC of the European Parliament and of the Council of 16 December 1996 concerning the posting of workers in the framework of the provision of services (as amended by Directive no. 2018/957) or in section 5(2) of the Labour Code. When the posting has exceeded twelve months (or eighteen months based on a particular notification of the visiting employer to the National Labour Inspectorate), the working conditions of the receiving country are applied in full, except for the regulation of termination of employment. So-called hardcore working conditions include:

(a) length of working time and rest;
(b) length of annual leave;
(c) minimum wage, minimum wage requirements, wage compensation for overtime work, wage compensation for working on a holiday, wage compensation for working on Saturday, wage compensation for working on Sunday, wage compensation for night work, wage compensation for rugged work performance, and other mandatory components wages and salary compensation for leave;
(d) safety and health protection at work;
(e) working conditions of pregnant women, mothers up to the end of the ninth month after giving birth, breastfeeding women and young employees;
(f) equal treatment of men and women and prohibition of discrimination;
(g) the conditions under which an employee can be temporarily assigned, the working conditions, including the wage conditions, and the conditions of employment of the temporarily assigned employee if it is a posting according to section 5(6)(c) of the Labour Code;
(h) accommodation conditions that the employer provides to employees;
(i) reimbursement of travel expenses, reimbursement of expenses for accommodation and meals during a business trip or when travelling to the usual place of work in the territory of the Slovak Republic; to apply a particular regulation or the relevant collective agreement, reimbursement of travel expenses, reimbursement of accommodation expenses and meals or other comparable benefits provided by the visiting employer according to the law of the state from which the employee is posted to perform work in the provision of services may also be included.

315. An employee who has been posted to the territory of the Slovak Republic may file a motion for a labour inspection or go directly to court and seek legal protection if he believes that his rights or interests protected by law have been affected by non-compliance with the conditions of posting to the territory of the Slovak Republic.

316. A visiting employee to whom the visiting employer, when sent to perform work in the provision of services in the narrower sense or during a group posting, did not provide the salary due in the scope of the hardcore or after the expiration of twelve, respectively eighteen months in the full scope of the wage conditions valid in the Slovak Republic, has the right to demand their payment from a natural person or a legal entity that is a supplier of services in the territory of the Slovak Republic, whose direct subcontractor is the visiting employer. The service provider is obliged to provide the guest employee with the due salary or its part in the amount in which it was not paid within fifteen days from the delivery of the guest employee's request, after deducting the deductions that the guest employer would have made from the salary if he had provided the due salary. In such a case, a guest employee posted under a temporary assignment regime has the right to pay the due salary or the difference between the salary of a comparable employee of the user employer and the salary of the user employer based in the Slovak Republic, provided to him by the employer, within fifteen days from the pay date of the temporarily assigned employee.

Chapter 4. Working Time, Annual Leave, Holidays

§1. Working Time

317. The legal regulation of working time mainly concerns its length and the principles of its distribution during a specific period; the determining factors for regulating working time are economic and social.

318. In Article 36, the Constitution grants employees the right to fair and satisfactory working conditions. He delegates the adjustment of these conditions to the law, which ensures them the highest permissible length of working time, adequate rest after work and the shortest permissible length of paid leave for recovery. These rights of employees guaranteed by the Constitution can be summed up in the right to adequate rest after work, which is a subjective right of the employee, defined by the time during which the employee is freed from work and which he can freely dispose of. This distinguishes it from the majority of the subjective rights of the employee, the implementation of which is carried out during the work process by the active fulfilment of obligations on the part of the obliged entity.

319. The general regulation of working time in the Slovak Republic consists of the Labour Code, which, when defining working time and its schedule, is based on ILO conventions and EU legislation. Article 3 of the basic principles of the Labour Code grants employees the right to wages for work performed, to ensure safety and health protection at work, and to rest and recover after work.

I. Definition

320. According to section 85(1) of the Labour Code, the working time is defined as a period in which the employee is available to the employer, performs work and fulfils obligations per the employment contract. It is not clear from the legal definition of working time whether the elements of working time (i.e., performance of work, instructions of the employer, the performance of activities or duties) are to be understood cumulatively (as it follows from the grammatical interpretation of the provision in question) or alternatively.

321. The employer can determine the time required for personal cleaning after the end of work in agreement with the employee representatives, which will also be included in the employee's working time. The following is also included in the working time:

- on-call duty at the workplace (section 96(2) of the Labour Code);
- breaks provided for reasons of ensuring the safety and health protection of employees at work (section 91(6) of the Labour Code);
- break for breastfeeding (section 170 of the Labour Code).

II. Length of Working Time

322. Considering the basic principles of adjusting the length of working time contained in the Labour Code, we distinguish:

- maximum weekly working time established by law (so-called statutory established in section 85(5) to (7) of the Labour Code);
- established weekly working time (working time determined by the employer following the provisions of the Labour Code);
- specified weekly working time (working time that the employee is obliged to work in the relevant week after scheduling the established weekly working time);
- shorter working time (section 49 of the Labour Code).

323. The Labour Code stipulates that an employee's maximum working time is forty hours per week. An employee who regularly performs work in a two-shift operation has a working time of no more than 38 and 3/4 hours per week, and in a three-shift or non-stop operation, has a working time of no more than 37 and 1/2 hours per week. A juvenile employee under 16 has a working time of no more than thirty hours per week, and an employee over 16 has a working time of no more than 37 and 1/2 hours per week, even if he works for several employers. This is the 'pure working time', the scope of which does not include breaks at work.

324. The working time in twenty-four hours may not exceed eight hours, and an employee's average weekly working time, including overtime, may not exceed forty-eight hours. An employee's average weekly working time, including overtime, may exceed forty-eight hours for four consecutive months in the case of a medical employee under a special regulation if the employee agrees to such a range of working time. Such an employee's average weekly working time, including overtime, may not exceed fifty-six hours.

325. The Labour Code does not define the lowest range of working time. It can be negotiated in the collective agreement, or it is possible to agree on shorter working time in the employment contract.

III. Scheduling of Working Time

326. The employer schedules the working time according to the principles established in the Labour Code. The employer must, therefore, decide whether the working time will be distributed evenly or unevenly or whether flexible working time or a working time account will be applied. When creating a shift schedule, the employer must establish the length of working time (established weekly working time), the employee's work schedule, the beginning and end of work shifts, and the beginning and end of the rest period. The employer must consider the needs of pregnant women and women and men taking care of children when assigning employees to work shifts. Certain restrictions also apply to the length and scheduling of working time of juvenile employees.

327. The employer decides on the schedule of weekly working time after negotiation or after agreement with employee representatives and notifies the employee at least one week in advance, valid for at least one week. The Labour Code does not specify how the employer will exercise authorization. However, it should be based on a five-day working week, with the fact that it can divide the working time of the same work shift and must take into account the peculiarities of work performance on non-working days. For the scheduling of working time, the scheduling period established for four weeks is essential, within which the average working time must not exceed the limit for the established weekly working time, even if, e.g., within one or two weeks, the limit for the established weekly working time will be exceeded. Overtime work is not included in this range of established working time. Working time can be distributed evenly or unevenly. The beginning and end of working time and the schedule of work shifts will be determined by the employer in agreement with the employee representatives and will be announced in writing at the employer's place that is accessible to the employee.

328. In the case of domestic work and telework, it is necessary to decide on the organization of working time. In the case of domestic work or telecommuting, the Labour Code allows for an agreement between the employee and the employer, according to which the employee will schedule his working time during the entire week, or the domestic work or telework will be carried out during the flexible working time. An employee performing domestic work or telecommuting has during his continuous daily rest and continuous rest in the week, if he is not ordered or agreed with him at this time to work emergency or work overtime while taking annual leave, a holiday for which work was cancelled, and obstacles in the so-called work the right to disconnect. Such is the employee's right not to perform work outside of working time (if it is not overtime or on-call duty) during work obstacles or holidays, as well as the employer's prohibition to qualify such non-performance of work as a violation of work discipline.

A. Even Scheduling of Working Time

329. An even scheduling of working time for individual weeks is when the difference in the length of working time falling on individual weeks does not exceed three hours. At the same time, the working time on individual days does not exceed nine hours. This mandatory provision cannot be deviated by the parties' agreement. At the same time, the average weekly working time must not exceed the established weekly working time limit in the relevant schedule period. The Labour Code limits the length of the scheduled period to a maximum of four weeks.

330. According to section 86 of the Labour Code, the employer decides on the equal distribution of working time after consultation with employee representatives. The Labour Code does not specify how the employer performs the right to distribute working time evenly.

B. Uneven Scheduling of Working Time

331. Uneven working time scheduling will be considered in cases where the difference in the length of working time attributable to individual weeks exceeds three hours and/or the working time on individual days exceeds nine hours. The employer may schedule the working time unevenly only if the nature of the work or the operating conditions do not allow the working time to be scheduled evenly over individual weeks. The nature of work or operating conditions is determined by the subject of the employer's activity; the legal regulation does not specify these concepts in more detail. Therefore, unevenly distributed working time does not have to be set for all the employer's employees; it can also be set for a specific part of the employer's workforce, such as relevant organizational units or types of work. However, the employer can schedule working time unevenly only after agreement with employee representatives or with the employee.

332. In an uneven work schedule, the average weekly working time may not exceed the established weekly working time in no more than four months. In order to protect the employees' health, the working time may not exceed twelve hours or twenty-four hours in case of an uneven work schedule.

333. Depending on the length of the schedule period, the Labour Code distinguishes between two situations in the case of uneven scheduling of working time – uneven scheduling of working time with a schedule period of no more than four months and uneven scheduling of more than four months.

1. Uneven Scheduling of Working Time with a Scheduling Period of No More than Four Months

334. The employer decides on an uneven working schedule with a schedule period of up to four months after the agreement with employee representatives or after the agreement with an affected employee. It is up to the employer to agree with his social partner or directly with the employee. If the employer agrees only with an affected employee, the agreement applies only to this employee. When the employer agrees with employee representatives, the agreement applies to all employer employees or the relevant group of employees or organizational units defined in the agreement. From a formal point of view, no conditions are imposed on the agreement on uneven working time. If four months have passed since the uneven working schedule, the employer can again unevenly schedule the working time with the same period for a maximum of four months.

2. Uneven Scheduling of Working Time with a Scheduling Period of More than Four Months

335. In the case of an uneven working schedule with a schedule period longer than four months, several requirements must be fulfilled cumulatively. First, jobs must show a different need for work during the year (e.g., in construction). Extending the scheduled period is not considered if there is no different need for work during the year. The second condition is an agreement with employee representatives on unevenly distributed working time, which cannot be replaced by the employer's decision or an individual agreement with the employee. If the employer does not have employee representatives, uneven working time with a more than four-month schedule is impossible.

3. Uneven Scheduling of Working Time for Special Categories of Employees

336. An employer may give an employee with a disability, a pregnant woman, a woman or a man who permanently takes care of a child under the age of three, a single employee who permanently takes care of a child under the age of 15, schedule working time unevenly only based on an agreement with the employee, even if there is an agreement on uneven scheduling of working time between the employer and employee representatives.

C. Working Time Account

337. The working time account represents a method of uneven scheduling of working time, which should solve the temporary inability of the employer to fulfil his primary obligation – to assign work to the employee according to the employment contract.

338. The essence of the working time account is that, in case of a greater need for work, the employee will work more hours than his established weekly working time, and in case of a minor need for work, the employee will work fewer hours than his established weekly working time, or he will not perform the work at all. This results in a separation of working time and remuneration for work performed. It also applies that an employee's average weekly working time may not exceed the established weekly working time in no more than twelve consecutive months. Thus, if an employee works fewer hours than his established weekly working time, he receives a salary. Conversely, if an employee works more than the established weekly working time, his work will not be considered overtime.

339. The employer can only introduce the working time account after agreement with the employee representatives. The employer's decision cannot replace the conclusion of an agreement on introducing a working time account, nor is an individual agreement with a specific employee possible. If the employer intends to establish a working time account for an employee with a disability, a pregnant woman, a woman or a man who permanently cares for a child under the age of three, a single employee who permanently cares for a child under the age of 15, he must, in addition to the general conditions, also achieve a special agreement on account of working time with such employee.

340. In the collective agreement or the agreement with the employees' representatives, an equalization period of the working time account must be agreed upon, in which the difference between the established weekly working time and the actual hours worked by the employee is equalized. The purpose of introducing an equalization period is to settle mutual obligations between employer and employee, depending on whether a positive or negative account was reached at the end of the period. The maximum period for which an equalization period can be agreed upon is thirty months.

341. When using the working time account, the employer is obliged to provide the employee with a basic wage component that corresponds to the established weekly working time of the employee and to keep a working time account, which records the difference between the established weekly working time and the actual time worked by the employee and the difference between the provided basic wage component and the basic wage component to which the employee would be entitled to the time worked. However, the provision of the basic wage component does not affect the employer's obligation to provide other wage components if this obligation results from the employment contract, collective agreement or the Labour Code.

342. When a lower wage than the employee was entitled to according to the working time account was paid before the termination of the employment relationship, the employer is obliged to pay the employee the remaining part of the wage.

343. When the employment relationship has been terminated, and the employee has not worked the full range of working time that falls within the period in which the working time account is applied, the employer can apply to the court for the right to return the paid wages only if the employment relationship with the employee has ended by dismissal or immediate termination due to the employee's reasons. The employer can exercise this right in court no later than two months after the employment relationship ends.

D. Flexible Working Time

344. Flexible working time represents a progressive method of even or uneven working time scheduling, in which the employee determines the beginning and end of the work shift, and thus the length of the work shift, within the framework of established or agreed rules. Thus, the employee can organize his working time, or part of it, according to personal needs within specific rules, which should increase work efficiency.

345. If the employer has employee representatives, the employer can introduce flexible working time only through a collective agreement or after agreement with the employee representatives. Flexible working time can be introduced for all employer operations or only for some. However, it cannot be introduced at the employer as a whole if the nature of the subject of its activity does not allow it or at its organizational units if the nature of these units does not allow it.

346. Flexible working time consists of optional working time and basic working time. The basic working time is the period established by the employer during which the employee must be at the workplace. Unlike in the past, the employer is no longer obligated to determine the basic working time. Optional working time is when the employee is entitled to choose the beginning and possibly the end of working time. If, for this period, the employer determines to the employee that he must be present at the workplace, this period cannot be qualified as optional working time. During the optional working time, the employee must be at the workplace to the extent that he works the operating time. Working time is the total working time the employee is obliged to work in a flexible working period determined by the employer.

347. A flexible working period shall be applied as a working day, working week, four-week or another working period. With daily flexible working time, the employee must work the specified length of the entire work shift every day. The employee only chooses the start of the work shift. With flexible weekly working time, the employee chooses the start and end of the work shift. With flexible weekly working time, the employee does not have a fixed length of daily shift, only the period of mandatory presence at the employer's workplace (primary working time). The employee works the rest of the weekly working time according to his decision. However, he must work the entire designated weekly working time within the week. With a flexible four-week working period, the employee chooses the start and end of the work shift. He is obliged to be present at the workplace during primary working time. The working time determined by the employer for four weeks must be worked within four weeks. In all three mentioned cases, the length of the work shift when applying flexible working time can be no more than twelve hours.

E. Work Shift and Work Modes

348. 'Work shift' must be distinguished from 'working time'. A work shift is that part of the established weekly working time that the employee is obliged to work within twenty-four consecutive hours (not during a calendar day) based on a predetermined work shift schedule and a break at work. A work shift is, therefore, a part of the established weekly working time without overtime, which the employee is obliged to work according to a pre-established schedule of work shifts. However, the work shift also includes a break at work to rest and eat.

349. 'Shift work' is a way of organizing working time in which employees alternate with each other at the same workplace according to a specific schedule and work at different times during a certain period of days or weeks. An employee working in shifts is any employee whose working regime is organized as shift work. The employee is obliged to work in the shift regime specified by the employer in the shift schedule in agreement with the employee representatives, except in cases where the parties to the employment relationship have, for example, agreed in the employment contract that the employee will perform work exclusively in morning shifts. In such a case, the employer must respect the agreement with the employee.

350. Determining the schedule of work shifts is the employer's right and obligation, but the employer can do so only after agreement with the employee representatives. If the employer does not have employee representatives, the employer is entitled to act independently. The employee must respect the designated start and end of working time and the schedule of work shifts. In addition, the employer also has a notification obligation towards the employee when he is obliged to notify the employee in writing of the working schedule at least one week in advance and with validity for at least one week. The employer can change the work shift schedule after agreement with the employee representatives, subject to compliance with the notification obligation. When assigning employees to work shifts, the employer must also consider the interests of pregnant women and women and men taking care of children. When a pregnant woman and a woman or a man permanently caring for a child under 15 request shorter working time or another appropriate adjustment of the designated weekly working time, the employer must comply with their request unless serious operational reasons prevent it.

351. For the schedule of work shifts, the morning shift must not start before 6 am; the afternoon shift must not end after 10 pm. The morning shift is the work shift, the majority of which falls between 6 am and 2 pm; the afternoon shift is the work shift, the majority of which falls between 2 pm and 10 pm; and the night shift is the work shift, the majority of which part falls between 10 pm and 6 am. The term night shift must be distinguished from the term night work, performed between 10 pm and 6 am.

352. If the working time is divided into two working shifts, it is a two-shift working regime; if the employer divides the working time into three working shifts, it is a three-shift working regime, a working regime in which the work activity takes place continuously on all days of the week is a continuous working mode.

353. When the employer does not agree otherwise in writing with the employee, the employer cannot schedule the working time so that the employee works night shifts for two consecutive weeks unless the nature of the work or the operating conditions do not allow to schedule the working time differently.

354. Although the Labour Code is based on the so-called clean working time and breaks for rest and eating are not included in working time, upon agreement with employee representatives, it allows the employer to determine the time needed for personal cleaning after work, which is included in the employee's working time. If the employer does not have employee representatives, the employer is entitled to act independently.

355. Labour Code in section 90(11) also allows individual adjustment of working time when the employer can allow the employee, at his request for health reasons or other severe reasons on his part, a suitable adjustment of the specified weekly working time or agrees it with him under the same conditions in the employment contract. The prerequisite for such a working schedule is the nature of the operation, which allows such a schedule. Similar to the case of shorter working time, in this case, too, it is necessary to distinguish between permitted and other suitable adjustments to the working time agreed in the employment contract.

F. On-Call Duty

356. On-call duty refers to a situation where, in justified cases and in order to ensure necessary tasks, the employer orders or agrees with the employee to stay for a specified time outside the framework of the work shift schedule and beyond the specified weekly working time, resulting from the pre-determined working schedule agreed place and was ready to perform the work according to the employment contract. The basic concept of working readiness is that the employee stays for a specific time in a particular place and is ready to perform work. In the case of on-call duty, this is time outside the framework of the work shift schedule and above the specified weekly working time resulting from the pre-determined work shift schedule.

1. The Inactive Part of the On-Call Duty

357. The time during which the employee stays at an agreed place outside the workplace and is ready to perform the work but does not is an inactive part of the on-call duty, which is not included in the working time. For each hour of the inactive part of on-call duty outside the workplace, the employee is entitled to a compensation of at least 20% of the minimum wage in euros per hour according to a special regulation.

358. When the employee stays at the workplace and is ready to perform work but is not working, this is the inactive part of on-call duty, which is considered working time. For each hour of the inactive part of on-call duty at the workplace, the employee is entitled to a wage equal to a proportional part of the basic wage component, but at least in the minimum wage. When the employer and the employee agree on compensatory time off for the inactive part of the on-call duty at the workplace, the employee is entitled to a salary in the amount of a proportional part of the basic salary component, at least in the minimum wage amount, for one hour of this on-call time, there is one hour of compensatory time off – the time of compensatory time off leave does not belong to the employee's salary.

2. The Active Part of the On-Call Duty

359. When an employee performs work while on on-call duty, it is considered overtime; since the performance of work during standby is considered overtime work, if the performance of work occurred during standby, the employee is not entitled to compensation for on-call duty but is entitled to overtime pay according to section 121 of the Labour Code. When ordering on-call duty, the employer must also pay attention to the limits of the possible ordering of overtime work. When the employee has already reached the legal limit of overtime work in the relevant calendar year, which can be ordered by the employer, and did not agree to further overtime work or has also exhausted the legal limit for agreed overtime work, for this employee, the on-call order has no meaning, even if this on-call was ordered within the agreed scope of on-call. It would not be possible to assess the employee's refusal to perform work as a violation of work discipline.

3. Extent of On-Call Duty and Prohibition of On-Call Duty

360. The Labour Code distinguishes between two types of on-call duty: ordered and agreed on-call duty. The significance of this distinction lies precisely in the establishment of annual limits for the performance of on-call work, in which the protective function of labour law is manifested. The employer can order a maximum of eight hours per week and a hundred hours per calendar year; above this extent, on-call duty is permissible only after agreement with the employee.

361. The protective function of labour law to on-call duty is also manifested in specific categories of employees. An employer cannot order a pregnant woman, a woman, or a man permanently caring for a child under three, or a single woman or a single man who is permanently caring for a child under 15 to be on standby; employers can only agree on on-call duty with them. The employer may not order on-call duty even for minor employees; in this case, on-call duty cannot be agreed upon.

G. Overtime

362. The employee must perform the agreed work during the specified working time. However, the Labour Code allows the performance of the agreed work outside of this time. The Labour Code refers to such work as overtime work while also providing a positive definition of it – overtime work is work performed by an employee at the employer's command or with his consent beyond the specified weekly working time resulting from a pre-determined working schedule and performed outside the framework of the work shift schedule. Overtime work can be performed not only after the end of the work shift but also before it begins.

363. The Labour Code also contains a negative definition of overtime work when it does not consider overtime work in those cases where the employee works overtime with work performed above the specified weekly working time, work time off that the employer provided him at his request, or working time that was lost due to adverse weather conditions.

364. The Labour Code distinguishes between ordered and agreed overtime work and establishes the conditions under which the employer can order overtime work. The employer can order overtime work only in the temporary and urgent increased need for work or if it is in the public interest.

1. The Highest Permissible Length of Overtime Work

365. Overtime work may not exceed an average of eight hours per week in no more than four consecutive months unless the employer and employee representatives agree on a more extended period, but no more than twelve consecutive months. Overtime should not be performed regularly but when there is an objective reason for overtime work.

366. In a calendar year, an employee can be ordered to work overtime for a maximum of 150 hours. Upon agreement, an employee may work overtime in a calendar year for a maximum of 400 hours. The stated highest permissible range of overtime work is not final. The scope of overtime work does not include overtime work for which the employee received compensatory leave or overtime work performed during urgent repair work or work, without the execution of which there could be a risk of an occupational accident or damage of a large scale, or extraordinary events according to a special regulation, where there was a danger threatening life, health or large-scale damage.

2. Overtime for Special Categories of Employees

367. A pregnant woman, a woman or a man permanently caring for a child under three, or a single woman or a single man permanently caring for a child under 15 may work overtime only with their consent.

368. Overtime cannot be ordered for an employee who performs risky work. Overtime can be agreed upon with this employee only exceptionally and for work that does not fall under the overtime limit. With the employee who performs risky work, after the prior consent of the employee representatives, it is possible to exceptionally agree on overtime work to ensure a safe and smooth production process.

369. Furthermore, overtime work cannot be ordered for an employee who performs a medical profession according to a special regulation and who has reached the age of 50; however, overtime work is permissible upon agreement with this employee.

3. Overtime for Employees with Shorter Working Time

370. Exceptions to the above overtime regulation are employees with shorter working time, for whom overtime work exceeds their weekly working time. An employee with shorter working time cannot be ordered to work overtime; it can only be agreed upon with him. When the employee and the employer have already agreed on a shorter working time in the employment contract, the employer cannot even order him to work within the established range of weekly working time.

H. Night Work

371. Night work is work performed between 10 pm and 6 am. An employee working at night is considered an employee who performs work that requires that it be regularly performed at night for at least three consecutive hours or is likely to work at least five hundred hours a year at night.

372. The employer is obliged to ensure that the employee working at night undergoes an assessment of the medical fitness for night work:

- before being assigned to night work;
- regularly as needed, at least once a year;
- at any time during assignment to night work for health disorders caused by the performance of night work;
- if requested by a pregnant woman, a mother up to the end of the ninth month after giving birth, and a breastfeeding woman.

373. The employer is obliged to equip the workplace, where work is done at night, with means for providing first aid, including the provision of means that enable quick medical assistance to be called. The employer is also obliged to provide employees working at night with safety and health protection at work corresponding to the nature of their work and to ensure that protective and preventive services or facilities related to safety and health at work are always available for employees working at night and that they are equivalent to those available to other employees.

374. The employer is obliged to regularly discuss the organization of work at night with employee representatives. An employer who regularly employs employees at night is obliged to notify the relevant labour inspectorate and employee representatives of this fact if they require it.

375. The prerequisite for the performance of night work by an employee who performs the medical profession of nurse and midwife according to a special regulation and who has reached the age of 50 is the employee's consent to the performance of work at night.

376. The employer is obliged to schedule the established weekly working time for an employee working at night so that the average length of a work shift does not exceed eight hours in a period of no more than four consecutive calendar months, while the calculation of the average length of a work shift of an employee working at night is based on a five-day work week.

377. The working time of an employee performing heavy physical, mental, or work that could endanger life or health may not exceed eight hours in twenty-four hours.

§2. Rest Periods

378. In addition to the maximum weekly working time, the Labour Code guarantees employees specific rest periods during which the employer may not require the employee to perform work. Rest time is any time that is not working time. Labour Code recognizes:

– breaks in work for eating and rest;
– rest between two shifts (daily rest after work);
– uninterrupted weekly rest.

I. Breaks in Work for Eating and Rest

379. The employer must provide an employee whose work shift is longer than six hours with a thirty-minute break for eating and rest. The employer must provide a thirty-minute rest and meal break to a juvenile employee whose work shift is longer than four and a half hours. If work cannot be interrupted, the employee must have adequate time to rest and eat, even without interrupting operations or work. The break for eating and rest cannot be granted at the beginning of working time or after its termination.

380. Breaks for rest and eating are not included in working time; this does not apply in the case of breaks provided to ensure the safety and health of employees at work, which are included in working time. Mothers breastfeeding their children have a special break in work for breastfeeding. They are entitled to two thirty-minute breaks up to the sixth month of the child's age and one thirty-minute break up to the ninth month of the child's age per shift. Breaks in work for breastfeeding are also considered part of working time (section 170 of the Labour Code).

II. Continuous Daily Rest

381. The employer must schedule working time so that between the end of one shift and the beginning of the second, the employee has a minimum rest period of twelve consecutive hours in twenty-four hours, and a juvenile employee at least fourteen hours in twenty-four hours.

382. Rest may be reduced to eight hours for an employee over 18 years of age in continuous operations and shift work, in urgent agricultural work, in urgent repair work, if it is to avert a danger threatening the life or health of employees, and in extraordinary events. If the employer shortens the minimum rest period, he must provide the employee with an equivalent continuous rest period within thirty days.

383. An employee who has returned from a business trip after twenty-four hours will be given time for necessary rest from the end of the business trip to the start of work in the amount of eight hours, and if this time falls within the employee's working time, also wage compensation in the amount of his average earnings.

III. Continuous Rest During the Week

384. The employer must schedule working time so that the employee has two consecutive days of continuous rest once a week, which must fall on Saturday and Sunday or Sunday and Monday.

385. When the nature of the work and the conditions of operation do not allow the schedule of the working time of an employee older than 18 years, two consecutive days of continuous rest per week shall be provided on other days of the week. When the nature of the work and the operating conditions do not make it possible to schedule the working time in such manner, the employer may schedule the working time of an employee who is older than 18 years old after agreement with the employee representatives or, if the employer does not have employee representatives, after agreement with the employee, in such a way that the employee had at least twenty-four hours of continuous rest once a week, which should fall on a Sunday, with the employer being obliged to additionally provide the employee with a replacement continuous weekly rest within eight months from the day on which the continuous weekly rest should have been provided.

386. When the nature of the work and the operating conditions do not make it possible to schedule the working time in the ways mentioned above, the employer can schedule the working time for an employee over the age of 18 after agreement with employee representatives or, if the employer does not have employee representatives, after agreement with the employee, so that the employee has once a week at least thirty-five hours of continuous rest, which falls on Sunday and part of the day before Sunday or part of the day after Sunday.

387. The Labour Code also distinguishes between non-working days, the days the employee has continuous rest during the week, and holidays. Work on non-working days can only be ordered after discussion with employee representatives. Work on Sundays and other days of rest is not permitted on principle. However, section 94 of the Labour Code provides exceptions from this rule in selected types of working activities:

- in urgent repair works;
- in loading and unloading operations;
- in taking inventories;
- in the works intended to avert a danger posing a risk to life or health;
- during natural disasters or other similar extraordinary events;
- to replace an employee who has not turned up for work in a continuous operation;
- during feeding and attending to domestic animals;
- during work indispensable for the satisfaction of living, health and cultural needs of the population;
- urgent agricultural work in plant production and the processing of food crops.

388. In the case of the abovementioned works, the employer is entitled to order work on rest days unilaterally. The employer must consult with employee representatives concerning such instructions on rest days.

§3. Holidays

389. The holidays are codified in section 94 of the Labour Code under 'non-working days'. Holidays are regulated by Act no. 241/1993 Coll. about national holidays, days off and memorial days.

390. On holiday, an employee can only be ordered to do work that can be ordered on the employee's days of continuous rest in the week, work in continuous operation and work necessary for guarding the employer's facilities.

391. On 1 January, 6 January, Good Friday, Easter Sunday, Easter Monday, 1 May, 8 May, 5 July, 29 August, 1 September, 15 September, 1 November, 17 November, 24 December afternoon, 25 December and 26 December, an employee may not be ordered or agreed to work, which is the retail sale of goods to the final consumer, including related work. An exception to this prohibition applies to retail sales at fuel and lubricant filling stations, retail sales and dispensing of medicines in pharmacies, retail sales at airports, ports, other public transport facilities and hospitals, sales of travel tickets, sales of souvenirs and sale of flowers on 8 May and sale of flowers and items intended for the decoration of the grave site on 1 November.

§4. LEAVE

392. The right to leave is a citizen's constitutional right exclusively bound to the employee's person. The primary purpose of the leave is to regenerate employees' physical and mental strength, which contributes to realizing employees' right to rest after work. We can define it as a legally guaranteed exemption from the employee's work duties, which serves for the employee's recovery after the work performed, during which the employee is provided with wage compensation in the amount of his average earnings. That means that during the leave period, the employee is financially protected by a wage compensation in the amount of the average earnings. The employee's right to leave includes two essential content elements: provision of work leave and material security during work leave. The Slovak labour law provides three types of leave. Apart from the standard annual leave and the leave for effective days worked, there is also additional leave.

I. Annual Leave

393. Annual leave is an employee's 'classic' leave. It is a continuous leave to which the employee is entitled on the condition that during the continuous duration of the employment relationship with the same employer, he performed work for at least sixty days in the calendar year. The employee is entitled to a proportional part of annual leave if the employment relationship did not last continuously during the entire calendar year. The day worked is the day the employee worked most of his shift. The parts of the shifts worked on different days are not added.

394. The basic amount of annual leave is at least four weeks. The annual leave of an employee who will be at least 33 years old by the end of the relevant calendar year and an employee who permanently cares for a child is at least five weeks. Annual leave is at least eight weeks in a calendar year for:

- teaching staff and professional staff according to a special regulation;
- university teacher;
- researcher and artistic staff of a public university or state university; and
- an employee with at least a second-level university education who carries out research-pedagogical activity or scientific activity, research activity and development activity at the research workplace of the organization of the Slovak Academy of Sciences, a public research institution or a state budget organization or a state contribution organization carrying out research established by a central body of state administration.

395. A longer length of leave can be agreed upon in collective agreements and employment contracts.

396. When an employee with unevenly distributed working time takes leave for individual weeks or the entire calendar year, he is entitled to as many days of leave as there are for his leave in the annual average.

II. Leave for Days Worked

397. An employee who is not entitled to annual leave or its proportional part because he did not work for the same employer for at least sixty days in a calendar year is entitled to leave for days worked in the length of one-twelfth of the leave for the calendar year for every twenty-one days worked in the respective calendar year. For example, a probationary employee is entitled to leave if he has worked for at least twenty-one days.

III. Additional Leave

398. Additional leave includes those who work underground for the entire calendar year to extract minerals or when digging tunnels and tunnels and employees who perform particularly difficult or health-damaging work. The additional leave is one week. If the employee works only part of the calendar year under these conditions, he is entitled to one-twelfth of the additional holiday for every twenty-one days worked in this way. Wage compensation cannot be provided for unused additional leave; this leave must be used up as a matter of priority.

IV. Shortening of Leave

399. For an employee who has fulfilled the condition of having worked at least sixty days in the calendar year for which the leave is granted, the employer may reduce the leave by one-twelfth for the first hundred missed working days and by one-twelfth for each additional twenty-one missed working days, if in this calendar year, he did not work for a reason:

- performing extraordinary service during a crisis or alternative service in times of war and martial law;
- taking parental leave according to section 166(2);
- long-term release for the performance of a public function and the performance of a trade union function;
- significant personal obstacles at work according to section 141(1) and (3) (c).

400. When shortening the leave, an employee whose employment relationship with the same employer lasted the entire calendar year must be granted a leave of at least one week and a juvenile employee of two weeks.

401. For each unexcused missed shift (working day), the employer can shorten the employee's leave by one to two days; unexcused missed periods of shorter parts of individual shifts count together.

402. An employee who did not work while serving a prison sentence shall have his leave for the calendar year reduced by one-twelfth for every twenty-one working days missed in this way, as well as his leave for serving his detention.

403. Leave for days worked and additional leave can only be shortened due to unexcused work absences. The employee's leave is not deducted for temporary incapacity for work resulting from a work accident or occupational disease for which the employer is responsible and for the period of maternity and paternity leave.

V. Taking Leave

404. A week of leave is seven consecutive days. The employer determines the use of leave after negotiation with the employee according to the leave plan determined with the prior approval of the employee representatives. The employee can use the leave as a rule in its entirety and by the end of the calendar year. If leave is granted in several parts, at least one part must be at least two weeks unless the employee and the employer agree otherwise. The employer is obliged to notify the employee at least fourteen days in advance of taking leave.

405. The employer is obliged to compensate the employee for costs incurred through no fault of the employee because the employer changed the use of leave or revoked leave. The employer may not determine the taking of leave when the employee is recognized as temporarily unable to work due to illness or injury and for the period during which the employee is on maternity and parental leave. During other obstacles to work on the part of the employee, the employer can determine the employee to take leave only at his request. If, during the employee's leave, a holiday falls on a day that is otherwise his usual working day, it is not included in his leave. When the employer assigns an employee additional time off for overtime work or for work on a holiday in such a way that it would fall on leave, he is obliged to assign him additional time off for another day.

406. The employer may, in agreement with the employees' representatives, determine collective leave if it is necessary for operational reasons. Collective leave may not be designated for more than two weeks unless otherwise stipulated; if it is for severe operational reasons notified to employees at least six months in advance, it may be designated for three weeks.

407. The employer can determine the employee to take leave, even if he has not yet met the conditions for the entitlement to leave, if it can be assumed that the employee will meet these conditions by the end of the calendar year in which the leave is taken, or by the end of the employment relationship.

408. When an employee cannot use up his leave in a calendar year because the employer does not determine its use or because of obstacles to work on the part of the employee, the employer is obliged to provide the employee with leave so that it ends no later than the end of the following calendar year. When the employer does not determine the employee's leave by 30 June of the following calendar year at the latest so that the employee uses up the leave by the end of this calendar year, the employee may determine the leave. The employee must notify the employer of this leave in writing, at least thirty days in advance; the specified period can be shortened with the employer's consent.

409. When an employee starts service in the armed forces during the leave, his leave will be interrupted if he has been recognized as temporarily unable to work due to illness or injury, treating a sick family member, or taking maternity or parental leave.

410. When the employee cannot use up the leave for taking maternity, paternal or parental leave even by the end of the following calendar year, the unused leave will be granted to her (him) by the employer after the end of the maternity or parental leave. When the employee cannot use up his leave because he was recognized as temporarily unable to work due to illness or injury, even by the end of the following calendar year, the employer will provide him with unused leave after the employee's temporary incapacity for work ends. When the employee cannot use up his leave because he was released for a long time to perform a public function or trade union function, the employer will grant him the unused leave after the performance of the public function or trade union function has ended.

411. The right to leave is a personal right of the employee, which is not transferable to other persons and, therefore, cannot be transferred to the heir. The right does not pass to the heir if the employee dies before taking the leave. However, the claim for compensation of wages for unused leave (or a proportional part thereof) is a monetary claim of the employee, which must be assessed like other wage claims from the employment relationship. As a result of the death of the employee, the persons mentioned in section 35(2) of the Labour Code, a claim to the extent established in this provision, which they can exercise themselves.

412. The employee is entitled to wage compensation for his average earnings for the used leave. For the part of leave that exceeds four weeks of the basic amount of leave, which the employee could not use even by the end of the following calendar year, the employee is entitled to a wage compensation in the amount of his average earnings. For the unused four weeks of the basic amount of leave, the employee cannot be paid compensation, except if he could not use this leave due to the termination of the employment relationship.

Chapter 5. Remuneration and Benefits

§1. Notion of Wage

413. Work performance in exchange for remuneration, in a relationship of subordination between employer and employee, is the essential attribute of an employment relationship. The right to remuneration for the work performed sufficient for a decent standard of living of employees is stipulated by Article 36 of the Constitution of the Slovak Republic. Article 3 and section 118(1) of the Labour Code also guarantee employees the right to wages for work performed. Wages are one of the forms of remuneration for work in an employment relationship. Compared with wages, therefore, remuneration for work is a broader notion. In labour law relations based on agreements on work performed outside the employment relationship, the employer grants the employee the agreed remuneration for the work performed.

414. The term wage can be defined positively (what is considered a wage) and negatively (what is not considered a wage). Under section 118(2) of the Labour Code, a wage is a payment or payment of monetary value (wages in kind) that the employer provides to the employee for work. The payment provided by the employer to the employee for work on the occasion of his work anniversary or life anniversary is also considered salary if it is not provided from profit after taxation or from the social fund.

415. However, wage compensation, severance pay, severance pay, travel allowances including non-entitlement travel allowances, contributions from the social fund, contributions to supplementary pension savings, contributions to employee life insurance, income from capital shares (shares) or bonds, are not considered wages, tax bonus, compensation of income in case of temporary incapacity for work of the employee, supplements to sickness benefits, compensation for work emergency, monetary compensation according to section 83a(4) and other performance provided to the employee in connection with employment according to the Labour Code, special regulations, collective agreement or employment contract, which is not of a wage nature. Further payment provided by the employer to the employee from the after-tax profit is also not considered a salary.

§2. Guaranteed Monthly Wages

416. According to the current legal situation, the wage is set for employers who carry out business activities in the Labour Code, according to which the remuneration of employees is carried out exclusively on a contractual basis. The Labour Code does not establish any upper limits for the provision of wages. However, it limits the contractual freedom of the participants of the employment relationship by the legal minimum wage because the wage must not be lower than the minimum wage established by Act no. 663/2007 Coll. on the Minimum Wage. A higher than the legal minimum wage can be agreed upon in the collective agreement. The wage of a specific employee is regulated under these regulations in an employment contract or a collective agreement. The Labour Code does not regulate or determine the wage structure. Its agreement is within the competence of the contracting parties during individual or collective negotiations. The amount of statutory minimum wage is adjusted every calendar year, and it is always effective from 1 January.

417. Wage conditions must be agreed upon without any discrimination based on gender; women and men have the right to equal pay for equal work or work of equal value.

418. Remunerating the same wage for work of different qualification requirements contradicts justice and the principle of equal treatment, which has its reverse side. Just as it is contrary to this principle to provide unequal pay for the same work or work of equal value, it is also contrary to the principle of equal treatment to provide equal pay for work of different complexity and skill requirements. Such a practice is still common among many employer entities. Therefore, minimum wage claims establish the lowest possible wage limit between participants in the employment relationship, depending on its complexity and demands, and in practice, lead employers whose remuneration is not agreed upon in a collective agreement to create their wage systems so that their employees are not entitled to a lower wage than are these minimum wage claims, or restricts the employer similarly to the minimum wage when negotiating the amount of wages with individuals in the employment contract. An employer whose remuneration of employees is not agreed in a collective agreement is obliged to pay the employee at least the amount of the minimum wage claim determined for the level of work demands of the relevant job. The Labour Code guarantees a minimum tariff wage limit depending on the qualification level of the work performed and does not allow the employer to provide the same wage to an employee performing the most straightforward work and an employee performing work that is difficult in terms of qualification.

419. The minimum wage requirements in section 120 of the Labour Code establish the lowest possible wage limit between participants in the employment relationship, depending on its complexity and demands. They apply only to employees whose remuneration for work is governed by the Labour Code and whose remuneration is not agreed in a collective agreement. The minimum wage claims represent a minimum wage limit depending on the difficulty of the work performed and guarantee an employee performing complex jobs a higher minimum wage than an employee performing the most straightforward jobs. For the participants of the employment relationship, the minimum wage claims are binding only concerning the lowest permissible limit of the negotiated wage, depending on the nature of the work performed. Above the level of these minimum wage claims, the Labour Code does not set the upper limits of the negotiated wage for the participants, nor does it exempt them from the obligation to negotiate a specific wage in terms of the difficulty of the work performed by placing them in the relevant tariff class.

420. Minimum wage claims do not exempt the participants of the employment relationship from the obligation to negotiate wage conditions in the employment contract under section 43 of the Labour Code. In order to comply with the primary purpose of the provision of minimum wage claims, the employer, unless the remuneration of employees is agreed in a collective agreement, is obliged to evaluate each job and assign a grade to each job following the characteristics of the degree of demands of the jobs, which are listed in Annex no. 1 of the Labour Code according to the most demanding work activity required of the employee within the agreed type of work in the employment contract. The specifics of the minimum wage claims are that after the employer assigns the degree of work difficulty to individual jobs, a separate minimum wage level is created, below which the minimum wage for the given job must not fall.

421. The system of remuneration in public administration is qualitatively different. Since employers of this type have budgets tied to public funding, Act no. 553/2003 Coll. lays down precise introductory pay rates and bonus regulations.

§3. Wages Payment

422. According to the Labour Code, wages are paid by the employer. It is one of the essential obligations of the employer towards the employees in the employment relationship. The wage is paid on the payment dates agreed in the employment contract, in the collective agreement or the payment dates announced according to section 47a(1)(d). With an employee performing domestic work, it is possible to agree on the payment of wages even for the delivery of each completed assigned work. At the employee's request, the wage due during the leave must be paid before the leave starts. The employer can provide an advance payment on the agreed terms between the payment terms. Wages are paid during working time and at the workplace unless otherwise agreed upon in the employment contract. If, for serious reasons, the employee cannot appear after the payment of the salary or if he works at a remote workplace, the employer shall send him the salary so that it is delivered to him on the day designated for its payment or at the latest on the next working day, at his own expense and risk, if they will not agree otherwise. Upon termination of the employment relationship, the employer shall pay the employee the salary due for the monthly period on the day of termination, unless otherwise agreed, but at the latest on the next payment date following the day of termination of the employment relationship.

423. The employer does not have the right to limit the employee's free disposal of the paid salary in any way.

§4. Mandatory Surcharge to Wages

I. Overtime Pay

424. The employee is entitled to the earned wage and a wage surcharge of at least 25% of his average earnings for working overtime. Employees who perform risky work are entitled to overtime wages and a wage surcharge of at least 35% of their average earnings. The employer can agree with the employee to take compensatory leave for overtime work. The employee is entitled to compensatory time off to the extent that the overtime work lasted; in such a case, the employee is not entitled to a wage benefit.

425. In the collective agreement, the employer can agree on a range of employees with whom it is possible to agree that any overtime work will be considered in the amount of wages, but no more than 150 hours in a calendar year. An employer who does not have such a range of employees agreed in the collective agreement can agree in writing with a senior employee in the direct management of a statutory body or a member of a statutory body or with a senior employee who is under the direct management of this senior employee, with an employee who performs conceptual, system, creative, methodical or business activities, manages, organizes or coordinates complex processes or extensive sets of very complex devices, that the salary will take into account possible overtime work, but no more than a total of 150 hours in a calendar year. In these cases, the employee is not entitled to wages for overtime work, including the wage surcharge, and cannot take compensatory time off for this period.

II. Wage and Compensation for Holiday

426. For working on a holiday, the employee is entitled to the earned salary and a wage surcharge of at least 100% of his average earnings. The wage benefit also applies to work performed on a holiday that falls on the employee's continuous week rest day.

427. When the employer and the employee agree to take compensatory time off for working on a holiday, the employee is entitled to one hour of compensatory time off per hour. In that case, he is not entitled to the wage surcharge. When the employer does not provide the employee with compensatory leave no later than three calendar months following the month the work was performed on a holiday or in another agreed period after the work was performed on a holiday, the employee is entitled to a wage surcharge. For taking compensatory time off, the employee is entitled to wage compensation in the amount of his average earnings. For an employee who is remunerated with a monthly salary, the time taken for compensatory leave for work on a holiday is considered time worked for which he is entitled to a wage; this employee is not entitled to compensation for the time spent on compensatory time off for work on a holiday.

428. An employee who did not work because the holiday fell on his usual working day is entitled to wage compensation in the amount of his average earnings if he missed the wage due to the holiday. For an employee paid a monthly salary, a holiday that falls on his usual working day is considered a day worked for which he is entitled to a salary. This employee is not entitled to compensation for the holiday.

429. Wage compensation for a holiday or salary does not belong to an employee who unjustifiably misses a work shift immediately preceding or following a holiday, a work shift ordered by the employer for a holiday, or part of any of these shifts.

430. In the employment contract, the employer can agree on the salary with the senior employee, considering possible work on a holiday. In this case, the senior employee does not receive a wage discount or compensatory time off for work on a holiday.

III. Wage Surcharge for Working on Saturdays

431. For work on Saturday, in addition to the wage earned for each hour of work on Saturday, the employee is entitled to a wage surcharge of at least 50% of the minimum wage in euros per hour. With an employer who, due to the nature of the work or the conditions of operation, requires that the work be regularly performed on Saturdays, a lower amount of wage surcharge can be agreed upon, but at least 45% of the minimum wage in euros per hour according to a special regulation, in a collective agreement, or an employment contract, if it is an employer that does not have a trade union and that employed less than twenty employees as of 31 December of the previous calendar year.

IV. Wage Surcharge for Working on Sundays

432. For work on Sunday, in addition to the wage earned for each hour of work on Sunday, the employee is entitled to a wage surcharge of at least 100% of the minimum wage in euros per hour. With an employer who, due to the nature of the work or the conditions of operation, requires that the work be regularly performed on Sundays, a lower amount of wage surcharge can be agreed upon, but at least 90% of the minimum wage in euros per hour, in a collective agreement or an employment contract, if it is an employer that does not have a trade union and that employed less than twenty employees as of 31 December of the previous calendar year.

V. Wage Surcharge for Night Work

433. In addition to the wage achieved for each hour of night work, the employee is entitled to a wage surcharge of at least 40% of the minimum wage in euros per hour. If an employee performs risky work, he is entitled to a wage surcharge of at least 50% of the minimum wage in euros for an hour. With an employer who, due to the nature of the work or the conditions of operation, requires that the majority of the work be performed as night work, it is possible to agree, if it is not an employee performing risky work, a lower amount of the wage surcharge, but at least 35% of the minimum wage in euros per hour, in a collective agreement, or an employment contract, if it is an employer that does not have a trade union and that employed less than twenty employees as of 31 December of the previous calendar year.

434. The wage can be agreed with the senior employee in the employment contract, taking into account possible night work. In that case, the wage surcharge does not belong to the senior employee.

VI. Wage Compensation for Rugged Work Performance

435. The employee is entitled to wage compensation for rugged work performance when performing work activities in an environment in which chemical factors, carcinogenic and mutagenic factors, biological factors, dust, and physical factors (e.g., noise, vibrations, ionizing radiation) operate, if these work activities are performed by the relevant public authority of the health sector in the third or fourth category according to a special regulation, and when performing them, the intensity of the work environment factors, despite the technical, organizational and specific protective and preventive measures taken according to the particular regulations, requires the employee to use personal protective work equipment to reduce the health risk. For each hour of such work, in addition to the earned wage, the employee is entitled to wage compensation for rugged work performance of at least 20% of the minimum wage in euros per hour according to a special regulation.

§5. Deductions from Wages

436. The Labour Code allows wage deductions based on an agreement on wage deductions or a unilateral action by the employer for precisely defined reasons. The employer can make precisely defined wage deductions based on section 131 of the Labour Code.

437. From the employee's wage, the employer will preferentially deduct social insurance premiums, advance premiums for public health insurance, arrears from the annual settlement of public health insurance advances, contributions to supplementary pension savings, which the employee pays according to a special regulation, deduction of advance tax or taxes, arrears of advance tax, tax arrears, the arrears, which arose due to the taxpayer's fault for advance tax and tax, including accessories, and arrears from the annual settlement of advance tax on income from the dependent activity.

438. After making the deductions according to the previous one, the employer can only deduct from the wage:

- a wage advance, which the employee is obliged to return because the conditions for awarding this wage were not met;

- sums affected by the execution of a decision ordered by a court or an administrative body;
- monetary penalties and fines, as well as compensation imposed on the employee by an enforceable decision of the competent authorities;
- unlawfully received amounts of social insurance benefits and old-age pension savings pensions or their advances, state social benefits, benefits in material need and contributions to benefit in material need, cash contributions to compensate for the social consequences of severe disability, if the employee is obliged to return them to based on an enforceable decision according to a special regulation;
- unbilled travel reimbursement advances;
- compensation of income in case of temporary incapacity for work of the employee or its part to which the employee lost the right or did not have the right;
- wage compensation for leave to which the employee has lost his entitlement or to which he was not entitled;
- wage compensation according to section 142(5) or its part to which the employee was not entitled;
- the amount of severance pay or its part, which the employee is obliged to return;
- unaccounted advances for the employer's allowance for meals or a purpose-bound financial allowance for meals.

439. The employer can only make additional deductions from wages beyond those mentioned above based on a written agreement with the employee on deductions from wages or if the employer's obligation to make deductions from wages and other employee income results from a particular regulation.

Chapter 6. Incapacity to Work

440. Although the essence of every labour law relationship is the contractual obligation of the employee to perform the agreed work and the corresponding obligation of the employer to assign the agreed work, the Labour Code defines the facts when the parties cannot fulfil their obligation. These are facts foreseen by law that prevent the employee from performing the agreed work and the employer from assigning the agreed work. These facts can be both objective and subjective and temporary or permanent. If these facts are only transitory (temporary), they can collectively be characterized as work obstacles. If it is a permanent impossibility to perform or assign work, termination of the employment relationship is considered.

441. An obstacle at work prevents the employee from fulfilling his work obligations towards the employer and temporarily prevents the employer from fulfilling his obligations towards the employee, especially if it concerns the assignment of work according to the employment contract. It is not an obstacle to work if this fact falls on a day the employee is not obliged to work. The existence of an obstacle at work establishes legal consequences foreseen by law. Since the legislator considers these facts legally significant without terminating the employment relationship, there is only a suspension or temporary suspension of fulfilling the stated obligation. The existence of an obstacle gives the employee the right not to perform the work (work leave) agreed with the employer in the employment contract, and at the same time, the right to wages for the work performed expires.

442. The legal basis of obstacles at work and their classification can be found in the Labour Code, which enshrines various obstacles. However, the Labour Code simultaneously creates a relatively broad framework for their more favourable adjustment, either through collective agreements (by expanding the types of obstacles to work regulated by law or by expanding obstacles to work with wage compensation beyond the framework established by law), or individually by agreement with the employee under section 141(3) of the Labour Code.

443. Obstacles at work can be divided from several points of view, either from the point of view of the entity on whose side the reason for the obstacle arose, depending on the material security of the employee, according to the nature of the obstacle or from the point of view of the employer's ability to decide on the provision of work leave.

444. The most common division is the division from the subject's point of view, i.e., depending on which of the participants in the employment relationship the reason for the obstacle arose. Accordingly, we recognize obstacles to work on the part of the employee and obstacles to work on the employer's side.

445. According to the material security of the employee, we distinguish between obstacles to work with wage compensation or another form of material security from the entity for the benefit of which the employee is working, obstacles to work with the right to material security according to social security regulations, and obstacles to work without the right to material security.

446. According to the nature of the obstacles at work, obstacles can be divided into justified and unjustified obstacles. If the employee's entitlement to work leave is directly defined by law, his absence from work is considered excused. In practice, however, there may also be cases when the employer is not obligated to justify the employee's absence. If he does not do so, such absence can be considered an unjustified obstacle to work.

447. According to the employer's ability to decide on the provision of work leave, we can distinguish between situations where the employer is obliged to provide work leave and must justify an obstacle to work and obstacles to work when the provision of work leave depends on the employer's assessment.

§1. Obstacles at Work on the Part of the Employee

I. Obstacles for Reasons of General Interest

448. In the case of obstacles at work due to the general interest, the reason for the creation of the obstacle does not lie in the person of the employee or his interest but in the interest of the company, the fulfilment of which justifies the employer's obligation to provide the employee with time off. The performance of public functions, the fulfilment of civic duties and other actions in the general interest can be considered obstacles to work due to public interest, per section 136 of the Labour Code. Since voluntary activity (section 138a), the performance of voluntary military training (section 138b) and the fulfilment of military service and regular exercise or the fulfilment of the tasks of the armed forces (section 139) also bring benefits to society, in our opinion there is no doubt that even these obstacles are obstacles for reasons of general interest.

449. In the case of obstacles to work due to the performance of public functions, the fulfilment of civic duties and other actions in the general interest, the Labour Code limits the scope of the provided work leave to the vital time.

450. In the case of several obstacles to work of this type, the Labour Code does not determine their maximum extent. According to the general provisions on obstacles to work, they must be drawn on for the necessary time. The employer should reflect a more specific regulation, mainly in the collective agreement or work regulations. When an employee performs a public function or fulfils civic duties or other actions in the general interest, he is obliged to do so as a matter of priority outside his working time. It is true that for obstacles at work due to the performance of public functions, the fulfilment of civic duties and other actions in the general interest, the employer is obliged to provide the employee with time off work only if the activity that is the subject of the obstacle at work cannot be performed outside of working time. The impact of an obstacle at work on the employee's working time results from the employer's pre-determined schedule of work shifts.

451. Leave from work due to the performance of public functions, the employer provides the fulfilment of civic duties and other actions in the general interest without compensation of wages, if the Labour Code (specifically in the case of participation in rehabilitation stays, participation in mandatory medical examinations, participation of employee representatives in education, participation in donations blood, participation in apheresis and participation in the donation of other biological materials), a particular regulation or collective agreement does not stipulate otherwise or unless the employer and employee agree otherwise.

A. *Long-Term Release of an Employee*

452. Provision of section 136(2) and (3) of the Labour Code regulates the long-term release of an employee. During this period, the employment relationship is suspended.

453. According to paragraph 2, a long-term release is due to the performance of a public function and a trade union function. The performance of a trade union function is the performance of a trade union function outside the employer (e.g., in the committee of the relevant trade union). Wage compensation from the employer with whom the employee is employed does not belong to him.

454. In this case, paragraph 3 is a long-term release for the performance of a function in a trade union body operating at this employer under the conditions agreed upon in the collective agreement and for the performance of a works council member after the agreement with the works council. Even if during the long-term layoff of the employee directly from the Labour Code, the employee is not entitled to wage compensation, the trade union can agree with the employer in a collective agreement on the terms of the agreement on the performance of the function.

B. *Work Leave of Employee Representatives*

455. In connection with the activity of employee representatives, it is necessary to distinguish whether the employer has released the employee for the long-term activity of the employee representative or not. In addition to the provisions of section 136, the activity of employee representatives whose employer has not released them for a long time to perform their duties is also governed by the provisions of section 240.

456. In the case of an employee whose employer has not released him for a long time to perform the function of an employee representative, it is necessary to distinguish between the performance of the function, which is directly related to the performance of the employer's tasks, and that part of the performance of the function, which is not directly related to the performance of the employer's tasks. Section 240(1) of the Labour Code considers it the performance of work the employee is entitled to pay. On the contrary, the part of the performance of the function of employee representatives, which is not directly related to the performance of the employer's tasks, is necessary according to section 240(2) to be considered another obstacle to work in the public interest, for which the employer – except for the training of employee representatives according to section 138 – does not provide wage compensation.

457. Labour Code, in the provisions of section 240(2), enshrines the conditional legal right of employee representatives to work leave to perform the function of employee representatives or to participate in their training, which is provided by the relevant trade union body, the works council and the employer, when the employer provides this work leave under the regime of the provisions of section 136(1) if important operational reasons on the part of the employer do not prevent this.

458. When there is no need for a long-term release of an employee for the performance of a trade union function, a member of the employee council, or an employee confidant, but the employee representative has the right to take time off, section 240(3) provisions apply. The employer provides a member of a trade union body for the activities of a trade union organization, a member of the works council for the activities of a works council or an employee confidant for his activities with work leave with compensation for the time agreed between the employer and the trade union or the employer and the works council or the employee confidant. If the employees' representatives and the employer disagree on the scope of work, leave, and the amount of the wage compensation, the employees' representatives are entitled to the monthly wage compensation as the product of the number of employed employees and the period of fifteen minutes. It is based on the number of employees employed by the employer in the previous calendar year.

459. The Labour Code allows the employer to check whether the employee uses the provided work leave according to section 240(3)for the purpose for which it was provided. The conditions for the performance of this control can be agreed upon in a collective agreement or an agreement between the employer and employee representatives, depending on the applicable legal status.

460. According to section 250, members of a particular negotiating body, members of the European Works Council and employee representatives ensure a different procedure for informing employees and negotiating with them at the employer or an organizational unit of the employer with headquarters in the territory of the Slovak Republic are adequately covered by section 240 when performing their duties. In the same way, the members of the particular negotiating body and the members of the European Works Council are provided with training and compensation to the extent necessary to perform their function as an employee representative.

C. Performance of a Public Function

461. The definition of the term performance of a public function for the Labour Code contains the provisions of section 137(2), according to which the performance of a public office is the fulfilment of obligations arising from the office, which is defined by a term of office or a period and is filled based on direct election or indirect election or exchange according to special regulations. A public function for the Labour Code is when the employee's activity fulfils the content mentioned above features, either according to the Labour Code or according to a special regulation. The Labour Code itself does not define the range of public functions. However, the term public functionary can be found, for example, in Constitutional Act no. 357/2004 Coll. on the Protection of the Public Interest in the Performance of the Functions of Public Officials, according to which public interest for this constitutional act is anyone who performs the function specified in Article 2(1).

462. The performance of a public function is an obstacle to work due to the general interest if the employee performs the activity and fulfils his work tasks arising from the employment relationship. In the event of an obstacle to work due to the performance of a public function, the employee is entitled to leave without compensation from the employer.

463. An employee can carry out the performance of a public function during a continuing employment relationship, or the employee is released from the performance of work duties from the employment relationship for a short period (according to section 137(2)), or it can be a long-term release of an employee whose employment relationship is suspended during the performance of a public function (according to section 136(2)). Unless a special regulation provides otherwise, an employee who performs a public function and fulfils the duties arising from the employment relationship may be granted work leave for a maximum of thirty working days or changes in a calendar year due to the performance of a public function.

D. Fulfilment of Civic Duties

464. The Labour Code provides an exemplary calculation of activities classified as civil duties. The obligation to fulfil civil obligations results primarily from particular regulations that impose this obligation on citizens; therefore, if special regulations result in another civil obligation for the employee not listed in the Labour Code, this is also considered an obstacle to work.

E. Other Actions in the General Interest

465. The Labour Code does not define other actions in the general interest. However, he gives examples of activities that can be considered an act in the general interest. However, it can also be other activities based on particular regulations that do not perform a public function or fulfil a civic duty.

F. *Obstacles at Work Due to Volunteering*

466. The Labour Code regulates the relations between the employee and the employer in matters of volunteering, thereby expressing the public interest in supporting volunteering. Voluntary activity is performed in free time without the right to remuneration and with the consent of the recipient of the volunteer activity, either for the benefit of this recipient, if it is a natural person or a legal entity, or for the public benefit if it is an activity performed for the benefit of the state or authorities territorial self-government. The rules for the performance of volunteer activities are set so that the volunteer does not have any claims arising from the performance of volunteer activities.

467. According to the Labour Code, it is up to the employer to assess the possibility of granting work leave to the employee while considering its operational capabilities and the public interest in supporting the volunteer's activities. The Labour Code allows the provision of work leave to an employee to perform volunteer activities if the employee requests it; this is not a legal right to the provision of work leave. The granting of work leave is subject to the employer's consent. Upon his request, the employer may grant an employee time off to perform activities based on a contract for voluntary activity in working time. In contrast, such employees do not receive wages or compensation for the time off. The leave from work granted in this way is not considered work performance.

468. The employer can also agree with the employees' representatives on the conditions for providing work leave due to voluntary activity. However, even in this case, the social partners cannot agree on providing wage compensation. The subject of the agreement should only be the conditions for providing work leave for volunteer activities.

G. *Obstacles at Work Due to Voluntary Military Training*

469. Voluntary military training is under Act no. 378/2015 Coll. on Voluntary Military Training, the activity by which a soldier of voluntary military training in a state of security prepares for the defence of the Slovak Republic. Voluntary military training is an obstacle to work, for the performance of which the employer can grant the employee a leave of absence based on the employee's request. In contrast, the employee is not entitled to wages or compensation during the leave of absence unless the employer and the employee agree otherwise. There is no legal right to the provision of work leave, and the work leave granted in this way is not considered work performance.

H. Obstacles at Work Due to the Fulfilment of Military Service and Due to Regular Exercise or Fulfilment of the Tasks of the Armed Forces

470. According to Act no. 570/2005 Coll. on Conscription, which also regulates the creation and termination of conscription, it is obligatory to submit to conscription unless the act provides otherwise and to perform extraordinary service or alternative service.

471. In connection with obstacles to work due to the fulfilment of military service and due to regular exercise or the fulfilment of the tasks of the armed forces, the Labour Code regulates three situations:

- the employee is obliged to appear in person in connection with the fulfilment of military service at the relevant district office in the seat of the region or for a medical examination;
- the employee is obliged to appear in person at the designated military unit of the armed forces for regular training or to fulfil the tasks of the armed forces;
- the employee has to go to regular training or perform the tasks of the armed forces in a place so far from his residence or workplace that the journey by public transport takes more than six hours.

472. When an employee must appear in person in connection with the fulfilment of military service at the relevant district office in the region's seat or for a medical examination, the employer will provide him with work leave for the necessary time. For this time, the employee is entitled to wage compensation from the employer in the amount of his average earnings. The costs of wage compensation are reimbursed to the employer by the relevant district office in the regional headquarters.

473. When the employee is required to appear in person at a designated military unit of the armed forces for regular training or to perform the tasks of the armed forces, the employer will grant him a leave of absence for the necessary time. The mentioned activities can be carried out within thirty calendar days in a calendar year. For this time, the employee is entitled to wage compensation in the amount of his average earnings, which the employer will provide to him after the end of regular training or the performance of the tasks of the armed forces, no later than the end of the following calendar month. The costs of wage compensation are reimbursed to the employer by the military unit of the armed forces in which the employee performed regular exercises or performed the tasks of the armed forces.

474. When an employee has to go on a regular exercise or to fulfil the tasks of the armed forces in a place so far from his place of residence or workplace that the journey by public transport takes more than six hours, he is entitled to one day off work and at the same time he is also entitled to one day for the journey back work leave. For this time, the employee is entitled to wage compensation in the number of his average earnings, which the employer will provide to him after the end of regular training or the performance of the tasks of the armed forces, no later than the end of the following calendar month. The costs of wage compensation are reimbursed to the employer by the military unit of the armed forces in which the employee performed regular exercises or performed the tasks of the armed forces.

II. Obstacles Due to Increasing Qualifications

475. The Labour Code allows the employer to support his employee in improving his qualifications. The employer can provide the employee with work leave and wage compensation in the amount of his average earnings, mainly if the anticipated increase in qualifications follows the employer's needs. Therefore, it is up to the employer to decide whether to grant the employee a leave of absence. The employer can agree with the employee on increasing qualifications, the details of which are regulated by section 155 of the Labour Code. By agreeing to increase the qualification, the employer not only ensures the stabilization of the employee for a certain period specified in the agreement but at the same time ensures the return of its costs spent on the qualification process if the employee does not comply with his stabilization obligation and does not remain with the employer after the agreed time.

476. If the employer agrees to the employee improving his qualifications, the employee is entitled to paid leave. Specifically, the employer will be obliged to provide him with leave from work at least:

- to the extent necessary for participation in classes;
- two days for the preparation and execution of each test;
- five days to prepare and perform the final exam, matriculation exam and discharge;
- forty days in total for the preparation and execution of all state exams or dissertation exams at individual levels of higher education;
- ten days to prepare and defend the final thesis, diploma thesis or dissertation.

477. Wages are not compensated for time off work granted to an employee to take a remedial exam.

478. Employees who practice the medical profession represent a particular group in providing work leave for further education. The Labour Code grants them a five-day leave of absence during the calendar year for continuing education and wage compensation in the amount of their average earnings.

III. Significant Personal Obstacles at Work

479. Significant personal obstacles represent a group of obstacles in the work consisting of the employee's person. Even though they express the employee's interest, the employer must justify the employee's absence.

480. In general, we can classify them from several points of view. The most common division is the material security of the employee during an obstacle at work. Accordingly, we distinguish obstacles in which the employee is not entitled to wage compensation but is provided with a material security benefit from another entity during the leave of absence and obstacles in which the employee is entitled to wage compensation during the leave of absence or in which he is only granted work leave without any monetary compensation.

481. The employer must justify the obstacles to work listed in section 141(1) of the Labour Code, regardless of their duration. These are cases of temporary incapacity for work due to illness or injury, maternity leave, paternity leave and parental leave, quarantine, personal and all-day care of a sick family member under a special regulation, personal and all-day care of a natural person under a special regulation and during the period when the person, who otherwise takes care of the child until the child reaches the age of eleven or until the child reaches the age of eighteen, if it is a child with a long-term adverse health condition, underwent an examination or treatment in a medical facility that could not be provided outside of the employee's working time. The Labour Code obliges the employee to promptly inform his employer of an obstacle at work. In the case of the mentioned obstacles, the employee is not entitled to wage compensation unless a particular regulation, which is most often a regulation of social security law, provides otherwise.

482. Section 141(2) of the Labour Code contains the regulation of obstacles to work, in which work leave is provided either for the necessary time or in a precisely defined range. This provision includes obstacles to work due to the examination and treatment of an employee in a medical facility, the birth of a child to an employee, accompanying a family member to a medical facility for examination or treatment in the event of a sudden illness or injury and for pre-determined examination, treatment or cure, accompanying a disabled child to the facility social care or a special school, death of a family member, wedding, inability to travel to work for an employee with a disability, unforeseen interruption of traffic or delay of regular public transport, relocation of the employee and finally finding a new place before the end of the employment relationship.

483. Wage compensation belongs to the employee in the case:

- examination or treatment of an employee in a medical facility – for the first seven calendar days of taking work leave; after exceeding the range of seven days in a calendar year and upon meeting the condition that the examination or treatment could not be carried out outside working time, the employee is entitled to additional work leave, but no longer without compensation;
- preventive examinations of a pregnant woman related to pregnancy – if examination or treatment cannot be carried out outside working time;
- birth of a child to an employee – work leave with wage compensation is provided only for the necessary time, which means for the transportation of the child's mother to the medical facility and back;

- accompanying a family member to a medical facility for examination or treatment in a medical facility – for the first seven calendar days of taking work leave; after exceeding the range of seven days in a calendar year and upon meeting the condition that the examination or treatment could not be carried out outside working time, the employee is entitled to additional work leave, but no longer without compensation;
- accompanying a disabled child to a social care facility or special school – for no more than ten days in a calendar year;
- death of a family member;
- employee's wedding;
- impossibility of travel to work by individual means of transport for an employee with a disability due to weather reasons – for the necessary time, at most one day;
- relocation of the employee, if it is a relocation in the interest of the employer;
- finding a new place before the end of the employment relationship.

484. On the part of the employee, there may also be other obstacles at work, the purpose of which is the arrangement of other necessary personal, family and other things and which cannot be handled during working time; therefore, in addition to the above cases, the employer can also provide the employee with additional work leave. Additional work leave can be granted for the same reasons as those listed in section 141 paragraph 2 of the Labour Code, but to a greater extent than the law provides, also for reasons other than those listed in section 141 paragraph 2 of the Labour Code, with or without wage compensation, then work leave at the request of the employee with or without wage compensation without the obligation to work it, and finally leave regardless of the employee's request, which the employee takes later. However, the employee has no legal right to take leave in these cases.

485. The employer cannot consider as an obstacle to work a situation where he cannot assign work to an employee due to obstacles to work on the part of the employer (e.g., if an employee who was not entitled to leave to the required extent does not work due to the mass taking of leave determined by the employer). In such a case, the regime of obstacles to work on the employer's part is applied.

IV. Temporary Suspension from Work

486. A particular type of obstacle at work is temporary suspension from work, which serves as a specific preventive institute in case of suspicion of the employer of a serious violation of work discipline by the employee. Until a severe violation of labour discipline is proven, the employer cannot apply actions leading to the termination of the employment relationship (e.g., immediate termination of the employment relationship) since the suspicion of a violation of labour discipline is not sufficient for their application and it must be proven that the culpable violation of labour discipline occurred. However, to avoid frustrating the employer's interest due to the impossibility of terminating the employment relationship, the employer may suspend the employee's work temporarily after one month of prior consultation with the employee's representatives.

487. An employee proven to have committed a severe violation of work discipline is entitled to compensation of wages of at least 60% of his average earnings during the temporary suspension of work performance. However, if a severe violation of work discipline is not proven, the employee is entitled to a supplement up to his average earnings.

V. Strike

488. The employer is obliged to justify the employee's absence from work during his participation in the strike in connection with exercising his economic and social rights. In this case, participation in a strike before the legality of a court decision on the illegality of a strike is considered an excused absence. In contrast, participation in an illegal strike after a court decision on the illegality of a strike is considered an unexcused absence from work. The employee does not receive wages or compensation for the duration of the strike.

489. The employer must allow employees who are not participating in the strike to perform their work. If these employees cannot perform work due to a strike, this is already an obstacle to work on the employer's part.

VI. Obstacles to Work and Agreements on Work Performed Outside the Employment Relationship

490. According to the provisions of section 223(2), the Labour code applies only to significant personal obstacles to work on the part of the employee according to section 141(1) and (2) (a) to (g), if they interfered with the time for which the employer determined the performance of the work. In the case of these obstacles at work, the employer is obliged to excuse the employee's absence from work, but the employee is not entitled to compensation for this time of absence from work.

§2. Obstacles at Work on the Part of the Employer

491. These are facts foreseen by law, in which the employer does not or cannot assign work to the employee. The time of obstacles to work on the employer's side is considered work performance. During the duration of the obstacle to work on the employer's side, the employee is entitled to financial security in the form of wage compensation in the amount of average earnings or part thereof.

492. Obstacles to work on the part of the employer can be divided into the following groups: downtime, adverse weather effects, obstacles to work based on operational severe reasons on the part of the employer, other obstacles to work that are not explicitly regulated by law, but the law allows for their existence, obstacles due to an extraordinary situation, state of emergency or state of emergency and finally limitation of the employer's activity due to an external factor. In addition to the mentioned obstacles, the Collective Bargaining Act also allows lockouts to be an obstacle to work.

I. Downtime

493. As it follows from the text of the law, downtime is in the case of a temporary shortage caused by a malfunction in machinery, in the supply of raw materials or motive power, faulty work documents or other similar operational causes. These are unforeseeable organizational or technical reasons on the part of the employer. In the case of downtime, it should be an obstacle to work that is sudden, unpredictable and transient in nature, which distinguishes it from other obstacles to work on the part of the employer, among which it is necessary to include such obstacles as regular or planned shutdowns due to repairs and revisions.

494. Due to downtime, the employer can transfer the employee to another job only if the employee agrees; however, if the transfer is within the scope of the employment contract, consent is not required. If the employee agrees to be transferred to another job, the obstacle in the form of downtime does not arise. When there is no agreement on a temporary transfer to another job, the employee is entitled to wage compensation in average earnings during the downtime.

495. If the employee schedules his/her own working time during domestic work or telework, the provisions on downtime do not apply except for downtime for which the employer is responsible. When a home-based employee cannot perform work according to the conditions agreed in the employment contract due to a limitation in production due to a decrease in the purchase of goods, it is not an obstacle to work on the part of the employer due to downtime, but another obstacle to work on the part of the employer.

II. Adverse Weather Effects

496. Adverse weather conditions constitute such an obstacle to the work as to prevent the performance of the work in such a way that its commencement or continuation cannot be expected. Unlike downtime, the existence of an obstacle does not lie in the work process but has an objective nature. The obstacle primarily concerns employees who work outdoors or whose work is dependent on weather conditions.

497. If the employee cannot perform the work due to adverse weather conditions, the employee is entitled to a wage compensation of at least 50% of his average earnings. The stated amount of wage compensation is only minimal; it is possible to agree on a more favourable adjustment for the employee in the collective or employment contract.

498. According to section 144a(1)(d) of the Labour Code, obstacles to work due to adverse weather conditions are assessed as the time of work performance. The employee is thus not obliged to make up such missed working hours. At the same time, however, the Labour Code allows the employer to agree that the employee will work the working time missed due to adverse weather conditions at another time. If the employee works overtime with work performed more than the specified weekly working time, working time lost due to adverse weather conditions is not overtime work.

III. Other Obstacles to Work on the Part of the Employer

499. In the case of other work obstacles on the employer's part, it is the non-allocation of work by the employer for reasons other than downtime or adverse weather conditions. The reason for such an obstacle lies on the employer's side, while it is irrelevant whether the employer can influence the occurrence and duration of the obstacle. In application practice, it can be, for example, a situation where an employee does not perform work due to an illegal act by the employer (the employer imposed a work task that is contrary to legal regulations or the employment contract) due to an inappropriately chosen moment of the effects of organizational changes (the employer cancelled the position, but the employment relationship with the employee has not yet been terminated), or if, as a result of organizational changes, a specific function at the employer has been abolished, and the employee has been invalidly transferred from this function to another function while declaring that he does not agree to the transfer.

500. Since the employer does not fulfil one of the essential obligations arising from the employment relationship – to assign the employee work according to the employment contract – the employee is entitled to wage compensation in the amount of his average earnings. Wage compensation to the employee belongs from the moment when the employer does not assign work or from the moment when the employer is unable to assign work per the employment contract and has the nature of the equivalent of the wage that the employee could not earn as a result of the employer not allowing him to perform work, to which he committed himself according to the employment contract.

IV. Operational Severe Reasons for Which the Employer Cannot Assign Work to the Employee (Defined in the Agreement with the Employee Representatives)

501. In a written agreement with employee representatives, the employer can define operational severe reasons for which the employer cannot assign work to the employee; this is an obstacle to work on the part of the employer, in which the employee is entitled to compensation of wages in the amount determined by the agreement of at least 60% of his average earnings. The employer's decision cannot replace the agreement.

V. Obstacles Due to Emergency or State of Emergency

502. In connection with the solution to the effects of the COVID-19 pandemic, the legislator adopted an amendment to the Labour Code, which introduced several changes in the eleventh part of the Labour Code, representing deviations from the generally applicable provisions of the Labour Code. These deviations apply only during a state of emergency and two months after revocation. Concerning obstacles at work, this is a situation where the employee cannot perform work in whole or in part due to the stoppage or restriction of the employer's activity based on the decision of the competent authority or due to the stoppage or restriction of the employer's activity as a result of the declaration of an extraordinary situation, state of emergency or state of emergency. According to section 250b(6) of the Labour Code, it will not be a case of force majeure, which is not an obstacle either on the part of the employee or on the side of the employer, but an obstacle to work on the part of the employer, in which the employee is entitled to compensation of wages in the amount of 80% of his average earnings, but at least in the amount of the minimum wages.

503. Therefore, if the state prohibits or restricts, for example, the operation of certain shops and restaurants for the public, as a result of which employers have to limit their activities, in such a situation, all employers, including those with no employee representatives, to provide wage compensation in a lower amount than the employee's average earnings, but at least 80% of his average monthly earnings. At the same time, the amount the employee receives when entitled to wage compensation cannot be lower than the minimum wage.

504. The mentioned regulation does not affect the existing agreements of the employer with the representatives of the employees, in which they have defined operational severe reasons for which the employer cannot assign work to the employee, in which the employee is entitled to compensation of wages in the amount determined by the agreement of at least 60% of his average earnings, as well as agreements on the request the employer on the provision of support during short-time work.

VI. Limitation of the Employer's Activity Due to an External Factor

505. In order to ensure that during the duration of an external factor, which is of a temporary nature, which the employer could not influence or could not prevent, and which harms the allocation of work to employees, there is no threat or loss of jobs, a special regulation – Act no. 215/2021 on Support During Short-time Work – allows the employer to use support during short-time work (so-called kurzarbeit). Support during short-time work serves to partially reimburse the employer's costs for partial compensation of the employee's wages during the duration of the external factor, due to which the employer's activities were restricted.

506. The time of short-time work means the time from the beginning of the limitation of the employer's activity due to the influence of an external factor to the end of the limitation of the employer's activity. Restriction of the employer's activity means an obstacle to work on the part of the employer to the extent that the employer cannot assign work to at least one-third of the employer's employees or part of the employer's employees to the extent of at least 10% of the established weekly working time. An external factor is a temporary factor that the employer cannot influence or prevent. It harms the employer's work assignment to employees, especially in an extraordinary situation, exceptional state or emergency, extraordinary circumstance, or force majeure circumstances. It is impossible to consider the time of war and martial law, the seasonality of the activity, restructuring, planned shutdown or reconstruction as an external factor.

507. Support during short-time work is provided as a claim after fulfilling the conditions established by law. Support is provided to an employer who:

(a) is on short-time work;
(b) paid social insurance premiums and mandatory old-age pension savings contributions for the entire period of the obligation to pay social insurance premiums and mandatory old-age pension contributions as of the date of applying support pension savings that lasted for at least twenty-four calendar months immediately preceding the calendar month for which the employer is applying for support;
(c) did not violate the prohibition of illegal employment for two years before applying for support;
(d) has a written agreement with employee representatives or with employees, if no employee representatives are at the employer, about the fact that the employer requests the provision of support or the arbitrator's consent according to the Labour Code to the submission of a request for the provision of support; and
(e) requests the provision of support no later than the end of the calendar month following the calendar month for which he is requesting providing support.

508. Support during short-time work is provided for the workplace of an employee:

(a) to whom the employer cannot assign work to the extent of at least 10% of the established weekly working time;
(b) whose employment relationship lasted at least one month as of the date of applying the provision of support;
(c) to whom the notice period does not expire on the day of applying the provision of support;
(d) who, on the day of applying the provision of support, has exhausted leave for the previous calendar year and the exhausted positive account of the working time account if the employer has established a working time account, and the employer cannot transfer it to another job within the agreed type of work, which is not affected by the limitation of the employer's activities; and
(e) for which the employer has the exact authorized costs or does not contribute according to special regulations for the same purpose.

VII. Lockout

509. Lockout means a partial or complete stoppage of work by the employer. Lockout is a last resort for resolving a dispute over the conclusion of a collective agreement. A lockout can be declared under the condition that the collective dispute over the conclusion of a collective agreement will not be resolved even in the proceedings before the mediator. At the beginning of the lockout, its scope, reasons, goals and the list of employees against whom the lockout is applied, the employer must notify the relevant trade union body in writing at least three working days in advance.

510. In contrast to participation in a strike, for employees locked out, this is an obstacle to work on the employer's part. For the duration of the lockout, employees are entitled to a salary of half of their average earnings. If the court decides on the illegality of the lockout, the employee is entitled to wage compensation in the amount of the average earnings.

Chapter 7. Job Security

511. According to Article 35(3) of the Constitution, citizens are guaranteed the right to work; the state materially provides persons who cannot exercise this right through their fault to an adequate extent. The right to work obliges the state, as a mandatory subject, to an active employment policy that creates the essential prerequisites for the economic security of its citizens. The content of the right to work also includes the right to protection against arbitrary dismissal from employment and the right to protection against discrimination in employment.

512. In Slovak labour law, the Labour Code exhaustively regulates how to terminate an employment relationship. Provisions of Slovak labour law governing termination of employment are mandatory. An employment relationship cannot be validly terminated in ways other than legal. Under section 59 of the Labour Code, the employment relationship may be terminated based on:

(a) legal act, namely:
  (i) by agreement;
  (ii) by notice;
  (iii) by immediate termination;
  (iv) by ending in the probationary period.
(b) a legal event, which can be:
  (i) the expiration of the time for which it was agreed or;
  (ii) death of the employee.
(c) official decision (e.g., with nationals of third countries);
(d) of the Act – the termination of the employment relationship of an employee when temporarily assigned to an employer or a temporary employment agency and the creation of an employment relationship with a user employer under section 59(5) of the Labour Code or also the employment relationship of university teachers according to the Act on Universities).

513. The employment relationship can also be terminated by several legal acts simultaneously or successively when the legal acts must be assessed separately, including the resulting legal effects.

514. All this refers to the termination of a valid employment relationship. In the case of an invalid, i.e., only de facto, employment relationship, the employment relationship can only be terminated de facto, i.e., by not assigning work without any legal action leading to its termination.

§1. Termination of the Employment Relationship Based on a Legal Act

515. The legal act of termination of employment regulated in a particular part of the Labour Code is governed by the provisions of the Civil Code, which apply to legal acts in addition to the provisions of the Labour Code. The validity of a legal act is also examined based on section 17 of the Labour Code (a legal act is invalid if the employee waived his rights in advance; if the law expressly provides for this; if the employee representatives did not give the required consent to the legal act or did not discuss it, or if the legal act does not perform in the prescribed manner).

I. Termination of the Employment Relationship by Mutual Agreement

516. Formally, the simplest and most common way to terminate an employment relationship is an agreement – a consensual expression of the employer's and the employee's will to end the existing employment relationship. The agreement is a bilateral legal act, which, based on the mutual expression of the will of the employee and the employer, results in the termination of the employment relationship on a specific date.

517. The agreement is concluded as soon as the participants agree on its content. The participants must first agree on the employment relationship's termination date because the employment relationship will end on the agreed date. Even though the Labour Code requires a written agreement on the termination of the employment relationship, its non-compliance does not lead to the legal consequence of the invalidity of the legal act; therefore, even an oral agreement on the termination of the employment relationship is valid.

518. The Labour Code stipulates that the reasons for the termination of the employment relationship must be stated in the agreement if the employee requests it or if the employment relationship was terminated by agreement for organizational and health reasons. This provision is essential to the employee's possible entitlement to severance pay. When the employment relationship is terminated by agreement, it is not required to be discussed with employee representatives.

519. In case of a planned termination of the employment relationship by mutual agreement with a juvenile employee (i.e., a person under 18 years of age), section 172 of the Labour Code stipulates that the employer must obtain the opinion of the juvenile's legal guardian. However, the negative opinion of the legal guardian on the employment termination agreement does not influence its validity because section 11 of the Labour Code recognizes the entire legal personality of natural persons in labour relations already upon the attainment of 15 years of age.

II. Termination of the Employment Relationship by Notice

520. Notice is a unilaterally addressed legal act which becomes legally effective when it arrives within the sphere of personal disposition of the other party to the employment relationship. An employment relationship ends with a termination based on a unilateral expression of will by the employer or the employee. Legal effects occur upon delivery to the other party. Any termination must be in writing and delivered to the other party; otherwise, it is void; the proper delivery of the notice is essential from the point of view of the beginning of the notice period, which always begins on the first day of the calendar month following the delivery of the notice. Upon expiry of the notice period, the employment relationship ends.

A. *Notice Period*

521. The notice period is at least one month unless the Labour Code provides otherwise. The Labour Code thus provides in three cases:

- when the employer gives notice to the employee for organizational reasons or because the employee has lost the long-term ability to perform the previous work due to his health condition according to a medical opinion, the notice period is at least:
  - two months if the employee's employment relationship with the employer lasted at least one year and less than five years as of the date of delivery of the notice or;
  - three months if the employee's employment relationship with the employer lasted at least five years as of the date of delivery of the notice.
- when the employer gives notice to the employee for other reasons, the notice period is two months; if the employee's employment with the employer lasted at least one year as of the date of delivery of the notice;
- when the notice is given by an employee whose employment relationship with the employer lasted at least one year as of the date of delivery, the notice period is at least two months.

522. By determining only the minimum notice period without determining its maximum length, the Labour Code creates a natural space for collective bargaining and enacts a more favourable exercise of these rights arising from labour law in a collective agreement. The notice period is the same for all categories of employees.

523. A particular notice period of fifteen days applies to the agreement on students' part-time work and agreement to perform work (sections 227 and 228(a) of the Labour Code).

524. During the notice period, both parties must adequately fulfil their obligations arising from the employment relationship.

525. When the notice period of the employee or employer is incorrectly stated in the notice or is not stated there at all, this does not result in the notice being invalid; however, the employment relationship ends upon the expiration of the statutory notice period.

526. The notice delivered to the other participant can only be revoked with his consent. Revocation of the termination and consent to its revocation must be done in writing. However, given that this provision does not link the invalidity of the legal act with the lack of a written form, it can be assumed that both the revocation of the termination and the consent of the other party to the revocation of the termination can also be done verbally, or implicit action. However, the lack of a written form may make it difficult to prove whether such a statement was made in the event of a dispute.

527. According to the current labour legislation, the notice period cannot expire if certain qualified legal events provide a so-called protective period. When the employer has given notice to the employee before the start of the protective period so that the notice period should expire during this protective period, the protective period is not included in the temporarily interrupted notice period. However, this does not apply if the employee declares that he does not insist on extending the notice period.

528. The duration of the employment relationship for counting the notice period also includes the duration of repeatedly concluded employment relationships for a certain period with the same employer, which immediately follow each other.

B. Notice Given by the Employee

529. The legal regulation of termination by the employee is significantly more straightforward than the possibility of termination by the employer.

530. An employee may resign for any reason or no reason. The Labour Code does not establish any other special conditions for the validity of a notice. It is enough for the employee to express his will in writing and deliver it to the employer; otherwise, it is invalid. An employee can revoke a delivered notice only with the employer's consent.

C. Notice Given by the Employer

531. The Labour Code establishes some facts that are a condition for the validity of a termination by the employer:

- the employer may give notice to the employee only for the reasons expressly stated in section 63(1) of the Labour Code;
- the employer cannot give notice to the employee during the protective period according to section 64 of the Labour Code;
- for the termination of an employee with a disability or an employee representative, the employer needs the prior consent of the competent authorities in the established cases (sections 66 and 240(9) of the Labour Code);
- the employer must discuss the termination in advance with the employee representatives if they act at the employer; otherwise, the termination is invalid (section 74 of the Labour Code);
- in selected cases, the employer must offer the employee a suitable job (section 63(2) of the Labour Code);

– the employer must give the notice in writing and deliver it to the employee; otherwise, it is invalid.

1. Reasons for Notice

532. The employer's exhaustively established grounds for termination include organizational, health, and legal reasons based on the quality of work or disciplinary reasons.

533. The grounds for termination are mandatory. Their purpose is that the participants in the employment relationship are adequately protected against termination so they can defend themselves if the reason for termination is not given. Therefore, it is necessary to state the reason for termination so that the legal reason is clearly stated. Because the reason for termination is an inevitable fact that shows the signs of a legal reason for termination, the reason in the written termination must always be stated. They cannot be expanded in the employment contract or the collective agreement. In the same way, no reason for termination can be subsequently changed. The indication of the reason for termination must be sufficiently definite and understandable so as not to raise doubts that it is a termination for a specific reason explicitly stated in the Labour Code so that the addressee of this expression of will is explicit on which of the legal grounds for termination is based.

534. Accumulation of several reasons for termination in one termination is generally permissible. The stated fact has the effect that in the proceedings initiated at the employee's suggestion, it is necessary to examine each of the reasons for termination separately, and it is also necessary to separately assess their effects on the further duration of the employment relationship. If the employment relationship ends based on one, the other reasons applied become obsolete.

535. In a dispute, the court is not bound by the legal qualification that the employer states in the notice. It must be based on how the termination is justified and whether this factual fulfilment is a prerequisite for any grounds for termination listed in the Labour Code. In the same way, the additional specification of the notice cannot be considered a part of the notice. In this way, it would be possible to circumvent the provision that the reason for termination cannot be subsequently changed.

Organizational reasons

536. It is a situation when the employer or part of it is cancelled or relocated, and at the same time, the employee does not agree to the change of the agreed place of work performance, or the situation when the employee becomes redundant due to the written decision of the employer or the competent authority to change his tasks, technical equipment or to reduce the number of employees in order to ensure work efficiency, or about other organizational changes and an employer who is a temporary employment agency, even if the employee becomes redundant due to the termination of the temporary assignment according to section 58 before the end of the period for which the fixed-term employment relationship was agreed.

537. In order to decide on organizational changes, the law does not require that these changes be implemented when the notice is given. However, they must already be decided on in a specified manner. Such a decision must always be made (issued) in writing and announced or communicated by the employer to the employee concerned; however, it is also sufficient if the employee learns about it first from the notice of termination. In a dispute, the court is not authorized to review the decision on organizational change. In the case of a reason for notice based on an employee's redundancy, the employer decides on the selection of a redundant employee; the court cannot review the employer's decision in this regard. In the case of assessing the justification of the use of this statutory reason for termination, the content of the employment contract must be based on the content of the employment contract, and it must be examined whether there has been any organizational change at the employer that would make the employee redundant for him in terms of the function for which the employment contract is written. The prerequisite for using this reason for termination is the existence of an organizational change, an employee's redundancy and a causal connection between the employer's decision to change his tasks and technical equipment or to reduce the employee's redundancy.

Health reasons

538. This covers situations when the employee, due to his health status, according to a medical opinion, has long lost the ability to perform his previous work or if he is not allowed to perform it due to an occupational disease or because of the threat of this disease, or if he has reached the highest permissible exposure at the workplace determined by the decision of the competent public health authority. A prerequisite for a valid termination of employment is a medical opinion that does not allow a professional conclusion other than that the employee has long-term lost the ability to perform the previous work. Therefore, a simple doctor's recommendation to change the type of work performed, justified by the unsuitability of the current work from the point of view of the employee's health, is not enough, just as an opinion that does not clearly show that the employee's incapacity for work is of a long-term nature (not just temporary) cannot be the basis for termination of employment.

Legal reasons

539. Legal reasons cover situations when the employee does not meet the prerequisites and requirements established by legal regulations or the employer's internal regulations for the performance of the agreed work (e.g., when the employee's working position is a driver and his driver's licence was legally revoked, or if the employee resigns or is dismissed from his position, does not wear the prescribed uniform through no fault of the employer).

Reasons based on the quality of work

540. These reasons come into consideration when the employee performs work tasks unsatisfactorily, and simultaneously, the employer has asked him in writing to eliminate the deficiencies in the last six months, and the employee has not eliminated them in a reasonable time. The adequacy of the time provided to the employee to eliminate deficiencies in the work cannot be lumped in but must be assessed individually; it depends, above all, on the nature of the work the employee performs for the employer.

Reasons for violation of work discipline

541. These reasons include reasons for which the employer could immediately terminate the employment relationship or a less severe violation of work discipline.

542. In the case of a less severe violation of work discipline, its continuous violation is not required. After the second less serious violation of work discipline, the employer may give a notice if, in the last six months, the employee has been notified in writing of the possibility of termination. In the case of a repeated violation of work discipline, it is not required to repeat the same act or a violation of discipline in the same way and with the same intensity.

543. When examining whether an employee has violated work discipline in a less serious, severe or particularly gross manner, the court may take into account the employee's personality, the position he holds, his previous attitude towards the performance of work tasks, the time and the situation in which the work violation occurred discipline, to the degree of fault of the employee, to the manner and intensity of the violation of the employee's specific obligations, to the consequences of the violation of work discipline for the employer, to whether the employee's actions caused damage.

544. For a violation of labour discipline or for a reason for which the employment relationship can be terminated immediately, the employer can only terminate the employee within two months from the day he learned about the reason for the notice, and for a violation of labour discipline abroad within two months after his return from abroad, at the latest always within one year from the day when the reason for notice arose. When the breach of labour discipline forms the object of investigation by another authority, the employer may give the employee notice within two months from the day he has learned the investigation results. In order for the employer to find out the reason for the dismissal, it is enough for any of its employees to find out about it; who is the superior of the employee who violated the work discipline and is therefore authorized to impose work tasks on this subordinate employee and give him binding instructions for this purpose.

Reaching the age of 65 and the age determined to be eligible for an old-age pension

545. Act no. 76/2021 Coll. partly amended the Labour Code concerning the reasons for terminating the employment relationship by notice on the employer's part.

According to the amendment, the Labour Code allows for giving notice because the employee has reached the age of 65 and, simultaneously, reached the age for entitlement to a retirement pension. The amendment had to take effect on 1 January 2022. On 15 December 2021, the Constitutional Court of the Slovak Republic decided to suspend the effectiveness of the provision. The subject of the proceedings in the case is a constitutional assessment of whether the employer's option to terminate an employee who has reached the age of 65 and is the age determined to be entitled to a retirement pension is constitutionally compatible with the prohibition of discrimination based on age. Provision section 63(1)(f) of the Labour Code will come into effect only based on the result of the decision of the Constitutional Court.

2. Protective Period

546. The employer may not give notice to the employee during the protection period, namely:

(a) in the period when the employee is recognized as temporarily unable to work due to illness or injury, if he did not intentionally cause or cause this incapacity under the influence of alcohol, narcotic substances or psychotropic substances, and in the period from the submission of a proposal for institutional treatment or from the start of spa treatment to until the day they end;
(b) when called to perform extraordinary service in a crisis from the day when the employee was called to perform extraordinary service by delivery of a call-up order or when he was called to perform extraordinary service by a mobilization call or a mobilization notice, or if the employee was ordered to perform extraordinary service, until within two weeks of his release from that service; this also applies in the case of the performance of an alternative service according to a special regulation;
(c) during the period when the employee is released for voluntary military training, for regular exercises or the fulfilment of the tasks of the armed forces of the Slovak Republic according to a special regulation;
(d) during the period when the employee is pregnant, when the employee is on maternity leave, during the period from the notification of the expected date of commencement of paternity leave to the employee, but no earlier than six weeks prior to the expected date of birth, until the end of the paternity leave, during the period when the employee and the employee on parental leave or when a lone female employee is taking care of a child under the age of three;
(e) in the period when the employee is released for a long period to perform a public function;
(f) when an employee working at night is recognized as temporarily unfit for night work based on a medical opinion.

547. When the employee is given notice before the beginning of the protection period in such a way that the notice period should expire during the protection period, the employment relationship will end on the expiry of the last day of the protection period, except when the employee announces that he does not insist on the extension of the employment relationship.

548. The prohibition of notice does not apply to termination given to an employee:

(a) for reasons:
  (i) cancellation of the employer;
  (ii) relocation of the employer during the period when the lone employee is taking care of a child under the age of three from the notification of the expected date of commencement of paternity leave to the employee but no earlier than six weeks prior to the expected date of birth, until the day preceding the day of commencement for paternity leave, and when an employee working at night is recognized as temporarily unfit for night work based on a medical opinion.
(b) for a reason for which the employer can immediately terminate the employment relationship, if it is not an employee on maternity leave or an employee on paternity leave – if the employee is terminated for this reason before starting maternity leave or paternity leave in such a way that the notice period expired at the time of this maternity leave or paternity leave, the notice period ends at the same time as the maternity leave or paternity leave;
(c) for a less severe violation of work discipline, if it is not a pregnant employee or if it is not an employee on maternity leave, the employee in the period from the announcement of the expected date of starting paternity leave, but no earlier than six weeks before the expected day of birth, until the end of the paternity leave or an employee on parental leave;
(d) if, due to his fault, he lost the prerequisites for performing the agreed work according to a particular law.

3. Offering a Suitable Work

549. The employer may dismiss the employee – if it is not a dismissal for unsatisfactory performance of work tasks, for a less severe violation of work discipline or for a reason for which the employment relationship can be terminated immediately – only if:

- the employer cannot further employ the employee – even for a shorter working time – in the place that was agreed upon as the place of work performance;
- the employee is unwilling to switch to another work suitable for him, which the employer offered him in the place that was agreed upon as the place of work performance or to undergo prior preparation for this other work.

550. The impossibility of further employing the employee means that the employer has no work for the employee. However, the employer is not obliged to create new job opportunities for the employee who has become redundant as a result of the organizational change decision in order to be able to offer the employee suitable work. Other suitable work for the employee means work corresponding to his health, abilities and, if possible, his qualifications (section 55 of the Labour Code). From the fact that other suitable work should correspond as much as possible to the employee's qualifications, it must be reasoned that such work should be understood primarily as work corresponding to the employee's qualifications and only then (if a position corresponding to the employee's qualifications is not vacant) to the work that best corresponds to the qualifications employee, and finally (if no vacancy matches the employee's qualifications as closely as possible) a job for which no special qualification is required. It is, therefore, possible to consider a suitable job even if the employee's qualifications are not fully utilized. However, suitable work is not work that the employee is unable to perform due to his health condition, limited abilities or lack of qualifications unless the qualification can be obtained through prior training.

4. Notice to an Employee with a Disability

551. An employer may terminate an employee with a disability only with the prior consent of the relevant office of labour, social affairs and family; otherwise, the termination is invalid. This consent is not required if the notice is given to an employee who has reached the age determined to be entitled to an old-age pension for reasons of termination of the employer or disciplinary reasons.

5. Participation of Employee Representatives

552. The employer is obliged to discuss the notice by the employer with the employee's representatives in advance; otherwise, the notice is invalid. The employee representative is obliged to discuss the notice by the employer within seven working days from the date of delivery of the written request; if no discussion takes place within the specified period, it is considered that the discussion has taken place.

553. The employer may give a notice to a member of the relevant trade union body, a member of the work council or an employee's confidant only with the prior consent of these employee representatives. Prior consent is also considered if the employee representatives did not refuse to give the employer consent in writing within fifteen days from the day the employer requested it. The employer can use the prior consent only within two months of its granting. If the employee representatives refuse to give consent, the termination by the employer is invalid for this reason; if the other conditions for termination or immediate termination of employment are met and the court in the dispute finds that the employer cannot reasonably demand that the employee continue to be employed, the notice is valid.

III. Immediate Termination of the Employment Relationship

554. Immediate termination of the employment relationship is a specific way of ending the employment relationship that both the employer and the employee can apply. It differs from the termination of the employment relationship by mutual agreement of the parties in that it is a strictly formal unilateral legal act. Immediate termination of employment differs from notice in that it is effective by delivery without notice.

555. For the immediate termination of the employment relationship, the Labour Code establishes rigorous formal requirements for its validity:

- the expression of will must be in written form and must be delivered to the other participant within the period established by law;
- immediate termination is possible only for the reasons listed exhaustively in the Labour Code;
- the reason must be defined precisely, factually so that it cannot be mistaken for another;
- the reason cannot even be changed subsequently;
- for the immediate termination of the employment relationship given to the employee representative, the employer needs the prior consent of the relevant employee representative (section 240(9) of the Labour Code);
- the employer must discuss the immediate termination with the employee representatives if they are at the employer (section 74 of the Labour Code).

A. *Immediate Termination of the Employment Relationship by the Employee*

556. The provisions of section 69 of the Labour Code entitle the employee to immediate termination of an employment relationship if:

- according to a medical opinion, he cannot continue to work without severe threats to his health, and the employer has not transferred him to another job suitable for him within fifteen days from the date of submission of this opinion;
- the employer did not pay him wages, wage compensation, travel allowances, work emergency compensation, income compensation in case of temporary incapacity for work of the employee or part of them within fifteen days after their due date;
- his life or health is in immediate danger;
- a juvenile employee, even if he cannot perform work without endangering his morals.

557. The employee can immediately terminate the employment relationship only within one month from the day he learned about the reason for the immediate termination of the employment relationship. Even if notice periods do not apply in the case of immediate termination of the employment relationship, an employee who immediately terminated the relationship is entitled to wage compensation in the amount of the average earnings for the notice period of two months.

B. Immediate Termination of the Employment Relationship by the Employer

558. The employer may immediately terminate the employment relationship only if the employee:

- was legally convicted of an intentional crime;
- seriously violated work discipline (e.g., unexcused absence of an employee, drunkenness, property and moral offences at the workplace, bodily harm).

559. Before the immediate termination of the employment relationship with the employee, the employer must have established the reason for this immediate termination; it is not enough just to suspect that this reason is given. If, when reviewing the employer's decision, the court finds that one of several violations of labour discipline, for which the employment relationship with the employee was terminated by immediate termination, is not proven, it assesses itself whether the other violations of labour discipline still justify the termination of the employment relationship in this way.

560. The court is not bound by the legal qualification that the employer states in the immediate termination of the employment relationship but must be based on how this cancellation statement is factually justified and whether this factual description establishes any of the reasons for the immediate termination of the employment relationship. The specification of the reason for the immediate termination of employment may be different; in many cases, it is sufficient to state briefly the facts justifying the termination of the employment relationship in this way, identical to their statement in the Labour Code and establishing the legal reason for this disciplinary sanction, but always in such a way that it is clear to the employee which violations of labour discipline blames and is, therefore, the reason for the termination of the employment relationship.

561. The employer cannot immediately terminate the employment relationship with a pregnant employee, with an employee on maternity leave, with an employee on paternity leave, with an employee and an employee on parental leave, with a single employee or with a lone employee if they are taking care of a child under the age of three, or with an employee who personally cares for a close person who is a person with a severe disability. However, except for an employee on maternity and paternity leave, the employer may terminate the employment relationship with them for the stated reasons in the notice.

562. Immediate termination of the employment relationship by the employer requires negotiation with the employees' representatives, and if it is a representative of the employees, their prior consent is required; otherwise, it is invalid. Similarly, as in the case of termination, the immediate termination of the employment relationship with a minor employee must be notified to his legal representative.

563. The employer can immediately terminate the employment relationship only within two months from the day he became aware of the reason for immediate termination but no later than one year from the day when this reason arose.

IV. Termination of the Employment Relationship in the Probationary Period

564. The employee and the employer can terminate the employment relationship during the trial period without giving a reason.

565. The Labour Code requires a written form of termination of the employment relationship during the trial period, but non-compliance does not invalidate the legal act. The written notification of the termination of the employment relationship must be delivered to the other participant, as a rule, at least three days before the day the employment relationship ends; however, failure to comply with this deadline is also not sanctioned by invalidity. A legal act leading to the termination of a probationary employment relationship made after the agreed probationary period has expired is invalid.

566. Termination of the employment relationship during the trial period with a pregnant woman, a mother up to the end of the ninth month after giving birth, and a breastfeeding woman can only be terminated by the employer in writing in exceptional cases that are not related to her pregnancy or maternity and must be duly justified in writing; otherwise, it is invalid.

567. The prior consent of the Office of Labour, Social Affairs and Family is not required to terminate the employment relationship during the trial period with a disabled employee.

§2. Termination of the Employment Relationship Based on a Legal Event

I. Termination of the Employment Relationship by the Lapse of Time

568. An employment relationship concluded for a defined period will end upon the expiry of this period. However, when the employee continues to work with the employer's knowledge after the agreed period has passed, this employment relationship is changed to an employment relationship for an indefinite period unless the parties agree otherwise. Before the agreed period ends, the employment relationship can also be terminated in other ways.

II. Death of the Employee

569. The employment relationship is tied to the person of the employee, who must perform the work himself according to the employment contract. Employment cannot be gifted, inherited, sold or rented. Thus, the employment relationship ends with the death of the employee.

570. The employee's monetary claims do not expire upon his death. Up to four times his average monthly earnings, wage claims from the employment relationship gradually go directly to his spouse, children and parents if they lived with him in the household at the time of death. They become the subject of inheritance if these persons are not present.

571. The employer's monetary claims expire with the death of the employee, except for claims that have been legally decided or that the employee acknowledged in writing before his death in terms of reason and amount and claims for compensation for damage caused intentionally or for the loss of objects entrusted to the employee for written confirmation.

§3. Employment Relationship Termination Based on an Official Decision

572. In addition to the usual ways of terminating the employment relationship, the employment relationship of a foreigner or stateless person can also be terminated based on a decision of the competent state authority. The peculiarity of this method of termination of the employment relationship lies in the fact that if the termination of the employment relationship did not take place in another way, the employment relationship ends on the day on which:

- employee's stay on the territory of the Slovak Republic is to end according to an enforceable decision on the cancellation of the residence permit;
- a judgment imposing the penalty of expulsion from the territory of the Slovak Republic on this person becomes final;
- the period for which the residence permit was issued in the territory of the Slovak Republic has passed;
- the period for which the employment permit was granted has passed;
- the employment permit was revoked.

§4. Termination of Employment Ex Lege

573. The employment relationship also expires by law when an employee is temporarily assigned to a user employer if the temporary assignment violates the Labour Code (section 59(5)). In these cases, the employment relationship ends with the employer or with the temporary employment agency, and an indefinite employment relationship is established with the user employer.

574. Even though reaching a certain age is not a reason for termination of employment according to the current legislation, an exception to the abovementioned principle applies to teachers and scientific employees of universities. According to Act no. 131/2002 Coll. on High-Grade Schools, the employment of teachers and scientific employees of universities ends at the end of the academic year in which they reached 70 unless their employment ended earlier for another reason. When a university teacher is in the position of rector or dean, and during his term of office in this position, his employment relationship is to end due to reaching 70, his employment relationship will end upon the expiration of the relevant term of office. A university teacher is entitled to severance pay upon termination of employment after reaching 70, as upon termination of employment due to redundancy.

§5. Obligations of the Employer Related to the Termination of Employment

575. In connection with the termination of the employment relationship, the Labour Code imposes on the employer, above all, other obligations.

I. Collective Dismissals

576. In addition to the substantive legal conditions the employer is obliged to fulfil with each termination, the labour regulation of collective dismissal imposes on him other obligations concerning the employees' representatives and the relevant labour office. The legislation does not interfere with employers' freedom to carry out mass redundancies. However, he must consult with the social partner and inform the relevant authority before this mass redundancies. The purpose of consultation procedures is to reach an agreement, especially concerning other measures to prevent mass layoffs or to limit them. Negotiating collective dismissals aims to find options for placing employees in suitable work and discuss measures to mitigate the consequences of mass layoffs. It is a collective dismissal if the employer or a part of the employer terminates the employment relationship by giving notice for the reasons specified in section 63(1)(a) and (b) (organizational reasons) or if the employment relationship is terminated in another way for a reason that is not the employee's fault, within thirty days:

(a) with at least ten employees at an employer that employs more than twenty and less than a hundred employees;
(b) with at least 10% of employees from the total number of employees at an employer that employs at least 100 and less than 300 employees;
(c) with at least thirty employees at an employer with at least 300 employees.

577. If the employer violates the consultation and information obligations, the employee with whom the employer terminates at least the employment relationship as part of the collective dismissal is entitled to compensation of wages twice his average earnings.

II. Working Review and Confirmation of Employment

578. The employer is obliged to issue the employee a work review within fifteen days of its request. However, the employer is not obliged to give the employee a working review earlier than two months before the end of the employment relationship. A work review is all documents related to the evaluation of the employee's work, qualifications, abilities and other facts related to the performance of the job. The employee can inspect the personal file and make extracts, write-offs and photocopies.

579. In addition to evaluating the employee's work, qualifications and abilities, the work review may also contain any other facts if they are related to the job performance. It can, therefore, include an assessment of the employee's overall relationship with co-workers and work, as well as an assessment of those personal qualities that are directly related to the performance of his work, such as conscientiousness, initiative, compliance with work discipline, the ability to manage and organize the work process, the ability to involve into teamwork with other employees. The work review does not express the employer's subjective evaluation opinion; however, it must be limited to a specific work evaluation of the employee's activity at the employer and cannot express his subjective evaluation opinion (recommended) on a general level about the suitability of the employee's future work in a specific range of work activities.

580. At the end of the employment relationship, the employer is obliged to issue a confirmation of employment to the employee and state in it, in particular, the duration of the employment relationship, the type of work performed, whether deductions are made from the employee's salary, in whose favour, in what amount and in what order is the claim for which should continue to make deductions, data on the salary provided for the work performed, on the salary compensation provided and on-call compensation, on income tax advances withheld and on other facts decisive for the annual settlement of tax advances from dependent activity and from functional benefits and for the calculation unemployment benefits, information on the agreement to remain in employment with the employer for a certain period of time, after taking the final exam or matriculation exam, or after completing studies or preparation for a profession, including information on when this period ends, information on the provision of severance pay.

581. The employer can provide other information about the employee only with consent unless a special legal regulation stipulates otherwise.

582. If the employee disagrees with the content of the employment report or employment confirmation and the employer does not correct or supplement the employment report or employment confirmation at the request of the employee within three months from the day on which he learned about their content, he may demand in court that the employer be obliged to adjust them accordingly. If the court finds that the proposal to correct the report on work activity is justified, it will impose on the employer how to modify the report; that is, it will determine to the employer exactly how the report should read in the part that the employee objects to being incorrect. For proceedings to amend the report on work activity, the court is bound by the participants' proposals. If the employee suggests that specific data be omitted from the report, the court can only deal with whether they should be omitted but cannot replace them with something else the employee did not suggest.

583. If the employee was not hired due to a false review of his work activities, the employer who issued such a report is liable for the damage caused by it.

III. Severance Allowance and Compensation

A. *Severance Allowance*

584. Severance allowance is a particular benefit (a certain 'satisfaction') provided to the employee by the employer for the fact that the employment relationship ends earlier than the participants in the employment contract anticipated and that the reason for the termination of the employment relationship does not lie in the person of the employee, but in the person of the employer, in his economic problems, which to the employee appear as a social risk for which he is not at fault.

585. An employee with whom the employer terminates the employment relationship by notice for organizational reasons or because the employee has lost the long-term ability to perform the previous work due to his health condition according to a medical opinion, upon termination of the employment relationship is entitled to severance allowance in the amount of at least:

- his average monthly earnings, if the employee's employment lasted at least two years and less than five years;
- twice his average monthly earnings, if the employee's employment lasted at least five years and less than ten years;
- three times his average monthly earnings, if the employee's employment lasted at least ten years and less than twenty years;
- four times his average monthly earnings if the employee's employment lasted at least twenty years.

586. Upon termination of the employment relationship by agreement for organizational reasons or because the employee has lost the long-term ability to perform the previous work due to his health condition according to a medical opinion, the employee is entitled to severance allowance at least in the amount of:

- his average monthly earnings, if the employee's employment lasted less than two years;
- twice his average monthly earnings, if the employee's employment lasted at least two years and less than five years;
- three times his average monthly earnings, if the employee's employment lasted at least five years and less than ten years;

– four times his average monthly earnings, if the employee's employment lasted at least ten years and less than twenty years;
– five times his average monthly earnings if the employee's employment lasted at least twenty years.

587. An employee whose employment relationship has been terminated by the employer or by mutual agreement because the employee is no longer allowed to perform work due to an occupational disease or because of the danger of such a disease, or if the maximum permissible level of exposure has been reached at the workplace, as determined by a binding decision of the competent health protection authority, is entitled to a severance allowance amounting to at least ten times his/her average monthly earnings.

588. If, after the end of the employment relationship, the employee rejoins the same employer or his legal successor in the employment relationship before the expiration of the time determined according to the severance pay provided, he is obliged to return the severance allowance or its proportional part, unless otherwise agreed with the employer.

B. Discharge Benefit

589. Severance pay, unlike allowance, has a different function. Discharge benefit is a legal entitlement of the employee, which belongs to him only at the first termination of the employment relationship after the entitlement to an old-age pension or disability pension if the decrease in the ability to perform gainful activity is more than 70%, severance pay at least in the amount of his average monthly earnings, if he requests the provision said pension before the end of the employment relationship or within ten working days after its end.

590. The employer is not obliged to provide the employee with severance pay if the employment relationship ends with immediate termination by the employer. A higher amount of severance pay and severance pay than stipulated in the Labour Code can also be agreed in the collective agreement or employment contract.

§6. Claims from Invalidly Terminated Employment

591. A participant in an employment relationship against whom a legal act has been applied, leading to the termination of the employment relationship by notice, immediate termination or termination during the probationary period, can exercise his right in court by filing a lawsuit for the invalidity of the termination of the employment relationship. In case of invalidity of the termination of the employment relationship, it is a relative invalidity, which can be invoked only by the participant affected by the invalidity. There is a two-month preclusion period for asserting a claim from the invalid termination of an employment relationship, which begins from the day the employment relationship was supposed to end based on the challenged legal act. The plaintiff in the proceedings to determine the invalidity of the termination of the employment relationship or the state employee relationship and, when asserting claims from the invalid termination of the employment relationship or the state employee relationship, is exempt from paying court fees in court proceedings.

592. When an employment relationship is invalidly terminated based on a legal act of the employee and the employer wants the employee to continue working for him, he must notify the employee that he insists that the employee continues to work, as well as file a lawsuit in the relevant court to determine the invalidity of the termination of the employment relationship. In this case, the employment relationship does not end, and the employee continues to be obliged to perform work. If he does not fulfil this obligation, the employer can demand compensation for the damage caused by this from the day he notified the employee that he insists on continuing to work. When the employment relationship was terminated invalidly, and the employer does not insist that the employee continue to work, it applies, unless the employer and the employee agree otherwise in writing, that the employment relationship was terminated by agreement, if an invalid notice was given, upon expiry of the notice period, the employment relationship was invalidly terminated immediately, the day the employment relationship was supposed to end, the employment relationship was invalidly terminated during the trial period, the day the employment relationship was supposed to end.

593. When the employer carries out the legal act of terminating the employment relationship against the employee, who considers the relevant termination act invalid, further behaviour depends on whether the employee wants to continue working for the employer or decides to work for another employer. Suppose the employee decides to remain with the employer in an employment relationship in order for the employment relationship to continue. In that case, the employee must notify the employer that he insists on continuing to employ him and, within two months, file a lawsuit with the competent court for the invalidity of the termination of the employment relationship. The notification does not require a written form, but the written form of the notification is vital from the point of view of evidence in a possible dispute. In such a case, his employment does not end unless the court decides that the employer cannot be fairly required to continue employing the employee. After notifying the employee that he insists that the employer continue to employ him, the employer either starts assigning him to work pending a final court decision or does not assign him to work. If the employer does not provide him with work, he must provide compensation to the employee; compensation belongs to the employee in the amount of his average earnings from the day he notified the employer that he insists on further employment until the time when the employer allows him to continue working or if the court decides on termination of employment. When the total time for which the employee should be compensated exceeds twelve months, the court may, at the employer's request, appropriately reduce his obligation to compensate the employee for the period exceeding twelve months or not award the employee compensation for the period exceeding twelve months. Wage compensation can be awarded for a maximum of thirty-six months.

§7. Protection of Employee's Representatives

594. During the term of office and six months after its end, employee representatives are protected against measures that could harm them, including termination of employment, and that would be motivated by their position or activity.

595. The employer may give notice to a member of the relevant trade union body, a member of the work council or an employee's confidant or immediately terminate the employment relationship with them only with the prior consent of these employee representatives. Prior consent is also considered if the employee representatives did not refuse to give the employer consent in writing within fifteen days from the day the employer requested it. The employer can use the prior consent only within two months of its granting.

596. If the employee representatives refuse to grant consent, the notice or immediate termination of employment by the employer is invalid for this reason; if the other conditions for termination or immediate termination of the employment relationship are met and the court finds in the dispute about the invalidity of the termination of the employment relationship that it cannot fairly demand from the employer to continue employing the employee, the termination or immediate termination of the employment relationship is valid.

Chapter 8. Protection of Specific Categories of Workers, Protection Against Discrimination in Employment

597. The category of employees with increased legal protection in labour relations includes young employees, employees with disabilities, pregnant women, breastfeeding women, mothers up to the end of the ninth month after giving birth, and employees with special obligations towards the family. The stricter employment conditions for young people are due to the need to protect their health, mental and physical development and moral integrity. Increased protection in the performance of their work results from Slovakia's obligations to international conventions and EU legal acts.

§1. Young Workers, Elderly Workers, Female Workers and Mothers, Employees with Parental Responsibilities, Disabled Workers

I. Young Workers

598. The working conditions of juvenile employees represent a summary of special authorizations on the part of juveniles and legal obligations on the part of the employer to ensure the development of juveniles' physical and mental abilities in employment relations. National protection of juvenile employees depends on constitutional guarantees. The Constitution also ensures the right to satisfactory working conditions under Article 36, which grants juveniles, women, and persons with disabilities the right to increased health protection and special working conditions (Article 38(1) of the Constitution). Juvenile people and persons with disabilities have the right to special protection in employment relationships and assistance in preparing for a profession (Article 38(2) of the Constitution).

599. The national regulation does not contain a definition of the term child or young person for employment purposes; it only includes the legal definition of a juvenile employee. According to section 40(3) of the Labour Code, a juvenile employee is an employee under the age of 18. The lower age limit for the definition of the term juvenile employee is derived from the moment of acquisition of labour law subjectivity of a natural person, which is reaching the age of 15.

600. The employer's most widely formulated obligation is to create favourable conditions for the all-around development of young employees' physical and mental abilities by uniquely adjusting working conditions (section 171(1) of the Labour Code). The legal regulation of juveniles' unique working conditions consists of determining the method of their employment and the type of work, the length of working hours, rest time, and the prohibition of specific jobs.

601. The employer must keep records of juvenile employees in an employment relationship. The employer is also obliged to keep records of concluded agreements on work performed outside the employment relationship, in the order in which they were concluded, and records of working time for these agreements so that the length of the period in which the work was performed was recorded on individual days.

A. *Interference of Legal Representatives Before the Establishment, During and at the End of the Employment Relationship*

602. It follows from the provisions of the Labour Code that a legal representative is not required to validate the labour law acts of a juvenile employee. The reason is the complete employment law subjectivity of a juvenile employee. Despite this, the form of participation of the legal representatives of the juvenile employee is reflected in the legislation. This is because the juvenile employee remains a minor natural person.

603. According to section 41(4) of the Labour Code, the employer is obliged to request the statement of a legal representative to conclude an employment contract. Labour Code does not establish any formal or content requirements for the form or content of the statement. The content of the legal representative's statement may be positive or negative (disagreeing), but even the negative statement should not affect the validity of the employment contract. The statement of the legal representative provides an opportunity to evaluate the performance of the minor's work for the employer or to influence the will of the juvenile employee or the employer to conclude an employment contract.

604. According to section 171(1) of the Labour Code, the employer closely cooperates with the juvenile's legal representatives when solving essential issues. The Labour Code does not further specify this cooperation during the duration of the employment relationship of the juvenile employee. It does not impose any special obligations on the employer with the legal representatives of the juvenile employee, except for the phase before the conclusion of the employment relationship and upon its termination. The intervention of legal representatives is given when the employment relationship is terminated by the juvenile employee or by the employer as follows: when the employer terminates the employment relationship by notice or immediate termination of the employment relationship, the employer is obliged to inform the legal representative of the juvenile of this legal fact, and when of employment is terminated by a juvenile employee, the employer is obliged to request a statement from the legal representative.

605. These requirements do not apply to establishing and creating employment relationships based on agreements on work performed outside of the employment relationship.

B. *Termination of Employment by the Employer and the Juvenile Employee*

606. When the employer or the juvenile employee terminates the employment relationship, the Labour Code does not establish any legal differences. As with other categories of employees, a juvenile employee has the right to protection against arbitrary dismissal from employment under the principle of equal treatment. The same substantive and procedural conditions as in the case of other employees apply to the employment relationship termination methods, except for the interference of legal representatives. The juvenile employee is not particularly protected even at the end of the employment relationship during the probationary period; he is not covered by increased protection in case of termination by the employer.

607. The only difference lies in the legal reasons for the immediate termination of the employment relationship on the part of the juvenile employee, who can also apply for the immediate termination of the employment relationship if he cannot perform the work without endangering his morals.

C. *Adequacy of Work Assigned to Juvenile Employees and Work Prohibited for Juvenile Employees*

608. The work the employer assigns to the juvenile employee must correspond to the generally formulated adequacy criterion. Assessment of the appropriateness of the assigned work is within the complete decision-making competence of the employer. However, it depends on the adequacy of the juvenile employee's physical development and intellectual maturity. Physical and mental development will be assessed from a general objective point of view, whether specific jobs usually correspond to the age limit of juveniles. However, it is also necessary to consider the subjective point of view involved in assessing the person of the juvenile (physical and mental development) and his abilities.

609. Physical maturity is related to the physical demands of work, which is the subject of an employment relationship and which is further detailed in the provisions of the Labour Code and Government Regulation no. 286/2004 Coll., which establishes a list of jobs and workplaces that are prohibited for minor employees, and which establishes certain obligations of employers when employing minor employees. These jobs entail the risk of various dangers and the resulting risks that potentially impact the juvenile employee's physical health and further development (e.g., handling heavy loads or monotonous work). The assessment of appropriate work, which should correspond to the mental maturity of a person under the age of 18, must be based on the complexity of the work and work procedures, the degree of independence, decision-making, and the legal consequences that may arise from the actions of a juvenile employee during the performance of work.

610. Another criterion for assigned work is work that does not endanger the morals of a juvenile employee. As work that conflicts with the criterion of morality, we can designate work that reduces the moral credit of a juvenile and even only potentially influences his further moral development.

611. Finally, a juvenile employee must not be employed in underground work to extract minerals or dig tunnels and tunnels. Considering this age's anatomical, physiological and psychological peculiarities, a juvenile employee may not be employed in disproportionate, dangerous or harmful work to his health. The employer may not employ juvenile employees in jobs exposed to an increased risk of injury or whose performance could seriously endanger the safety and health of fellow employees or other persons.

612. A government regulation establishes lists of jobs and workplaces prohibited for underage employees.

613. The employer is obliged to ensure the assessment of the health fitness for work based on the results of the preventive medical examination concerning the work of the juvenile employee before reassigning a juvenile employee to another job, and regularly, as necessary, at least once a year, unless a special regulation provides otherwise. A young employee is obliged to undergo prescribed preventive medical examinations concerning work. When assigning work tasks to a juvenile employee, the employer is also guided by medical reports.

D. Working Hours, Rest Periods and Remuneration of Juvenile Employees

614. Regulations regarding working time and rest periods protect juvenile employees' physical and mental integrity. Provisions regarding working time have a mandatory or relatively mandatory nature. They allow a deviation in favour of the employee, provided that the legal maximum or minimum limits are respected.

615. A juvenile employee under 16 has a working time of no more than thirty hours per week, even if he works for several employers. A juvenile employee over 16 has a maximum working time of 37 and 1/2 hours per week, even if he works for several employers. At the same time, the working time of a juvenile employee may not exceed eight hours in twenty-four hours.

616. The employer must provide a thirty-minute rest and meal break to a juvenile employee whose work shift is longer than four and a half hours.

617. The employer must schedule working time so the juvenile employee has a minimum rest between the end of one shift and the beginning of the second. Also, the employer must schedule working hours so the employee has a minimum rest period of at least fourteen hours in twenty-four hours between the end of one shift and the beginning of the second.

618. When shortening the leave, a juvenile employee whose employment relationship with the same employer lasted for the entire calendar year must be granted a leave of at least two weeks.

619. The employer may not employ juvenile employees for overtime or night work and may not order or agree with them on on-call duty. Exceptionally, juvenile employees over 16 may perform night work not exceeding one hour if necessary for their vocational training. The night work of a juvenile employee must immediately follow the work assigned to him according to the work shift schedule for the daytime.

620. The Labour Code does not establish special rules for remunerating young employees, except for the legal prohibition of using such a method of remunerating work that would lead to increasing work performance and endangering safety and health at work.

II. Elderly Workers

621. Slovak labour laws do not contain special provisions concerning elderly employees. The exception is section 63(1)(f) of the Labour Code regarding terminating an employee's employment by notice due to reaching 65 and the age designated for entitlement to a retirement pension. The Constitutional Court has so far only decided to suspend the effectiveness of the provision in question. He has not yet decided whether the given provision, which was supposed to be effective from 1 January 2022, is or is not following the constitution, and he should still make a decision on the matter.

622. Act no. 5/2004 Coll. on Employment Services considers a job seeker who is a citizen older than 50 to be a disadvantaged job seeker. In order to support the employment of a disadvantaged job seeker, a special allowance is granted based on the Act.

III. Female Workers and Mothers

A. Workplace Requirements

623. The general obligation of the employer to establish, maintain and increase the level of social and personal hygiene facilities (section 151(2) of the Labour Code) is followed by a special obligation to establish, maintain and increase the level of social and personal hygiene facilities for women. The details are governed by Regulation of the Government of the Slovak Republic no. 391/2006 Coll. on minimum safety and health requirements for the workplace. The general obligation of the employer to establish, maintain and increase the level of social and personal hygiene facilities (section 151(2) of the Labour Code) is followed by a special obligation to establish, maintain and increase the level of social and personal hygiene facilities for women. The details are governed by Regulation of the Government of the Slovak Republic no. 391/2006 Coll. on minimum safety and health requirements for the workplace.

1. Equipment for Personal Hygiene

624. Based on the Government Regulation, arrangements must be made for the separation of changing rooms or the separate use of changing rooms for men and women, as well as measures for the separation of shower rooms or the separate use of showers for men and women. Washbasins must be separated or used separately for men and women if necessary for privacy. The government regulation also envisages the implementation of measures for the separation of toilets or the separate use of toilets for men and women.

2. Rest Rooms for Pregnant Women and Breastfeeding Mothers

625. Rest rooms must be large enough, sufficiently lit, ventilated, and equipped with sufficient tables, chairs, backs, and hangers for the given number of employees. If they are used for eating and drinking, they must have a sink, a kitchen sink with a hot and cold water outlet, a stove for heating food and drinks, and a refrigerator. Pregnant women and breastfeeding mothers must have the opportunity to rest lying down in appropriate conditions in rest rooms.

B. Prohibition of Work

626. Pregnant women, mothers up to the end of the ninth month after giving birth, and breastfeeding women may not be employed in jobs that are physically inappropriate for them or harmful to their bodies. A general ban on work for pregnant women, mothers up to the end of the ninth month after giving birth and breastfeeding women and an individual ban on work for pregnant women, mothers up to the end of the ninth month after giving birth and breastfeeding women must be distinguished.

627. The general ban on work for pregnant women, mothers up to the end of the ninth month after giving birth and breastfeeding women states that these women may not be employed in work that is physically inappropriate for them or harmful to their organism. This general requirement is specified in Regulation of the Government of the Slovak Republic no. 272/2004 Coll., establishing a list of jobs and workplaces that are prohibited for pregnant women, mothers up to the end of the ninth month after giving birth and breastfeeding women, a list of jobs and workplaces associated with a specific risk for pregnant women, mothers up to the end of the ninth month after childbirth and breastfeeding women and which establish certain obligations for employers when employing these women.

628. The individual work ban does not apply to all pregnant women, mothers up to the end of the ninth month after giving birth, and breastfeeding women, but only to specific employees from this group of women (or jobs performed by them) for whom a medical opinion has been prepared that reflects their health condition. As for a pregnant woman, she must not be employed in work that, according to a medical opinion, endangers her pregnancy due to health reasons inherent in her person. These are jobs that are generally not forbidden to pregnant women (i.e., they are not covered by a general ban), but because of the health reasons that lie in the person of the pregnant woman, these jobs endanger her pregnancy. This allows each pregnant woman's health status to be considered individually.

629. When a pregnant woman, a mother up to the end of the ninth month after giving birth, or a breastfeeding woman performs work that is prohibited for pregnant women, mothers up to the end of the ninth month after giving birth, or breastfeeding women or which, according to a medical opinion, endangers her pregnancy, her biological condition in connection with the birth of a child or her special relationship with the child after his birth, the employer is first of all obliged to make a temporary adjustment to the working conditions. When a temporary adjustment of the working conditions is not possible, the employer must transfer the pregnant woman, the mother until the end of the ninth month after giving birth, and the breastfeeding woman to another job. At the same time, the employer is obliged to transfer the employee to another job if a pregnant woman, a mother up to the end of the ninth month after giving birth, and a breastfeeding woman performs work which these women may not be employed with or which, according to a medical opinion, endangers her pregnancy or motherhood. The employer has to transfer a pregnant woman, a mother up to the end of the ninth month after giving birth, and a breastfeeding woman to a job where she can earn the same income as her current job. If it were to happen that a woman in the job to which she was reassigned, through no fault of her own, earns a lower salary than in her current job from the health insurance under the conditions established by Act no. 462/2004 Coll. on social insurance provides this woman with an equalization benefit from the sickness insurance system.

630. If a pregnant woman, a mother until the end of the ninth month after giving birth, and a breastfeeding woman cannot be transferred to another suitable job, the employer must provide her with paid leave. It also applies if a woman cannot be transferred to daytime work. Night work is generally not prohibited for these women; however, if a pregnant woman, a mother up to the end of the ninth month after giving birth, and a breastfeeding woman working at night requests it, the employer is obliged to transfer her to another job.

C. *Maternity Leave*

631. Maternity leave belongs to a woman in connection with childbirth and the care of a newborn child. The provision in question sees the woman as the child's mother, who gave birth to the child and takes care of it. Maternity leave also belongs to a woman who took over a child based on a court decision to place the child in care, replacing parental care. A man does not have maternity leave; a man is entitled to paternity leave in connection with the care of a newborn child.

632. A woman is entitled to thirty-four weeks of maternity leave. A single woman is entitled to thirty-seven weeks of maternity leave. A woman who has given birth to two or more children simultaneously is entitled to a maternity leave of up to forty-three weeks. A woman starts maternity leave as a rule from the beginning of the sixth week before the expected day of delivery; the mentioned duration includes the time before and after delivery. If a woman uses up less than six weeks of maternity leave before giving birth, it is necessary to investigate why. If it is because the birth took place earlier than prescribed by the doctor, the woman's maternity leave is not shortened. It means a woman is entitled to maternity leave from the day she starts until the time established for the total scope of maternity leave expires. When a woman uses up less than six weeks of maternity leave before giving birth for any other reason, she will be granted maternity leave from the date of delivery only until the expiration of twenty-eight weeks. A single woman will be granted maternity leave until the expiration of thirty-one weeks. For a woman who has given birth to two or more children simultaneously, maternity leave will be granted until thirty-seven weeks have passed.

633. The woman is entitled to maternity leave for fourteen weeks if the child is stillborn. If the child dies while the woman is on maternity leave, this leave is still granted for two weeks from the day of the child's death, the longest until the day the child has reached one year.

634. It is not the woman's duty to use up the maternity leave to the full extent to which it belongs. A woman can end her maternity leave earlier and start working. However, she must respect the rule that maternity leave cannot be shorter than fourteen weeks and cannot end or be interrupted before six weeks have passed since the day of childbirth.

D. Breastfeeding Breaks

635. Breastfeeding breaks represent special breaks that the employer must provide to a mother who is breastfeeding her child, in addition to work breaks, according to section 91 of the Labour Code. A mother who works for the specified weekly working hours is entitled to two half-hour breastfeeding breaks for each child up to the end of the sixth month of his age and one-half hour breastfeeding break per shift in the following six months. These breaks can be combined and provided at the beginning or end of a work shift. If she works for a shorter working time but at least half of the designated weekly working hours, she is entitled to only one-half hour break for breastfeeding for each child up to the end of the sixth month of children's age. Breastfeeding breaks are included in the woman's working time and are compensated for in her average earnings.

IV. Employees with Parental Responsibilities

A. *Adjustment of Working Time*

636. The employer must consider the needs of pregnant women and women and men taking care of children when assigning employees to work shifts. The obligation to take into account the needs of these women and men does not mean that the employer must necessarily accommodate them. Determining the schedule of work shifts remains within the discretion of the employer. However, when exercising this authority, the employer must consider the needs of pregnant women and women and men taking care of children. If the employer does not intend to respect the needs of these women and men when assigning employees to work shifts, his decision must not be arbitrary.

637. From the issue of assigning employees to work shifts, we must differentiate between the issue of introducing an uneven schedule of working time and the working time account. A pregnant woman, a woman or a man who permanently takes care of a child under three, or a single employee who permanently takes care of a child under 15 may be assigned uneven working hours only after agreement with him. Similarly, a pregnant woman, a woman, or a man permanently caring for a child under three, a single woman, or a single man permanently caring for a child under age 15 may be employed by overtime only with their consent. On-call duty can only be negotiated with them.

638. When a pregnant woman and a woman or man permanently caring for a child under the age of 15 requests shorter working hours or another appropriate adjustment of the specified weekly working hours or, in justified cases, an earlier return to the original way of organizing work, the employer is obliged to comply with their request, if operational severe reasons do not prevent it. The employer must justify the rejection of the application in writing.

B. *Prohibition of Notice From the Employment Relationship*

639. The prohibition of termination of an employment relationship by the employer applies when the employee is pregnant, when the employee is on maternity leave, in the period from the notification of the expected date of commencement of paternity leave of the employee, but no earlier than six weeks before the expected date of birth, until the end of the paternity leave, when the employee is on parental leave or when a lone employee takes care of a child under the age of three. It also applies to substitute parental care. The prohibition of notice does not apply to termination due to the termination of the employer or the existence of a reason for the immediate termination of the employment relationship. In such a case, however, the employer has the right to give notice to these employees as well (except for an employee on maternity leave and an employee on paternity leave) if there is a reason for the immediate termination of the employment relationship.

640. Protection does not apply to the termination of the employment relationship within the probationary period (except for pregnant women, mothers up to the end of the ninth month after giving birth, breastfeeding women and men on paternity leave in exceptional cases not related to pregnancy, motherhood or caring for a newborn child) and termination of the employment relationship agreed for a definite period by the elapse of this period.

C. *Paternity Leave*

641. In connection with the care of a new child, a man is entitled to paternity leave of twenty-eight weeks from the day the child is born, a single man of thirty-one weeks, and in connection with the care of two or more children of thirty-seven weeks. To the same extent, paternity leave is granted to a man who has taken a child into the custody of his parents based on a valid decision of the competent authority, starting from the day of taking over the child. The expected date of commencement of paternity leave, the anticipated date of interruption, termination and changes regarding the commencement, interruption and termination of paternity leave shall be notified by the man in writing to the employer at least one month in advance.

D. *Parental Leave*

642. Parental leave for caring for a child belongs to a woman and a man (even both simultaneously) who request it. The employer must provide parental leave to the woman and man who request it until the child turns three years old. However, neither the woman nor the man are obliged to take all the parental leave that belongs to them (to which they have the right), and they are also not obliged to take the parental leave in one unit. This leave is granted to the extent the parent requests, but usually for at least one month. The employer must provide the employee parental leave to care for the child at their request. However, granting parental leave does not depend on the employer's will or the objectively existing conditions at the workplace; it depends solely on the parent whether he requests the provision of parental leave.

643. A different scope of parental leave is established in the case of the child's long-term adverse health condition requiring special care. In such a case, the employer must provide parental leave to the woman and man who request it until the child turns six years old.

644. The employer can agree with the employee that parental leave to take care of the child can be granted no later than the day on which the child turns five years old, and if it is a child with a long-term adverse health condition requiring special care, no later than the day on which the child turns eight years old. The total scope of parental leave for deepening the child's care remains preserved because this parental leave can be granted in this way at most to the extent that this leave is taken in a period of up to three or she did not pump until the child was six years old.

E. *Interruption of Maternity and Paternity Leave, Loss of Entitlement to Maternity and Paternity Leave*

645. If the child has been taken into the care of a medical institution for health reasons and the woman or man starts work, the maternity leave or paternity leave will be interrupted by this start of work. The unused portion of maternity or paternity leave is granted to a woman or a man from the day they took the child into their care from a medical facility and, therefore, stopped working at the latest until the day the child turns three years old.

646. A woman or a man from whom a child has been taken away from personal care by a court decision is not entitled to maternity leave or paternity leave for the period during which they are not taking care of the child.

F. *Entitlement to Maternity or Parental Leave When a Child Is Taken into Care Replacing Parental Care Based on a Valid Decision of the Competent Authority*

647. Maternity, paternity, and parental leave to take care of the child belong not only to the employed biological parent(s), including adoptive parents, on an equal footing with them but also to the surrogate parent(s). The Labour Code guarantees to a particular extent the right to maternity leave and parental leave to a woman and a man who, based on a valid decision of the competent authority, took over a child in the care, replacing the care of the parents, who was entrusted to him by the decision of the competent authorities for later adoption or foster care, or a child, whose mother died.

G. *Returning to Work After Maternity, Paternity or Parental Leave*

648. When an employee returns to work after a significant personal obstacle, such as maternity, paternity, or parental leave, the employer must assign them to their original job and workplace. If assignment to the original job and workplace is not possible, the employer must assign them to another job corresponding to the employment contract.

649. When returning to work after maternity and paternity leave, the employer is obliged to place the employee under conditions that will not be less favourable for them than the conditions they had when a significant personal obstacle to work arose. The employee has the right to benefit from any improvement in working conditions that they would have right if this personal obstacle at work had not occurred.

650. The employee has the right, after the end of the parental leave, to preserve all the rights that they had or that accrued to them at the time of starting this parental leave in the original scope; these rights shall apply, including changes resulting from legal regulations, the collective agreement or the usual procedures of the employer.

651. When the employee cannot use up the leave for taking maternity leave, paternity leave or parental leave even by the end of the following calendar year, the employer will provide them with unused leave after the end of the maternity leave, paternity leave or parental leave.

V. Disabled Workers

652. An employee with a disability for the Labour Code is recognized as disabled under the Social Insurance Act and submits a decision on a disability pension to his employer.

653. According to Article 8 of the basic principles of the Labour Code for employees with disabilities, the employer provides working conditions enabling them to apply and develop their skills for work concerning their health status. Provision of section 158 specifies some obligations of the employer to employees with disabilities. The employer must:

- employ an employee with a disability in suitable jobs;
- enable an employee with a disability to obtain the necessary qualification through training or study, as well as take care of its improvement;
- create the conditions for the employee to have the possibility of employment;
- to improve workplace equipment so that the employee can achieve, if possible, the same work results as other employees and to make his work as easy as possible.

654. The given calculation of the employer's obligations is not exhaustive. Additional obligations of the employer to an employee with a disability are regulated by other provisions of the Labour Code, which, in connection with the legal regulation of general labour law institutes, contain special rules applicable to employees with a disability (e.g., upon termination of employment – section 66 of the Labour Code or when scheduling working time – section 87 of the Labour Code). The employer should provide the employee with a disability with theoretical or practical training (retraining). It aims to preserve, increase, expand or change the existing qualification or adapt it to technical development to keep the employee in employment. The goal of keeping an employee with a disability in employment is formalized and institutionalized by the provisions of section 66 of the Labour Code, according to which the employer may terminate the employment of an employee with a disability only with the prior consent of the relevant office of labour, social affairs and family, otherwise, the termination is invalid.

655. The Labour Code does not represent a comprehensive regulation of the employment of employees with disabilities, as other legal regulations besides the Labour Code regulate this issue.

656. In this context, the Act on Employment Services regulates legal relations in the provision of employment services and also to citizens with disabilities. According to this law, a job seeker who is a citizen with a disability is considered a disadvantaged job seeker. These categories of persons are then bound by the regulation of legal relations in the provision of employment services, which, on the one hand, assumes financial incentives for the employment and practice of trade by these persons and, at the same time, anchors the so-called quota system and other obligations of the employer when employing citizens with disabilities.

657. It explicitly envisages the possibility of setting up a protected workshop or workplace. According to the Act on Employment Services, a sheltered workshop and a sheltered workplace are workplaces established by a legal entity or a natural person, where citizens with disabilities are employed in an employment relationship who are unable to find employment on the open labour market, or workplaces where citizens with disabilities with disabilities train or prepare them for work and where working conditions, including requirements for work performance, are adapted to the state of health of citizens with disabilities. To support the employment of citizens with disabilities, the Employment Services Act also provides for contributions from the Office of Labour, Social Affairs and Family.

§2. Measures to Promote Equal Treatment

658. The Antidiscrimination Act governs the principle of equal treatment and establishes the means of legal protection in case of violating this principle. The general part of this Act uniformly enshrines basic concepts related to the problem of discrimination for the entire legal system of the Slovak Republic. Compliance with the principle of equal treatment consists in the prohibition of discrimination on the grounds of sex, religion or belief, race, belonging to a nationality or ethnic group, disability, age, sexual orientation, marital and family status, skin colour, language, political or other opinion, national or social origin, property, gender or other status or because of reporting criminality or other anti-social activity. Compliance with the principle of equal treatment also involves taking measures to protect against discrimination.

659. Discrimination is direct discrimination, indirect discrimination, harassment, sexual harassment and unjustified discrimination; discrimination is also an instruction to discriminate and an incitement to discriminate. For discrimination on grounds:

- discrimination on the grounds of pregnancy or maternity, as well as discrimination on the grounds of sexual or gender identification, is also considered gender;
- racial, national or ethnic origin is also considered discrimination due to a relationship with a person of a specific racial, national or ethnic origin;
- religion or belief is also considered discrimination due to a relationship with a person of a specific religion or belief, as well as discrimination against a physical person without a religion;
- disability is also considered discrimination due to a previous disability or discrimination against a person who, based on external symptoms, could be assumed to be a person with a disability.

660. Discrimination is not such differential treatment justified by the nature of the activities carried out in employment or the circumstances under which these activities are carried out if this reason constitutes a fundamental and decisive requirement for employment provided that the aim is legitimate and reasonable.

661. Following the principle of equal treatment, discrimination against persons for the stated discriminatory reasons is prohibited in employment relations, similar legal relations, and related legal relations. The principle of equal treatment applies only in connection with the rights of persons established by special laws, especially in:

(a) access to employment, occupation, other gainful activity or function, including requirements for employment and the conditions and method of selection for employment;
(b) performance of employment and conditions of performance of work in employment, including remuneration, functional advancement in employment and dismissal;
(c) access to vocational training, further vocational training and participation in programmes of active measures on the labour market, including access to counselling for choosing a job and changing jobs or;
(d) membership and activity in the organization of employees, the organization of employers and organizations bringing together persons of certain professions, including the provision of benefits that these organizations provide to their members.

662. The principle of equal treatment as a general principle should be reflected in all employer measures, decisions and instructions. The principle of equal treatment is applied not only in individual labour relations but also in collective labour relations.

663. Different treatment based on age is not discrimination if pursuing a legitimate goal, objectively justifies it and is necessary and appropriate for its achievement if a special regulation stipulates it. Discrimination on the grounds of age is not, in particular, the differential treatment that lies in the provision:

- minimum or maximum age limit as conditions for entry into employment;
- special conditions for access to employment or vocational training and special conditions for the performance of employment, including remuneration and dismissal, if it concerns persons of a specific age category or persons with caring responsibilities and if the purpose of these special conditions is to support the work integration of these persons or their protection;
- conditions of a minimum age limit, professional experience or years of service for access to employment or certain benefits.

664. In order to apply the principle of equal treatment concerning a person with a disability, employers shall take such measures as will enable such a person to have access to a specific job, to the performance of a specific activity at work, to a functional or other employment procedure or access to vocational training; this does not apply if the adoption of such measures would be disproportionately burdensome for the employer. Discrimination on the grounds of disability is not objectively justified differential treatment, which consists of establishing a condition of health capacity for access to employment or a condition for the performance of specific activities in employment if the nature of this employment or activity requires it.

665. Discrimination on the grounds of sex is not objectively justified differential treatment, the purpose of which is to protect pregnant women, mothers up to the end of the ninth month after giving birth, and breastfeeding women.

666. According to the Anti-discrimination Act, everyone has the right to equal treatment and protection from discrimination. Everyone can claim their rights in court if they believe that their rights, legally protected interests, or freedoms have been or have been affected by non-compliance with the principle of equal treatment. In particular, it can demand that the person who did not comply with the principle of equal treatment abandons his actions, if possible, corrects the illegal situation or provides adequate satisfaction; if it is a non-compliance with the principle of equal treatment due to the reporting of crime or other anti-social activity, the invalidity of the legal act, the effectiveness of which has been suspended, can also be sought.

667. If adequate satisfaction would not be sufficient, if the injured person's dignity, social respectability or social application was significantly reduced due to non-compliance with the principle of equal treatment, the injured person may also claim compensation for non-pecuniary damage in money. The amount of compensation for non-pecuniary damage in money will be determined by the court, taking into account the seriousness of the damage caused and all the circumstances under which it occurred.

668. In proceedings related to violating the principle of equal treatment, the participant may also be represented by a legal entity to which a special law grants such authorization or whose purpose or object of activity is protection against discrimination.

669. Proceedings in matters related to the violation of the principle of equal treatment are initiated at the request of a person who objects that his right has been affected by the violation of the principle of equal treatment. The plaintiff must indicate in the proposal that the person he claims violated the principle of equal treatment. The defendant must prove that he has not violated the principle of equal treatment if the plaintiff informs the court of facts from which it can be reasonably concluded that the principle of equal treatment has been violated.

670. The Labour Code provides that the employee has the right to file a complaint with the employer in connection with a violation of the principle of equal treatment, non-compliance with the conditions (according to which the exercise of rights and obligations arising from employment relations must be following good morals, as well as no one may abuse these rights and obligations for damage to the other participant in the employment relationship or co-employees) and violation of rights and obligations arising from the employment relationship; the employer is obliged to respond in writing to the employee's complaint without undue delay, to make corrections, to refrain from such action and to eliminate its consequences.

671. An employee may also not be persecuted or otherwise penalized in an employment relationship for filing a complaint against another employee or the employer, filing a complaint with the relevant labour inspection body, a lawsuit, a proposal to initiate criminal prosecution or other notification of criminality or other anti-social activity, or not maintaining confidentiality about his working conditions, including wage conditions and employment conditions, or that he is exercising rights and interests protected by law arising from the employment relationship.

672. An employee who believes his rights or legally protected interests have been violated can go to court and seek legal protection. When an employee in an employment law dispute informs the court of facts from which it can be reasonably concluded that the termination of the employment relationship by the employer occurred because the employee exercised his rights and legally protected interests arising from the employment relationship, the employer must prove that the termination of employment ratio occurred for other reasons.

Chapter 9. Covenants of Non-competition

673. The employer may not prohibit the employee from performing other gainful activities outside the working hours specified by the employer; this does not affect the limitation of other gainful activity according to section 83 of the Labour Code or according to special regulations (such as section 9 of the Act no. 552/2003 Coll. on the Performance of Work in the Public Interest or section 112 of the Act no. 55/2017 Coll. on the Civil Service).

674. According to section 83 of the Labour Code, employees may, in addition to their employment in an employment relationship, perform other gainful activities that are competitive with the subject of the employer's activity only with prior written consent. The employer's consent is not required to perform scientific, pedagogical, publishing, tutoring, lecturing, literary and artistic activities.

675. The legal regulation of the performance of an employee's competitive activity assumes that the employee must request in writing consent from his employer, with whom he is employed, for the performance of this activity. The employer can respond to the employee's written request by granting him consent to perform the competitive activity or not granting this consent. The Labour Code enshrines an alternative solution to an employee's request for consent to perform a competitive activity by formulating an irrefutable legal presumption of consent to the employee's gainful activity if the employer does not respond to the employee's written request within fifteen days of its delivery. The employee's request addressed to the employer must be in writing. The Labour Code imposes a fifteen-day deadline for its delivery if the employer does not respond to the employee's request. The Labour Code requires the employer to grant or withhold prior consent to gainful employment in writing.

676. According to the current legal status, the employer is not bound by any period within which he can revoke his prior consent to the performance of the employee's gainful activity. The employer can do so anytime during the employee's employment relationship. However, the Labour Code requires the employer to justify the revocation of his previous consent to the employee's gainful employment. After revoking the employer's consent, i.e., only after delivery of this appeal, does the employee have a legal obligation to terminate another gainful activity lawfully without undue delay. If the employee did not end his gainful activity, even if the employer revoked his previous consent to its performance, it would be a violation of labour discipline with all the resulting consequences, including the establishment of the employee's liability.

677. The Labour Code enshrines the possibility of limiting the competitive activity of the employee even after the end of the employment relationship, provided that the employee and the employer have agreed to this in the employment contract. The Labour Code explicitly stipulates that the duration of this limitation may not be longer than one year. An agreement on restricting the employee's competitive activity is permissible only if the employee could have access to information during the duration of the employment relationship, the misuse of which could cause substantial harm to the employer. The employer must provide the employee with adequate monetary compensation, at least 50% of the average monthly earnings for each month, in this limitation of the employee's earning activity. When the employee does not fulfil his obligation about the employee's gainful activity of a competitive nature, he is obliged to provide the employer with adequate monetary compensation, which was mutually agreed upon in the employment contract, but at most up to the amount of the monetary settlement that the employer was obliged to the employee to provide for limiting the competitive activity of the employee after the end of the employment relationship. Only the employer can withdraw from the obligation not to perform another gainful activity after the end of the employment relationship and only during the duration. The Labour Code explicitly requires a written withdrawal form from this obligation under penalty of invalidity. The employee may terminate the originally agreed commitment not to perform competitive activities after the end of the employment relationship if the employer has not paid him a monetary settlement within fifteen days of its due date.

678. The collective agreement can define the range of employees with whom the employer can agree on a restriction of gainful activity after the end of the employment relationship if it is of a competitive nature to the subject of the employer's activity, as well as the duration of this restriction, the minimum level of adequate monetary compensation, as well as the limitation of the highest amount of this monetary compensation.

Chapter 10. Inventions by Employees

679. Employee inventions are regulated in section 11 of Act no. 435/2001 Coll. on Patents, Supplementary protection certificates (the Patent Act). According to the Patent Act, if the inventor – an employee, created an invention as part of the performance of work tasks, the right to a solution belongs to his employer unless the parties to this relationship have agreed otherwise. An employee who has created an employee invention is obliged to notify the employer of this fact in writing without delay and, at the same time, to hand over to him all the documents necessary for the assessment of the invention. In the notification, the employee describes the technical problem, its solution, and the origin and essence of the employee's invention so that the expert can implement the invention.

680. The employer can exercise the right to a solution against the employee in writing within three months of notifying the employee. The submission of an application, a European patent application or an international application, the subject of which is an employee invention and in which the inventor who created the employee invention is listed as the originator, is considered an exercise of the right to a solution. When the employer exercises the right to a solution, it is obliged to immediately inform the employee in writing about the chosen method of protection of the employee's invention, particularly the submitted application, European patent application or international application. If, within the three months, the employer does not exercise the right to solution in the manner indicated or notifies the employee in writing within this period that he does not exercise the right to resolution, this right passes to the employee. Until the deadline for exercising the right to a solution expires, until the right to a solution is exercised, or until the right to a solution passes to the employee, whichever occurs first, the employer and the employee are obliged to keep the employee's invention confidential to third parties.

681. The employee against whom the employer has exercised the right to a solution has the right to adequate remuneration from the employer. When determining the amount of remuneration, the technical and economic significance of the employee's invention and the benefit that can be achieved through its use or other application are decisive, taking into account the employer's material contribution to the creation of the employee's invention and the scope and content of the inventor's work tasks. The reward is payable within one month of exercising the right to solution.

Chapter 11. Liability for Damage in Labour Law

682. Protecting property is one of the primary duties of employees and employers. Adequate property protection requires the application of a whole range of legal and non-legal instruments, which aim to prevent damage and, if damage does occur, to ensure its effective remediation. In the field of labour law, such a tool is primarily the legal regulation of liability for damage contained in the eighth part of the Labour Code. It is divided into the employee's responsibility and the employer's responsibility.

683. In order for a specific liability relationship to arise, particular prerequisites must be met; among the prerequisites for the emergence of liability for damage in labour law are:

- the existence of an employment relationship;
- illegal act or harmful event;
- existence of damage;
- the causal connection between the illegal act and the harmful event and the resulting damage;
- the connection between the damage and the performance of work tasks;
- fault (but only in the case of an employee).

684. The construction of the liability of employees for damage caused to the employer in the Labour Code is based on the principle of subjective responsibility. The employee is liable to the employer for the damage caused to him by the culpable breach of duties during work tasks or in direct connection with it. The employer must prove the employee's fault, except in exceptional cases of responsibility for the deficit and the loss of entrusted objects. The employee is also responsible for the damage caused by intentional actions against good morals.

685. Fault can be characterized as the psychological relationship of the actor to his action, which is illegal, and to the damage as a consequence of such action. Fault in the form of intent (intentional culpability) is given when the actor knows that he could cause damage and wants to cause damage (direct intent) or when the actor knows that he could cause damage if he causes it, he understood with it (intention indirect). Fault in the form of negligence (negligent culpability) is given if the actor knew that he could cause damage without adequate reasons, relied on not causing it (conscious negligence), or did not know that he could cause damage; however, given his circumstances and circumstances, he should and could have known (unconscious negligence).

686. The performance of work tasks is the performance of work duties arising from the employment relationship, other activities performed at the employer's order, and activities that are the subject of a business trip. In direct connection with the performance of work tasks, actions necessary for the performance of work and during work are customary or necessary before the start of work or after it ends. However, such actions are not the journey to and from work, meals, treatment or examination in a medical facility, nor the journey to and from them. The journey to and from work is from the employee's residence (accommodation) to the point of entry to the employer's premises or another place intended to perform work tasks and back. If it is an employer in agriculture, forestry and construction, it is also the journey from the residence to the designated assembly point and back. The journey from the municipality of the employee's residence to the workplace or to a place of accommodation in another municipality, which is the purpose of the business trip, if it is not the municipality of his regular workplace at the same time, and back is considered a necessary action before the start of work or after it ends.

§1. Preventing Damage

687. The employer must provide his employees with such working conditions that they can adequately perform their work tasks without endangering life, health and property; if he discovers deficiencies, he must eliminate them. In order to protect his property, the employer is entitled to carry out, to the extent necessary, the inspection of things that employees bring to the workplace or take away from the workplace.

688. The employee is obliged to act in such a way that there is no threat to life, health, damage to property or its destruction, nor unjust enrichment. If there is a risk of damage, the employee must notify the manager. If intervention is urgently needed to avert imminent damage to the employer, he is obliged to take action; he does not have this obligation if necessary circumstances prevent him from doing so or if he would expose himself or other employees or close people to grave danger.

§2. Liability of the Employee

689. Depending on the proof of general and specific assumptions, the responsibility of employees can be divided into:

- liability with proven fault (or presumption of innocence), which includes:
  - (a) general liability;
  - (b) liability for failure to fulfil obligations to prevent damage.
- liability with presumption of fault (also referred to as special liability):
  - (a) liability for the shortfall in entrusted values, which the employee is obliged to account for;
  - (b) liability for the loss of entrusted objects.

690. The extent of compensation for damage is adjusted differently depending on the type of liability on which the employee is liable to the employer.

I. General Liability of the Employee for Damage

691. The employee is liable to the employer for the damage caused to him by the culpable breach of duties during work tasks or in direct connection with it. The employee who caused it intentionally by acting against good morals is also responsible for the damage. The employer must prove all prerequisites for general liability when applying for damages.

II. Liability of the Employee for Damage Caused by Non-fulfilment of the Obligation to Prevent Damage

692. The employer may demand from an employee who knowingly did not warn a senior employee of imminent damage or did not take action against imminent damage, even though this would have prevented the immediate occurrence of damage, to contribute to the compensation of the damage to the extent appropriate to the circumstances of the case, if it cannot be compensated otherwise (e.g., because that no direct pest was detected). The employer demonstrates all prerequisites for this responsibility.

693. The employee is not obliged to take action against impending damage if necessary circumstances prevent him from doing so or if he would expose himself or other employees or close people to grave danger.

III. The Employee's Liability for the Shortfall in the Entrusted Values, Which the Employee Is Obliged to Account For

694. The fault of the employee is assumed in the case of this liability. The employer does not have to prove that the employee was at fault for the damage; the employer only proves the valid conclusion of the material liability agreement and the existence of a shortfall in the values the employee was obliged to account for. The subject of an agreement on material responsibility can only be values intended for circulation, with which the responsible employee can dispose of the object for the entire time entrusted to him. The material liability agreement must be concluded in writing; otherwise, it is invalid. It is impossible to conclude an agreement on material responsibility with an employee who has not yet reached the age of 18. Even his legal representative cannot conclude such an agreement on his behalf. With the agreement on material responsibility, the employee assumes responsibility for the shortfall at any workplace, in any function associated with this responsibility and in any group of jointly materially responsible employees, where he will be transferred, assigned or transferred at any time later. Therefore, when transferring to another job and transferring, it is not necessary to conclude a new agreement on material responsibility with the employee. The responsibility for the shortfall in entrusted values based on the material liability agreement remains with the employee at every employment relationship change. The agreement expires on the day of termination of the employment relationship or the day of withdrawal from this agreement.

695. The shortfall is understood as the difference between the actual state of entrusted values, which the employee is obliged to account for, and the data of the accounting records, for which the actual state is lower than the accounting state. For the determination of the shortfall, the inventory is of decisive importance, which is necessary both to determine the initial state of the values entrusted for accounting and their actual state during their management. At workplaces where employees with joint material responsibility work, the inventory must be carried out when concluding agreements on material responsibility with all jointly responsible employees:

- upon termination of all these agreements;
- in case of reassignment to another job or transfer of all jointly responsible employees;
- in the event of a change in the function of the manager or his deputy;
- at the request of any of the jointly responsible employees when there is a change in their team;
- when one of them withdraws from the material liability agreement.

696. The employee can absolve himself of responsibility in whole or in part if he proves that the shortfall arose in whole or in part through no fault of his. When the employee is to be entirely or partially relieved of responsibility for the shortfall in entrusted values, he must prove not only the existence of facts indicating that the shortfall could have arisen in whole or in part through no fault of his but also the causal connection between these facts and the occurrence of the shortfall. It must, therefore, demonstrate that without these facts, the deficit would not have arisen as it did. The employee is wholly or partially relieved of responsibility for the shortfall if he proves that the shortfall arose through no fault of his, either because the management of the company did not create working conditions that would enable him to perform his duties correctly or for objective reasons for which none of the participants is to blame. The reasons for the full or partial release of the employee's responsibility are generally considered by the courts to be the failure to carry out an inventory in the warehouse when the employee was unable to work, while the material for which he was materially responsible was handled by third parties, the employee's inability to work at a crucial time, the location of the store and warehouse in unsuitable rooms and premises, and insufficient number of employees in the store, or insufficient supervision, failure to take measures after the detection of a previous deficiency, if the employer did not ensure the closure of the space for storing packages that were freely stored in the yard, if the employer entrusted the function of materially responsible employee without the necessary competence and did not provide him with help in more qualified work tasks, if the employer entrusted the warehouseman with management warehouse without being properly instructed about his work, despite the fact that the warehouse worker worked at a different workplace, etc.

IV. Employee's Liability for Loss of Entrusted Objects

697. Similar to the case of shortfall liability, the employer does not prove the employee's fault. For the employee to be liable for this, it is sufficient if the employer proves that he entrusted the employee with the object based on a written confirmation and that the employee lost the object or did not return it.

698. The entrusted object can be an object that the employee himself and exclusively uses and has the possibility of qualification to ensure its protection. Entrusted items can only be things not consumed by use that can be assumed to be returned. The employee's responsibility for the loss of items entrusted for written confirmation assumes that it is an item that the employee uses exclusively and has the opportunity to take care of its protection in a qualified manner. It is not the case when the entrusted object is also used by other employees within the scope of their work activities, resulting from their work duties.

699. A particular prerequisite for this responsibility is a written confirmation of the entrustment of the subject, in which the subject entrusted to the employee is indicated and which contains confirmation of the receipt of the subject by the employee's signature. Therefore, the essential elements of the written confirmation are the unambiguous identification of the entrusted object and the employee's handwritten signature confirming receipt.

700. The employee shall be released from responsibility for the loss of the entrusted item in whole or part only if he proves that the loss occurred in whole or in part through no fault of his.

V. Scope and Method of Compensation for Damages on the Part of the Employee

701. The employer may demand compensation from the employee for which the employee is liable; the employer will determine the compensation. The employer shall discuss the requested compensation with the employee and notify him of it within one month at the latest from the date it was established that the damage occurred and that the employee is responsible for it. When determining damage to things, the price of the thing at the time the damage occurred is based on it. The employee responsible for the damage is obliged to compensate the employer for the actual damage, in money, if he does not remove the damage by returning it to the previous state and if the employer demands this damage from the employee.

702. Compensation for damage caused by negligence, which the employer demands from the employee, may not exceed an amount equal to four times the average monthly earnings of an individual employee before the breach of duty by which he caused the damage.

703. If it is a special responsibility of the employee (i.e., liability for the shortfall or loss of entrusted items) or if the damage was caused under the influence of alcohol or after consuming narcotic or psychotropic substances, the employer can demand actual damage from the employee. Actual damage means damage consisting of the reduction of the property status of the injured party and representing the property values that would have to be spent to restore things to their previous state.

704. If the damage was caused intentionally, in addition to the actual damage, the employer could also demand compensation for lost profit; if not paid, it would be contrary to good morals.

705. When the damage was also caused by the breach of duty by the employer, the employee shall pay a proportionate part of the damage according to the degree of his fault.

706. If the employee accepts the obligation to compensate for the damage in the specified amount and the employer agrees with him on the compensation method, the employer must agree in writing; otherwise, the agreement is invalid.

707. If several employees are liable to the employer for the damage, they will pay a proportional part of the damage according to the degree of their fault. In the case of joint responsibility for the shortfall, the share of compensation is determined for individual employees according to the average earnings ratio; their manager and deputy's earnings are counted double. The share of compensation for individual employees, except for the manager and his deputy, may not exceed an amount equal to their average monthly earnings before the damage occurred; if the share determined in this way does not cover the entire damage, the manager and his deputy are obliged to pay the rest according to the ratio of their average earnings. If it is found that the shortfall or part of it is the fault of one of the jointly responsible employees, this employee will cover the shortfall according to the degree of his fault; all jointly responsible employees in shares will cover the remaining part of the shortfall.

708. When employees who have concluded individual agreements on material responsibility without a negotiated clause on joint material responsibility were included in the workplace where they worked with such responsible employees, they are not responsible for the deficit incurred at the joint workplace in the amount calculated in proportion to the Labour Code. However, they are responsible for the shortfall only if it is proven that they have taken-over entrusted values, valuables, or goods and the shortfall has arisen from these individually taken-over values.

§3. Employer's Liability

709. The employer's responsibility is objective. This means that the employer is responsible for the damage caused to the employee during work tasks or in direct connection with them, regardless of fault.

710. We divide the employer's liability into:

- general liability,
- special liabilities, as:
  (a) liability for damage in the event of work accidents and occupational diseases;
  (b) liability for damage to stored items;
  (c) liability for averting damage.

711. Employees' claims for damages are adjusted depending on the type of employer's liability. In general, the principle also applies here that the responsible entity is obliged to compensate the injured party for the actual damage in money unless it is remedied by restoring the previous state.

I. General Liability of the Employer for Damage

712. The employer's general liability is the objective liability for damage that, under the established conditions, arises from the mere violation of a legal obligation or deliberate action against good morals; the employer is thus also responsible for such violations of legal obligations that occurred without his fault. The employer's general liability comes into consideration if the damage is:

- which was incurred by the employee during the performance of work tasks or in direct connection with the breach of legal obligations – it is not essential who caused the damage (the employer or a third party) or whether the damage was caused as a result of culpable conduct;
- which was incurred by the employee during the performance of work tasks or in direct connection with it by deliberate actions against good morals;
- caused to the employee by breach of legal obligations in the performance of the employer's tasks by employees acting on his behalf – this does not require the immediate performance of work tasks, nor a direct connection with this performance on the part of the employee, but the activity of the employer's employees.

713. However, the employer is not responsible to the employee for damage to the motor vehicle, tools, equipment, and objects necessary for the performance of work that the employee used in the performance of work tasks or directly connected with it without the employer's written consent.

II. Employer's Liability for Damage to Stored Items

714. The employer is obliged to ensure safe storage, especially of outerwear and personal items that employees usually carry to work; this obligation is also towards all other persons, if they are active for him at his workplaces, failure to fulfil the employer's obligation to ensure the Labour Code sanctions this safe storage with the special liability of the employer for damage to stored items.

715. In connection with the scope of damages, the legislation distinguishes between what employees usually carry to work and other things. The range of things that employees usually bring to work must be assessed from a general point of view (not only from the subjective point of view of an individual employee), i.e., taking into account what things are usually worn to work, as well as taking into account what is usual for which employee. In both cases, these are things that the employee has left with him while performing work tasks or in direct connection with him in a place designated for that purpose, and if no such place is designated, then in the place where they are usually put away.

716. The employer pays the actual damage in the case of liability for damage to stored items. For items employees do not usually bring to work, the employer is only liable for up to EUR 165.97. However, if the employer has taken these items into safekeeping, the employer will pay the damage without limitation. If the employer proves that the damaged employee also caused the damage, the employer's liability will be limited.

717. If the employee did not notify the employer in writing about the damage without unnecessary delay no later than fifteen days from the day he became aware of the damage, the right to compensation for the damage will expire.

III. Employer's Responsibility for Averting Damage

718. An employee who suffered material damage while averting imminent damage to the employer is entitled to compensation for it and for purposefully incurred costs if he did not intentionally cause the danger and acted appropriately to the circumstances. Employees who averted a danger to life or health are also entitled if the employer was responsible for the damage.

719. If he suffered damage to his health, this damage is considered an occupational accident.

IV. Employer's Liability for Damage in the Event of an Occupational Accident and Occupational Disease

720. When an employee suffers health damage or dies from an accident while performing work tasks or in direct connection with it, the employer with whom the employee was employed at the time of the work accident is responsible for the resulting damage. An occupational accident is an injury to the employee's health caused to the employee during work tasks or in direct connection with it, independently of his will, by the short-term, sudden and violent action of external influences. In the case of an occupational accident, a causal link between the health damage and the accident process must always be proven if the injury occurs when the employee is not performing a work task nor is he performing an activity that is directly related to the performance of work tasks, it cannot be an occupational accident. An occupational accident is not even an accident the employee suffered on the way to work and back.

721. In contrast to occupational accidents, occupational diseases are usually the long-term effects of a risky workplace on the employee. An occupational disease is specified in the Social Insurance Act if it arose under the specified conditions. The employer with whom the employee last worked before it was discovered in the employment relationship under the conditions that caused the occupational disease that affected him is responsible for the damage caused to the employee by an occupational disease.

722. Since the employer, in this case, is liable to the employee regardless of whether the damage was to blame, the Labour Code enshrines the possibility of full or partial liberation (release from responsibility) of the employer. In this way, the employer can get rid of responsibility even if all the prerequisites for liability for damage caused by an occupational accident or disease are met.

723. The employer shall be relieved of all liability if he proves that the sole cause of the damage was the fact that:

- the damage was caused by the fact that the affected employee, through his fault, violated legal regulations or other regulations for ensuring safety and health protection at work, or instructions for ensuring safety and health protection at work, although he was properly and demonstrably familiar with them and knew and followed them were consistently required and controlled; or
- the damage was caused by the disabled employee under the influence of alcohol, narcotic substances or psychotropic substances, and the employer could not prevent the damage.

724. The employer is relieved of responsibility in part if he proves that:

- the affected employee violated legal regulations or other regulations or instructions for ensuring safety and health protection at work through his fault, although he was properly and demonstrably familiar with them, and this violation was one of the causes of the damage;
- one of the causes of the damage was that the employee was under the influence of alcohol, narcotic substances or psychotropic substances;
- the employee suffered damage because he acted contrary to the usual way of behaviour in such a way that it is clear that, although he did not violate legal regulations or other regulations, or instructions for ensuring safety and health protection at work or special regulations, he acted recklessly and had to at the same time, due to qualifications and experience, be aware that may cause harm to health.

725. The employer could not absolve himself of responsibility if the employee suffered an occupational accident while averting damage to the employer or a danger directly threatening life or health if the employee did not intentionally cause this condition.

V. Scope and Method of Compensation for Damage on the Part of the Employer

726. The employer must compensate the employee for actual damage, namely in money, if he does not remove the damage by returning it to the previous state.

727. If the employer proves that the injured employee also caused the damage, his liability will be limited. However, this does not apply to work accidents and occupational diseases, which have a special exemption from liability.

728. The employer who compensated the injured party is entitled to compensation from the person responsible for such damage to the extent that corresponds to the extent of this responsibility towards the injured party.

729. The Social Insurance Agency pays out compensation for damages in case of work accidents and occupational diseases as part of the accident insurance.

§4. Unjust Enrichment

730. Unjust enrichment is property benefit obtained through performance without a legal reason, performance due to an invalid legal act, performance due to a legal reason that has lapsed, and property benefit obtained from dishonest sources. If the employee unjustly enriches himself at the employer's expense or if the employer does so at the employee's expense, they must release the enrichment.

731. The object of unjust enrichment must be given to the person at whose expense it was obtained. Everything acquired through unjust enrichment must be surrendered. If this is not possible, mainly because the enrichment consisted of performances, monetary compensation must be provided. The benefits of unjust enrichment must also be released if the person who received the enrichment did not act in good faith.

732. The person who issues the object of unjust enrichment has the right to compensation for the necessary costs that he has spent on the matter.

733. The employer may demand the return of wrongly paid amounts from the employee if the employee knew or had to assume from the circumstances that the amounts were wrongly determined or paid by mistake within three years of their payment.

Chapter 12. Settlement of Disputes

734. The protective function of labour law is reflected in the specific rights of the employee, which correspond to the employer's obligations. This does not mean that employees are not the bearers of obligations and that employers have no rights. However, the nature of the legislation results in a disparity between the rights of the employee and the employer. However, the purpose of the protective regulation is not to put the employer in a disadvantageous position (after all, for the functioning of the market and society as such, employers are just as important as employees) but to equalize an economically weaker position.

735. Protective legislation aimed at the employee as the weaker party does not only determine the catalogue of the employee's substantive rights and obligations of the employer but also in the forms of legal protection and the procedural procedure for its fulfilment. The guarantee of legal protection for the employee is implemented by:

- the activity of employee representatives;
- institutional protection – the labour inspection mainly provides institutional protection; in addition to the relevant labour inspectorates, other bodies carry out supervision and oversight within the scope of the authority defined by law; in particular, we can mention:
  (a) Personal Data Protection Office of the Slovak Republic.
  (b) Office for the Protection of Whistleblowers of Anti-Social Activities.
- judicial protection.

§1. Judicial Protection

736. Disputes between the employee and the employer regarding claims from labour relations are discussed and decided by the courts. The right to judicial protection is a fundamental right guaranteed by international conventions and the Constitution of the Slovak Republic. According to Article 46 of the Constitution of the Slovak Republic, everyone can claim their right in an independent and impartial court through the procedure established by law and, in cases established by law, in another body of the Slovak Republic. Anyone who claims that they have been deprived of their rights by a decision of a public administration body can turn to the court to review the legality of such a decision unless the law provides otherwise. However, reviewing decisions concerning fundamental rights and freedoms must not be excluded from the court's jurisdiction. Everyone has the right to compensation for damage caused by an illegal decision of a court, other state authorities, public administration bodies, or incorrect official procedures. The conditions and details of judicial and other legal protection shall be established by law. From the point of view of labour law disputes, such a regulation is, in particular, Act no. 160/2015 Coll. the Code of Contentious Civil Procedure.

I. Individual Labour Disputes

737. In general, the parties to the dispute have an equal position in the proceedings, with the same degree of possibility to apply procedural attack and defence. Equality of arms is a fundamental principle of litigation expressed in Article 6 of the Code of Contentious Civil Procedure. However, even the principle of equality of arms must give way in some disputes if the nature of the matter under discussion requires increased protection of the party to the dispute to balance the naturally unbalanced position of the parties. It is about the so-called disputes with the weaker party, among which the Code of Contentious Civil Procedure includes anti-discrimination disputes and individual labour disputes.

738. An individual labour law dispute is between an employee and an employer resulting from labour law and other similar employment relationships. A dispute arising from the principle of equal treatment is also considered an individual labour dispute if it is related to an individual labour dispute.

739. The natural unequal position of employer and employee is balanced by including individual labour law disputes among disputes with the weaker party, in which the adversary is not fully applied. The legislator believes that balancing the economic imbalance only by substantive legal provisions is insufficient and that the employee must also be provided with special protection by procedural standards.

740. Special procedural protection in individual labour law disputes manifests itself in the following aspects:

- special local jurisdiction;
- extended possibility of employee representation;
- manducation duty (teaching duty);
- not applying concentration of proceeding.

A. *Local Jurisdiction*

741. Causal local jurisdiction applies to labour law disputes, disputes from collective labour relations, strikes and lockouts. It means that only one district court determined by law is always competent for the hearing and decision of labour law disputes for the regional court district. It assumes higher specialization, ultimately leading to better and fairer decision-making. In addition to causal local jurisdiction, the Code of Contentious Civil Procedure also regulates particular local jurisdictions given a choice. In addition to the defendant's general court, the court in whose district the defendant has his place of work, according to the employment contract, has local jurisdiction over the proceedings.

B. Possibility of Employee Representation

742. The parties may be represented in the proceedings. A representative can be a natural person or a legal entity. If the representative is not a lawyer, the court examines the eligibility for representation, and the court is authorized to decide on the inadmissibility of the chosen representative if it finds that the representative is not qualified for proper representation or if he acts as a representative in several proceedings. The specificity of individual labour law disputes is that a trade union can represent an employee, while the court is not authorized to assess such representation.

C. Manducation Duty

743. Manducation duty is the court's duty to instruct. The duty to instruct and the right to be represented is an immanent part of the fundamental right to judicial protection – the omission of the manducation duty results in fundamental procedural defects. The general manducation duty of the court is regulated in section 160 of the Code of Contentious Civil Procedure. The court instructs the parties about their procedural rights and obligations to the extent established by law. The court always instructs the parties about their right to choose a lawyer and the possibility of turning to the Legal Aid Center. In general, it can be stated that the court is obliged to instruct the participants in the proceedings, in particular, what rights are granted to them and what obligations are imposed on them by the procedural regulations, how the procedural acts intended by them need to be carried out in order to monitor the procedural effects, or how it is necessary to eliminate the defects of the already performed procedural acts actions, what legal consequences are associated with the performed procedural actions and how it is necessary to fulfil the procedural obligation from the law or the court's decision. However, the manducation duty does not include instructions on what the participant should or could do in a given case; it only helps to clarify what he intends to do in the proceedings in a manner established by law. The court should not instruct the participant about his material rights.

744. In individual labour law disputes, the court has a special educational obligation. During the first procedural act to the employee, the court will appropriately instruct the employee about the options for representation and procedural rights and obligations, not only in the scope of the general educational obligation, but also instruct him on the evidence that needs to be presented, on the possibility of submitting a proposal for an urgent measure or a security measure, and on other options necessary for the purposeful exercise or defence of his rights.

745. The court does not have an obligation to instruct if the party is the state, a state body or a legal entity and the person acting on its behalf, or its employee or member acting on its behalf, has a second-degree university legal education or a natural person who has a university law degree second-level education, or if the party is represented by a lawyer, a legal entity founded or established for consumer protection, a trade union or a natural person who has a second-level university legal education.

D. Concentration of the Proceedings

746. According to the Code of Contentious Civil Procedure, one of the main principles of contentious proceedings is the concentration of proceedings, which is supposed to fulfil the requirement of speed and economy. The concentration of proceedings is the obligation of the disputing parties to apply means of procedural attack and defence in time. The Code of Contentious Civil Procedure distinguishes the legal concentration of proceedings and judicial concentration of proceedings.

747. The legal concentration of proceedings means that the means of procedural attack and the means of procedural defence can be applied no later than the announcement of the resolution, which ends the evidence. The judicial concentration of proceedings is conceived more strictly; it stipulates the obligation of the disputing parties to apply the means of procedural attack and the means of procedural defence on time, that is, as soon as it was objectively possible to apply them for the first time, taking into account the speed and economy of the proceedings. The court does not have to take into account the means of procedural attack and the means of procedural defence that the party did not submit in time, especially if this would require the ordering of another hearing or the execution of other acts of the court.

748. The rules of judicial concentration of proceedings and legal concentration of proceedings shall not be applied in individual labour law disputes. The employee can submit or mark all facts and evidence to prove his claims no later than announcing the decision on the merits. In addition, in the case of individual labour law disputes, the discovery principle is also applied, which is essentially the opposite of the general principle of adversarial proceedings. The court can also take the evidence that the employee did not propose if it is necessary to decide on the matter. Even without a motion, the court will procure or secure such evidence; for this purpose, the employer must cooperate if it can be fairly requested from him.

749. In individual labour law disputes, the provisions on default judgment will not apply if this judgment should be issued against the employee.

II. Anti-discrimination Disputes

750. An anti-discrimination dispute is a dispute that concerns a violation of the principle of equal treatment according to regulations on equal treatment and protection against discrimination. As mentioned, a dispute arising from the principle of equal treatment is also considered an individual labour dispute if it is related to an individual one. However, from the point of view of the procedural rules, this is not a fundamental difference; all the special rules that apply to individual labour law disputes are applied to anti-discrimination disputes as opposed to disputes with the weaker party. A special feature of anti-discrimination proceedings is transferring the burden of proof to the defendant.

751. If an employee feels discriminated against, applicable claims arise from the anti-discrimination law, referred to in section 13 of the Labour Code. Anyone who believes that his or her rights, interests or freedoms protected by law have been affected by non-compliance with the principle of equal treatment may demand in court that the person who has failed to comply with the principle of equal treatment:

– abandoned his action;
– corrected the illegal situation;
– provided adequate satisfaction, eventually compensated the non-property damage in money;
– replaced the damage.

752. In one lawsuit, individual means of legal protection can be applied simultaneously; for example, an employee who feels that his rights have been violated can simultaneously request to refrain from unauthorized intervention, apply for damages, and provide adequate satisfaction. Claims from discriminatory actions cannot be understood as an exhaustive calculation but as a demonstrative list.

III. Criminal Proceedings

753. The employee is also provided exceptional legal protection of his material rights through criminal proceedings. According to Act no. 300/2005 Coll. Penal Code non-payment of wages and severance pay is a criminal offence. In practice, filing a criminal complaint is frequently used by an employee to recover his wages, salary or other remuneration for work, compensation for wages or severance pay that was not paid to him within the due date. The effectiveness of such a procedure is enhanced by the fact that the criminally responsible person is always a natural person; in the case of an employer who is a legal entity, the statutory officer, a member of a statutory body, and a procurator bear criminal liability. Not every failure to pay wages is a crime; the employer does not bear criminal liability if it is proven that he did not have the funds on the due date of the payment or that he absolutely needed them to ensure the employer's activities.

§2. Arbitration

754. In labour law, the fundamental right to judicial protection is highlighted because disputes between participants in the employment relationship are decided exclusively by courts, and the jurisdiction of arbitration bodies is excluded. Any arbitration clause for deciding an employment dispute is void.

Part II. Collective Labour Relations

755. Collective labour law regulates the relations between the representatives of employees and the employer and relations originating between higher-order trade union bodies and the employers' associations. In recent years, collective labour law has been broadened substantially, mainly by Act no. 2/1991 Coll. on Collective Bargaining as amended.

756. Collective labour law concerns such legal relations as social partnership, tripartite and collective bargaining, strikes and lockouts, regulating legal relations between the employer or employers' organizations and the representatives of the employees in the enterprise, represented by trade union organizations, higher-order trade union bodies, works councils or employee confidants.

Chapter 1. Freedom to Establish and Join Unions

757. The existence of specific entities that would become authorized (necessary) participants in the existing interaction between the employer and employees becomes a necessary prerequisite for realizing collective labour relations. If the legal order did not recognize such forms of representation of employees or employers and did not grant them a favoured status for the performance of their activities compared to other entities appearing in the field of labour law, it would not be possible to implement a corresponding purposeful social dialogue in practice.

758. Freedom of association assumes that formal or less formal organizations (associations) established on its basis promote specific public or private interests of a group of persons. An association is considered a legal entity with two essential features – voluntary decision-making on joining and exiting the association and the existence of a common goal, which must be permitted and have a private law nature.

759. In collective labour law, freedom of association can be understood as citizens' right to freely associate to promote and protect their economic and social interests. Such a definition directly corresponds to the freedom of association on the general principle contained in Article 37(1) of the Constitution, which affects employee representatives in the field of labour law and applies to other groups of civil society. The specific feature of the freedom of coalition, unlike the general freedom of association, therefore further approaches at the moment of its identification with the rights of employees and employers; the coalition corresponds to a civil association of employers or employees, the purpose of which is to formulate, defend, promote their interests exclusively in the field of labour relations (labour law, social security law, labour market, social dialogue) in creating working, social and economic conditions. The content of freedom of association includes not only the right to establish various coalitions independently but also the right to autonomy of collective agreements, the right to establish supra-corporate associations, and free activity in such associations.

760. The general character of coalition freedom, as a remarkable expression of freedom of association, also corresponds to the method of creation of employee representatives as a civil association in the sense of Act no. 83/1990 Coll. on the freedom of association, similar to the case of other representatives of self-government of interest. The Act on Associations of Citizens also stipulates that no one may be forced to join, join associations or participate in their activities. Everyone can leave the association freely. It must not be a civil detriment to anyone he joins that he is a member of an association, participates in its activities, supports it, or stands outside of it.

Chapter 2. Subjects of Collective Labour Relations

761. The subject of labour law (also collective law) are natural or legal persons whose rights and obligations in labour relations are defined by labour law norms. These subjects are only potential subjects of these relations. At the same time, they become 'real' subjects of employment relations only based on a specific legal fact with which the legal norm connects the emergence of the relevant legal relationship. The subject (participant) of collective labour relations is the one who, in a given labour relation, is the bearer of the rights and obligations arising from it, according to the relevant legal standards. We include the subjects of collective labour relations in the Slovak Republic:

- employee representatives:
  (a) representatives based on section 11a of the Labour Code;
  (b) European Works Council;
  (c) specific methods of employee representation within European companies.
- representatives of employers:
  (a) a legal or natural person who employs other natural persons in an employment relationship;
  (b) the organization in which the employer is associated (employer's union).
- the State.

§1. Employee Representatives

762. The legal basis for the definition of employee representatives is found in the provisions of section 11a of the Labour Code, according to which we distinguish the following employee representatives:

- the relevant trade union body;
- employee council or employee confidant;
- employee representative for safety and health at work;
- in a cooperative society, where the member's employment relationship with the cooperative society is part of the membership, according to the Labour Code, the representative of the employees is a particular body of the cooperative elected by the members' meeting.

763. Based on the legislation in the Labour Code, these representatives can work side by side. From the legal diction in sections 229 and 232 of the Labour Code, it is clear that the cooperation of a trade union and the works council (or employee confidant) and several trade unions are permissible. Even if this is not directly reflected in the Labour Code, it should not be possible for several works councils to operate side by side at the same employer.

I. Trade Unions

A. The Concept and Establishment of a Trade Union

764. The trade union currently represents the only original form of employee representation in the Slovak legal order, primarily concerning the scope of recognized competencies and the historical-legal context. Only the trade union can access the essential authorization of employee representatives in the form of the right to collective bargaining and the conclusion of a collective agreement as an essential means of improving employees' working and social conditions with a generally binding legal effect. The exclusive position of a trade union is also manifested in the possibility of performing safety and health protection checks at the workplace, where the Labour Code grants authority only to a trade union body.

765. The formation of trade unions is directly linked to freedom of association and coalition. The law grants legal personality to trade unions; therefore, they are qualified to act in labour relations as legal entities, respectively, subjects of labour law. In practice, one can encounter two ways of acquiring legal personality through trade unions; however, in the end, both cases are based on the membership of natural persons in a trade union (trade union).

766. In section 230 of the Labour Code, the law directly determines the legal form of trade union activity and defines a trade union as a civil association according to a special regulation. The formation of a trade union corresponds to the legal regime of establishing a civil association with specific inherent differences in section 9a of Act no. 83/1990 Coll. on the Association of Citizens. In the case of the creation of trade unions, and similarly in the case of the creation of employers' organizations, the principle of registration is not applied, as in the case of classic civil associations, but the principle of registration. At least three citizens, of whom one must be over 18 (preparatory committee), can submit a proposal to register a trade union organization. Such a way of forming a trade union is used both for establishing a trade union operating at the level of a specific enterprise and for establishing trade unions operating at a supra-enterprise level.

767. Another way of establishing trade unions is the procedure when, under the Act on Associations of Citizens, only a trade union is registered as a civil association at the Ministry of the Interior of the Slovak Republic, and individual trade unions operating at the enterprise level derive their legal personality from the statutes of the thus registered trade union (trade union organization) under the Act on Associations of Citizens. The trade union is also based on the membership of individual natural persons in the trade union (it acts de facto as one trade union organization), and individual trade unions operating in companies act as organizational components of one trade union organization (in this case called a trade union), i.e., they primarily fulfil the organizational function of ensuring the activities of the union within the framework of the territorial and substantive principle. Thus, the classic method of formation was applied in the case of the establishment of the trade union itself (the first trade union organization) and individual trade unions, and the method of their constitution is derived from the association's internal documents (constitutions). Individual trade unions operating at the employer derive their legal personality from the trade union, and in legal relations, they act as separate legal entities alongside the trade union itself.

B. Conditions of Operation of Trade Unions at the Employer

768. The trade union is obliged to inform the employer in writing about the start of its activities with the employer and to submit a list of members of the trade union body as a statutory body of the trade union organization authorized to act on behalf of the organization. A written notice is necessary for the employer to know that he has a social partner with whom he is obliged to act in cases where the law stipulates. The employer is obliged to allow entry to the employer's premises, related to the purpose of entry, even to a person who is not an employee of the employer, if this person acts on behalf of a trade union in which his employee is associated, to exercise employee rights; this person is obliged to the extent necessary to comply with the duties and measures established for the field of safety and health protection, special regulations and internal regulations of the employer, given the purpose of entry.

769. The employer is obliged to enable the operation of a trade union at the workplace if there are members of this trade union among the employees. When a trade union applies to the employer and informs him that it wants to work for him but does not prove that it has members among its employees in an employment relationship (from the grammatical expression, it is assumed that it must have at least two members among the employer's employees), the employer is not obliged to accept such a trade union. If the employer or another trade union already operating at the employer has doubts as to whether among the employees in employment, there are members of the trade union that informed him in writing about the start of its operation, a dispute arises about the operation of the trade union at the employer, and Labour Code enables that these doubts were confirmed or removed by an independent arbitrator, on whose person the parties to the dispute agree. When the parties to the dispute do not agree on the person of the arbitrator, at the request of any of the parties to the dispute, the arbitrator will be appointed by the Ministry of Labour, Social Affairs and Family of the Slovak Republic.

770. Based on section 232 of the Labour Code, if several trade unions operate side by side with the employer, the employer must, in cases involving all or a more significant number of employees, if generally binding legal regulations or a collective agreement require negotiation or the consent of a trade union body, fulfil these obligations to the competent authorities of all participating trade unions, unless otherwise agreed with them. When the authorities of all participating trade unions do not agree within fifteen days of the request at the latest whether to grant consent or not, the opinion of the body of the trade union organization with the most significant number of members at the employer is decisive. If several trade unions operate at the employer, the competent trade union body of the trade union organization of which the employee is a member acts in labour relations and similar labour relations concerning individual employees. For an employee who is not unionized, the body of the trade union organization with the most significant number of members at the employer acts in labour relations and similar labour relations unless the employee specifies otherwise.

771. The trade union that operates at the employer has the right to approach the employee appropriately and offer him membership. The trade union and the employer agree on addressing the employee. If an agreement is not reached, the employer is obliged to provide the employee with written information about the trade union that works for him, to the extent of the primary data provided by the trade union to the employer, which includes, in particular, the name, registered office, website address, e-mail address, profile address on social networks, phone number and address of the reserved space within the employer's electronic information system, namely:

- no later than seven days from the date of commencement of her employment with the employer;
- no later than seven days from the day the employee's employment relationship was established, if the trade union started operating at the employer before the employee's employment relationship was established;
- no later than seven days from the day when the trade union requests it due to a change in primary data;
- once per calendar year, no later than seven days after the trade union requests it.

772. A trade union that operates at an employer can inform employees about its activities appropriately. The trade union and the employer will agree on the method of informing employees about its activities. If no agreement is reached, the employer is obliged to allow the trade union to publish notices of its activities in a place accessible to employees in an appropriate manner. If employees have access to the employer's electronic information system, the obligation is fulfilled if the employer reserves space in this system for the trade union.

II. Work Council and Employee Confidant

773. A work council is a specific form of alternative social partner to the trade union organization. Unlike a trade union, it is not based on a membership system but on an electoral basis. It is a kind of representative body of all employees that participates in labour relations, and the employer is obliged to allow it to operate in the workplace (the same applies to the employee confidant).

774. According to the applicable legislation, the work council is a body that represents all employer employees. The condition for its operation at the employer is that it employs at least fifty employees. In comparison, an employee confidant can be established at an employer that employs less than fifty employees but at least three employees.

775. Notably, the Labour Code and no other regulation grant legal subjectivity to the Works Council; therefore, it should not be a subject of law and should not enter into legal relations or perform legal acts. Nevertheless, the Labour Code assigns competencies, including joint decision-making.

A. *Conditions and Rules for the Creation of the Employee Council and the Employee Confidant*

776. The existence and operation of the works council and the employee confidant is not an obligation but a right of the employees, to which the employer's obligation belongs as an opposite enable not only action but also the holding of elections to the work council if at least 10% of the employees request the employer in writing, and at the same time pay the costs of paying for the election of the employees' council and the employees' confidant.

777. The Labour Code establishes the relevant number of members of the Works Council with the number of employees at the employer as follows:

- from 50 to 100 employees, has at least three members;
- from 101 to 500 employees, has at least one additional member for every 100 employees;
- from 501 to 1,000 employees, has at least one additional member;
- from 1,001 or more employees, there is at least one additional member for every 1,000 employees.

778. All employer employees have the active voting right to elect members of the staff council or staff trustee if they have been working for the employer for at least three months. Every employee of the employer over the age of 18 who is of good character, is not a close person of the employer and has worked for the employer for at least three months has the passive right to be elected as a member of the staff council or as an employee trustee (for a four-year term).

779. The first election of works council members at the employer is organized by an election committee consisting of at least three employees and no more than seven employees who signed the application to create a works council. The employer determines the number of election committee members depending on the number of employees and the internal structure of the employer. The work council organizes further elections. The conditions for the validity of elections are defined by the Labour Code as follows:

- elections are direct with a secret ballot based on a list of candidates proposed by at least 10% of the employees or the relevant trade union body;
- elections are valid if at least 30% of all employees who have the right to elect members of the staff council participate in the vote;

- those candidates who received the most significant number of votes become members of the staff council, while their number is determined in advance by the election committee in agreement with the employer;
- if the required number of work council members are not elected, the employer will allow another round of elections within three weeks;
- if the required number of work council members are not elected even after the repeated election, the employees' council will not be established;
- new elections to the staff council will take place only after twelve months have passed since the repeat election was held;
- the costs of paying for the elections of the employee council and the employee confidant shall be paid by the employer.

B. Demise of the Work Council and the Employee Confidant and Termination of Membership in the Work Council

780. The employee council (this employee confidant) is demised by:

- the end of the election period;
- resignation of the staff council, if the resignation was accepted at the staff meeting;
- dismissing the staff council by a majority of the employees present at the vote, if at least 30% of all employees participated in the vote;
- a decrease in the number of employees at the employer to less than fifty.

781. Membership in the work council (as well as the function of employee confidant) ceases for the following reasons:

- termination of the employment relationship with the employer;
- by giving up membership in the work council or by giving up the position of confidant;
- by dismissal of a member of the work council by a majority of employees if at least 30% of all employees participated in the vote.

III. Employee Representative for Safety and Health at Work

782. A particular employee representative is the employee representative for occupational health and safety. The definition of his position is not in the Labour Code but in Act no. 124/2006 Coll. on Safety and Health Protection at Work. According to this Act, the employer is obliged to appoint one or more employees as employees for health and safety at work, based on the proposal of the relevant trade union body, the works council or the election of the employees if the employer does not have a trade union body or a works council. The employee representative for safety and health at work is entitled, for example:

- carry out inspections of workplaces and verify the implementation of measures from the point of view of ensuring safety and health protection at work;
- require information from the employer about facts affecting safety and health protection at work;
- cooperate with the employer and submit proposals for measures to increase the level of safety and health protection at work;
- require the employer to eliminate identified deficiencies; if the employer does not eliminate the shortcomings pointed out to him, he is entitled to give suggestions to the relevant labour inspectorate or the relevant supervisory body.

783. The employee representative for health and safety at work enjoys all benefits and is entitled to the same working conditions and protection as other representatives.

IV. European Work Council (Including Representatives in European Company and European Cooperative Society)

784. The Labour Code enshrines employees' rights to transnational information primarily through European Works Councils or other procedures for informing employees. In addition to the participation of employees at the transnational level in the legal form of European Work Councils, the existing Slovak legal order also regulates the participation of employees in the legal form of a European Company and a European Cooperative Society. The Labour Code enshrines that this employee participation model will also be used in the case of transnational information and negotiations in a European company and a European cooperative, provided that a particular regulation stipulates this.

785. The participation of employees in the legal form of European works councils presupposes only a legal model of informing employees and a legal form of negotiation with employees.

V. Conditions of Activity of Employee Representatives and Their Protection

A. *Leave from Work to Perform the Function*

786. The activity of employee representatives, directly related to the performance of the employer's tasks, is considered the performance of work for which the employee – a member of the trade union body, member of the work council or employee confidant and employee representative for safety and health at work – is entitled to a salary. The employer shall release the employee on a long-term basis to perform a function in a trade union body operating at the employer under the conditions agreed in the collective agreement and to perform the function of a works council member after agreement with the works council. The performance of the function of employee representatives or participation in their training, provided by the authority of the relevant trade union body, the staff council and the employer, is considered an obstacle to work due to the general interest according to section 136(1) of the Labour Code.

787. The employer shall provide a member of a trade union body for the activities of a trade union organization, a member of the works council for the work of a works council, or an employee confidant for his activities with work leave with compensation for the time agreed between the employer and the trade union or the employer and the works council or the employee confidant. If an agreement is not reached, the employer will provide, based on the distribution of work leave, to the members of the trade union body for the activities of the trade union organization and to the members of the works council for the work of the works council or to the employee confidant for his work, work time off with compensation of wages per month in total to the extent determined as the product of the average number of employees working with the employer during the previous calendar year and a period of fifteen minutes. If the employer did not employ employees in the previous calendar year, it is based on the number of employees as of the last day of the calendar month that precedes the calendar month in which the work leave is granted. If more than one employee representative works for the employer, they will notify the employer in writing of the division of work leave. If the employee representatives disagree on the distribution of work leave, the division of work leave will be decided by an arbitrator whom they appoint; for the time until the written notification of the distribution of work leave to the employer, the employee representatives are not entitled to leave. The trade union body decides on the division of work leave between individual members of the trade union body, and the work council decides between individual members of the works council; the trade union body and the staff council shall notify the employer in writing of this division. In the collective agreement or the agreement with the employees' representatives, the conditions under which the trade union, the employees' council or the employee's representative are entitled to monetary compensation for unused work leave are agreed upon.

788. In connection with the provided work leave, the employer is entitled to check whether the employee is using it for the purpose for which it was provided. The conditions for performing this check can be agreed upon in the collective agreement or an agreement with the employee representatives.

B. Material and Technical Support for the Activities of Employee Representatives

789. According to its operational capabilities, the employer must provide the employee's representatives (trade union body, work council or employee confidant and employee representative for safety and health at work) with the necessary equipment and cover the costs associated with their maintenance and technical operation.

C. *Obligation to Maintain Confidentiality*

790. Employee representatives (members of the trade union body, members of the work council or employee confidant and employee representative for safety and health at work) and experts performing tasks for employee representatives are obliged to maintain confidentiality about facts they learned about in performing their duties and were designated as confidential by the employer. This obligation also lasts one year after the end of the function's performance unless a special regulation provides otherwise.

D. *Protection of Employee Representatives*

791. Employee representatives may not be disadvantaged or otherwise penalized by the employer for performing tasks arising from their duties.

792. During the term of office and six months after its end, employee representatives are protected against measures that could harm them, including termination of employment, and that would be motivated by their position or activity.

793. The employer may give a member of the relevant trade union body, a member of the works council, or an employee confidant or employee representatives for safety and health at work notice or immediately terminate the employment relationship with them only with the prior consent of these employee representatives. Prior consent is also considered if the employee representatives did not refuse to give the employer consent in writing within fifteen days from the day the employer requested it. The employer can use the prior consent only within two months of its granting. If the employee representatives refuse to grant consent, the notice or immediate termination of employment by the employer is invalid for this reason; if the other conditions for termination or immediate termination of employment are met and the court, in a dispute under section 77, finds that the employer cannot reasonably demand that the employee continue to be employed, the termination or immediate termination of employment is valid.

§2. Employers and Representatives (Organizations) of Employers

794. The subject of collective labour relations is the employer or employers' organizations, as opposed to employee representatives.

I. Employer

795. Based on valid legislation, the employer can be a legal entity or a natural person who employs at least one natural person in an employment relationship and, if provided for by a particular regulation, also in similar employment relationships.

II. Employers' Organizations

796. Employers' organizations also act as a subject of collective labour relations. According to the existing legal status, employers' organizations, together with the relevant higher trade union bodies or relevant higher trade union bodies, conclude a higher-level collective agreement. Employers' organizations also derive their legal personality from the freedom of association, the legal expression of which is the Act on Associations of Citizens. The same conditions apply to employers' organizations as in the case of registration of trade unions.

§3. The State as a Subject of Collective Labour Relations

797. The state plays a vital role in collective labour relations and several different levels that result from the generally defined functions of labour law.

798. First, the state creates a suitable legal environment for implementing relations and simultaneously determines the legal scope of the relations that arise in collective labour law.

799. The second level of state participation in collective labour relations is primarily at the level of the so-called tripartite negotiations. Negotiations of tripartite bodies, conclusion of agreements at different levels, negotiations, consultations and other activities between the state and its bodies on the one hand and the so-called social partners (representatives of employees and employers) on the other hand, we generally call social dialogue. At the highest level, social dialogue is regulated in Act no. 103/2007 Coll. on Tripartite Consultations at the National Level (Tripartite Law), which regulates the conditions of these tripartite negotiations on fundamental issues of economic and social development and employment development to reach an agreement on these issues, as well as the establishment, composition and principles of activity Economic and Social Council of the Slovak Republic.

800. The third level of state participation in collective labour relations is when the state acts as an employer that participates in collective bargaining at the enterprise or higher levels.

Chapter 3. Institutionalized Relations Between Employers and Employees

801. The forms and methods of collective labour relations are diverse, and only some are regulated by law. However, some are outside the framework of legislation. These are primarily forms and ways of implementing social dialogue at various levels, such as cooperation and discussion of important issues of a conceptual nature or organizing various professional conferences.

802. The most important form of collective labour relations is collective bargaining, which, based on legislation from international, European, or national sources of collective labour law, belongs only to trade unions or the relevant trade union body.

803. The Labour Code defines that, to ensure fair and satisfactory working conditions, employees participate in the employer's decision-making, which concerns their economic and social interests directly or through the relevant trade union body, work council or employee confidant. Section 229(4) of the Labour Code distinguishes the following forms of employee participation:

- co-decision-making;
- negotiation;
- the right to information;
- control activity.

804. The Labour Code also considers the cooperation of several employee representatives mentioned above. Specifically, section 229(7) defines that if a trade union, a work council or an employee confidant works side by side with the employer, then:

- A trade union has the right to:
  (a) collective bargaining;
  (b) co-decision-making;
  (c) control activity; and
  (d) information.
- Work council or employee confidant has the right to:
  (a) negotiation; and
  (b) information.

§1. The Right to Co-decision-making

805. Co-decision-making is the statutory authorization of employees to participate in the employer's decision-making, which concerns their economic and social interests, to ensure fair and satisfactory working conditions. Employees participate in co-decision-making directly or through the relevant trade union body, works council or employee confidant. In this case, it is a method of decision-making in which the employer can exercise his powers only on the condition that he is granted the consent of the representatives of the employees or if he reaches an agreement with the employee representatives. Co-decision-making authority of employees takes place, for example, when granting consent to issue work regulations by the employer (section 84), when adjusting and scheduling working time (section 87(2)), when determining the leave plan or collective leave-taking (section 111), or upon the termination of the employment relationship by the employer with a member of the relevant trade union body, a member of the staff council or an employee confidant (section 240(9)).

806. Based on section 12 of the Labour Code, if the consent of employee representatives or an agreement with them is required according to this law, an employer who does not have employee representatives may act independently; this does not apply if this law stipulates that a decision of the employer cannot replace an agreement with employee representatives. When the Labour Code stipulates that a decision of the employer cannot replace an agreement with employee representatives, this agreement cannot be replaced by an agreement with the employee either.

807. Co-decision-making is an essential form of employee participation for the validity of legal acts in labour relations. That is, based on section 17(2) of the Labour Code, it follows that a legal act for which the employee representatives did not give the prescribed consent is invalid only if the Labour Code or a special regulation expressly provides for it.

§2. The Right to Negotiate

808. By negotiation, we mean a particular form of employee participation in creating the conditions for work performance at the employer. During negotiations, there is an exchange of views and a dialogue between the representatives of the employees and the employer, and it is carried out in an understandable way and at an appropriate time, with adequate content, to reach an agreement. So, negotiation is understood as a form of cooperation between the relevant trade union body and the employer, which consists of the fact that the employer must present the listed areas of questions to the relevant trade union body for discussion or consultation before deciding on the matter; the form of negotiation is not determined by law; therefore it can take place orally, but also in writing. However, only the employer's unilateral notification of the intended decision is not considered such, as it usually happens in practice. The current legislation grants the right to negotiate with the work council or the employee confidant in the case of cooperation between both forms of employee representatives. In case of exclusive operation of the trade union at the employer, the right to negotiate belongs to the trade union. Section 237 of the Labour Code specifies which issues the employer is obliged to discuss in advance with employee representatives:

(a) the state, structure and expected development of employment and planned measures, especially if employment is at risk;
(b) fundamental issues of the employer's social policy, measures to improve hygiene at work and the working environment;
(c) decisions that may lead to fundamental changes in work organization or contractual conditions;
(d) organizational changes, which are considered to be the restriction or cessation of the employer's activity or its part, merger, fusion, division, or change of the employer's legal form;
(e) measures to prevent accidents and occupational diseases and protect employees' health.

809. Negotiation as a form of participation is also contained in many provisions of the Labour Code, such as participation of employee representatives at the end of the employment relationship (section 74), even distribution of working time (section 86), or temporary interruption of work performance (section 141a).

810. We cannot ignore that failure to reach an agreement during negotiations does not invalidate the negotiation act. However, there are cases in which the Labour Code punishes the absence of a negotiation with the invalidity of a legal act.

§3. The Right to Information

811. The current legislation does not distinguish between a works council and a trade union, and at the same time, it grants the right to information to both. If both types of employee representatives work at the workplace simultaneously, it is not excluded that they exercise their right to information separately. The employer thus provides information not only to the trade union but also to the works council.

812. The provision of information to employee representatives by the employer for familiarization with the content of the information is considered information by the Labour Code. The employer must inform the employee representatives about his economic and financial situation and the expected development of his activity. Provision section 229(2) of the Labour Code clarifies that employees can provide information about the employer's economic and financial situation and the expected development of its activities at the appropriate time. An example of the employer's information obligations is information obligation during the transfer of rights and obligations from employment relations (section 29) or to inform employees in a fixed-term employment relationship and employee representatives about open-ended jobs that have become vacant with him (section 48).

813. However, the Labour Code also establishes a negative definition of this right of employees in such a way that it allows the employer to refuse to provide information that could harm him. Also, the employer may require that this information be treated as confidential.

§4. The Right to Control

814. Within the framework of the legal order, we must distinguish between the exercise of the right of control according to section 149 of the Labour Code (exclusively the competence of trade unions) and the exercise of control according to section 239 of the Labour Code (belongs to both the trade union and the works council). Under section 239 of the Labour Code, the right to inspection mainly includes inspection of compliance with labour law regulations, including labour regulations, including wage regulations and obligations arising from the collective agreement; for this purpose, they are entitled in particular to enter the employer's workplaces at a time agreed with the employer, and if they do not agree with the employer, no later than three working days after notifying the employer about entering his workplaces, to demand the necessary information and documents from senior employees, to submit proposals for improvement working conditions, require the employer to give an instruction to eliminate identified deficiencies, propose to the employer or another body entrusted with the control of compliance with labour law regulations to apply appropriate measures against senior employees who violate labour law regulations or the obligations arising for them from collective agreements, or require from the employer, information on what measures were taken to eliminate deficiencies found during the inspection.

815. In the case of the simultaneous existence of a trade union and a works council at one workplace, current legislation grants the right to control. If only the works council were to operate at the employer's workplace, it would not have the right to control the area of health and safety protection at work (exclusive competence of a trade union under section 149 of the Labour Code) and could only exercise the right to control according to section 239 of the Labour Code. In the case of a trade union, it is not a question of competitive performance of control activities against the labour inspection, as a state body which, among other things, carries out control in the area of safety and health protection at work. The trade union organization's competence in the field of safety and health protection at work is the realization of its right, which is related to the mission of the trade union.

Chapter 4. Collective Bargaining

816. In addition to the mentioned methods of employee participation in creating fair and satisfactory working conditions, collective bargaining is probably the most essential institution of collective labour law. From a theoretical point of view, it is necessary to perceive collective bargaining as an effort to reach a consensus between individual social partners, within which certain concessions are made in exchange for achieving an advantage in another provision (another obligation). The right to collective bargaining can be considered a particular form of employee participation in the employer's activities. Under ILO conventions (e.g., Convention no. 154 on the Promotion of Collective Bargaining from 1981), this participation is entrusted exclusively to the competence of trade union bodies. The Constitution guarantees the constitutional right to collective bargaining in Article 36. The constitutional enshrining of this right refers to guarantees in the form of a law that will ensure the given right. In this case, the right to collective bargaining is regulated in Article 10 of the Basic Principles of the Labour Code, which guarantees employees and employers the right to collective bargaining and in a particular legal regulation in Act no. 2/1991 Coll. on Collective Bargaining.

817. The Act on Collective Bargaining regulates collective bargaining between the relevant bodies of trade unions and employers, aiming to conclude a collective agreement. The collective agreement, as one of the results of its negotiation at the company level, the sector level, or part of the sector, contributes significantly to fulfilling the principle of permanent and effective social dialogue and achieving social peace.

818. According to the Act on Collective Bargaining, the main goal of collective bargaining between the relevant bodies of trade unions and employers is the collective conclusion of a collective agreement.

819. Although the Collective Bargaining Act is primarily a procedural regulation, it also regulates particular substantive law institutions, such as provisions on collective agreements, their invalidity, the period of conclusion, and provisions on the subsidiary scope of the Labour Code.

§1. Levels of Bargaining

820. The Act on Collective Bargaining recognizes two types of collective agreements according to which we can also distinguish the levels of collective bargaining, namely:

– an enterprise collective agreement concluded by the relevant trade union body or relevant trade union bodies and the employer, which is also the service office; and

– a collective agreement of a higher level concluded for a more significant number of employers between the relevant higher trade union body or relevant higher trade union bodies and the organization or organizations of employers.

821. The enterprise collective agreement, by its nature and subject to regulation, corresponds to the classic standard contract type, which developed within the historical concept of collective labour law. The enterprise collective agreement regulates a specific issue, which is based on the specific conditions of the enterprise, in comparison with the collective agreement of a higher level, which solves many areas of adjustment of the working conditions of employees expressly as a framework.

822. From a procedural point of view, there is no significant difference in the collective bargaining process of an enterprise collective agreement and a higher-level collective agreement. The same principles and procedures govern collective bargaining of both types, and it can be stated that most of the above can be applied to higher-level collective agreements as well. As a rule, the contracting party of the enterprise collective agreement is the sole employer and the trade union or several trade unions. Multiple employer entities can never be a contracting party to an enterprise collective agreement, even in the case of their property connection, since, as a rule, they are separate business entities that represent separate legal entities in the sense of special regulations. In case of interest in concluding a collective agreement for a more significant number of business entities (even if they are connected by property), a higher level collective agreement would have to be concluded. The legal order does not further limit the nature of the concluded collective agreement; therefore, in practice, it is possible to encounter various differentiating criteria limiting their subject or scope, e.g., concluding a collective agreement for only one organizational component of the employer, concluding a collective agreement and adjusting the claims of only one objectively determinable group of employees.

823. According to the Act on Collective Bargaining, a higher-level collective agreement is a document concluded for a larger number of employers, namely between the relevant higher union body or higher trade union bodies and the organization or employers' organizations. In this case, the higher trade union body is the trade union. At the same time, the Collective Bargaining Act does not exclude several trade unions that collectively negotiate and conclude the higher-level collective agreement as a party to the contract. The provision's wording does not preclude several employers' organizations acting on the employer's side. A collective agreement concluded between a higher trade union body (trade union) or by several higher trade union bodies (trade unions) and one employer, which in this case is the state. The last type of collective agreement of a higher level is a collective agreement of a higher level concluded for employers who, when remunerating employees, proceed according to the Act on Remuneration of Certain Employees in the Performance of Work in the Public Interest, namely between the relevant higher trade union body, which is a trade union, or by several trade unions on the one hand and the other hand by government-appointed representative representatives of employers.

824. Collective bargaining for a higher number of companies, the goal of which is to conclude a collective agreement of a higher level, is no different from enterprise collective bargaining from the procedural point of view. The Collective Bargaining Act determines only some of the content requirements of a higher-level collective agreement in a different way, in contrast to an enterprise collective agreement (e.g., a list of employers), while considering their compliance as a condition for the validity of a higher-level collective agreement. The collective negotiation of a higher-level collective agreement does not end with signing the collective agreement but only with its deposit at the Ministry of Labour, Social Affairs and Family of the Slovak Republic. The right to conclude a collective agreement of a higher level is always the trade union and the employer's union, i.e., deviating from the corporate level, it will be a collective representative (organization) representing employees and several employers. The legal order does not establish any formal requirements for the content of the higher-level collective agreement itself, from the point of view of the requirement to adjust some defined areas of employees' working conditions quality (level of their adjustment).

825. A collective agreement of a higher level does not represent and does not have the character of a collective agreement oriented to the adjustment of working conditions in a specific economic sector.

§2. Content of Bargaining

826. From the point of view of labour law theory, a collective agreement is a legal act and a source of law in its normative part, an instrument of social reconciliation between employees and employers and a political, legal, economic and social document regulating the relations of the relevant entities and their content (rights and obligations of collectives and individual nature). Labour law theory is based on the assumption that the substantive legal prerequisites for collective bargaining and the conditions for concluding a collective agreement are contained in the Labour Code (as well as in other labour law regulations, e.g., in the Travel Reimbursement Act, in the Minimum Wage Act, or Act on the Social fund). Procedural issues of collective bargaining are regulated in the Act on Collective Bargaining. The obligations contained in the collective agreement can be divided into normative and contractual-legal obligations that do not give rise to claims for individual employees.

I. Normative Obligations

827. Obligations of a normative nature give rise to claims or provide optional benefits to individual employees; respectively, they regulate other individual rights and obligations of employees, i.e., they establish the subjective rights and obligations of individuals in the same way as in the case of generally binding legal regulations. In this part, the collective agreement has the nature of a legal regulation concerning its binding nature. Under the provisions of the relevant labour law regulations, the classic normative obligations mainly regulate the wage and labour rights of employees, a more favourable regulation of the provision of work leave, and the like. The possibility of moderating the regulation of labour law claims in terms of the principle of convenience naturally depends on the legal regulation of the selected labour law institute, i.e., whether the Labour Code allows deviations from the labour regulations (in the form of 'at most', 'minimum', 'least', and the like). The contracting parties' agreement must respect the agreement's minimum or maximum limits for these claims. At the same time, it is also possible to negotiate such claims that employees do not derive from any legal regulation and are only the result of an agreement between the contracting parties following the principle 'what is not prohibited is permitted'.

II. Contractual Obligations That Do Not Give Rise to Claims for Individual Employees

828. Obligations of the collective agreement, which do not give rise to claims for individual employees and do not result from individual rights and obligations of employees, can be negotiated based on authorization in a legal regulation or without it. It will primarily concern the adjustment of questions related to the scheduling of weekly working hours, the determination of the beginning and end of work shifts, the adjustment of working conditions of special categories of employees, the mutual relationship between the employer and the trade union organization (granting time off for the performance of trade union functions, ensuring the material conditions for the activities of employee representatives), scope of information provision and conditions of negotiations, joint decision-making, or control activities by the trade union, issues of corporate social policy, safety and health protection at work. Since the legal order does not exhaustively list all cases of trade union participation in the employer's decision-making, they can be agreed in a collective agreement.

§3. The Procedure of Collective Bargaining

829. The collective bargaining process is neither strictly formalized nor institutionalized; the Act on Collective Bargaining sets only the minimum formal rules of procedure for the collective negotiation of collective agreements; all other matters are left to the express agreement of the contracting parties or customary practices.

830. Collective bargaining begins with submitting a written proposal for the conclusion of a collective agreement by one of the contracting parties to the other contracting party. The Act does not specify in what form the draft collective agreement should be delivered, so it is up to the parties to the contract whether to deliver it personally or via a postal company. The contracting party is obliged to respond to the proposal in writing within thirty days at the latest, unless the contracting parties agree otherwise, and in response to comment on those parts that were not accepted.

Rejection of collective bargaining, or taking over the draft collective agreement, can be considered a dispute over the conclusion of a collective agreement, in which the institution of a mediator can be used, or arbitrator of collective disputes, in extreme cases even a strike. The contracting parties are then obliged to negotiate and provide each other with the required cooperation if it does not conflict with their legitimate interests. The final stage of the collective bargaining process is usually the signing of the agreed content of the collective agreement. Parties authorized to sign a collective agreement are persons simultaneously authorized by law to negotiate and conclude a collective agreement.

831. The contracting parties are also obliged to start negotiations on the conclusion of a new collective agreement at least sixty days before the expiry of the concluded collective agreement. The deadline has an orderly nature, which means that its non-compliance does not result in the invalidity of the collective bargaining process or the impossibility of starting collective bargaining, and in no case is non-compliance capable of invalidating the collective agreement.

832. The contracting parties can agree on changing the collective agreement and its scope in the collective agreement. The parties of the collective agreement usually want the conclusion of amendments in cases where the collective agreement is concluded for several years, and yearly wage growth and the budget of the social fund are negotiated in the form of an amendment. When the parties to the contract agree on the change and possible scope of the change to the collective agreement (i.e., which obligations may be subject to change) during the period of its validity, the law stipulates that the procedure for negotiating this change is the same as for the negotiation of a collective agreement.

§4. Extension of Collective Agreements

833. Collective agreements of a higher level are concluded at the sector level or part of the industry between the employers' association and the higher trade union body. The goal is to adjust working and wage conditions in a specific industry. This collective agreement is binding on the contracting party of the employers for the relevant union that concluded the collective agreement and the employers listed in the list of employers attached to such collective agreement. Thus, a collective agreement of a higher level does not automatically apply to all employers in the sector or part of the sector in which it is concluded but only to employers listed in the list of employers, which is an annexe to the collective agreement of a higher level.

834. With effect from 1 March 2021, provisions on extending higher-level collective agreements were deleted from the Collective Bargaining Act. Due to this fact, the Slovak legal system does not currently regulate the extension of collective agreements.

§5. VALIDITY AND BINDING OF COLLECTIVE AGREEMENTS

835. Collective agreements are valid if they are concluded in writing and signed on the same document by an authorized representative or authorized representatives of the relevant trade union bodies and employers or representatives of their organizations and supported by a list of employers if it is a collective agreement of a higher level.

836. A collective agreement is invalid in that part that conflicts with generally binding legal regulations and/or regulates employees' claims to a lesser extent than the collective agreement of a higher level.

837. The collective agreement is binding for the contracting parties. The collective agreement is also binding for:

(a) an employer associated with the employers' organization:
   - for whom a collective agreement of a higher level was concluded and for which a trade union associated with the trade union organization operates, whose higher union body concluded the collective agreement of a higher level;
   - which concluded the higher-level collective agreement, if the code of the statistical classification of economic activities of this employer at the division or group level is the same as the designation of the branch or part of the industry for which the higher-level collective agreement is concluded, and if it is not binding for this employer another collective agreement of a higher level.

(b) employees for whom the relevant trade union body or the relevant higher trade union body concluded a collective agreement;
(c) trade union body for which the relevant higher union body concluded the collective agreement.

838. A collective agreement of a higher level is also binding for an employer who is not associated with the employers' organization that concluded the collective agreement of a higher level if the employer requests the contracting parties to accede to the collective agreement of a higher level and the contracting parties agree to the accession. The contracting parties of a higher-level collective agreement shall notify the Ministry of the employer's accession to the higher-level collective agreement according to the first sentence within fifteen days of the employer's accession to the higher-level collective agreement at the latest. The employer's accession to a higher-level collective agreement is announced at the request of the Ministry in the Collection of Laws of the Slovak Republic.

839. The relevant trade union body concludes a collective agreement also for employees who are not unionized. The collective agreement is concluded for a period that is expressly determined in it. If this period is not determined, it is assumed that it was agreed upon for one year. The effectiveness of the collective agreement begins on the first day of the period for which the agreement was concluded and ends with the expiration of this period unless the period of effectiveness of some obligations is not negotiated differently in the collective agreement.

Chapter 5. Settlement of Industrial Disputes, Protection of Vital Needs

840. There is no exact definition of the term 'collective dispute' in the Slovak legal order. Provision of section 10 of the Act on Collective Bargaining, as collective disputes, refers only to disputes about the conclusion of a collective agreement and disputes about the fulfilment of collective agreement obligations, which do not give rise to claims by individual employees. Nevertheless, in the Act on Collective Bargaining, we also find a dispute about the determination of the trade union authorized to conclude a collective agreement, to which the Act no longer grants the adjective 'collective'. In the Labour Code, we find three more disputes in which employee representatives are parties, namely the dispute about applying for support during short-time work (section 142a), the dispute about the operation of a trade union at the employer (section 230a), and finally a dispute over the distribution of work leave provided by the employer for the performance of the function of employee representatives (section 240(3)).

§1. Dispute Over the Operation of a Trade Union at the Employer

841. A dispute over the operation of a trade union at the employer concerns the case when the employer or the trade union that operates at the employer has doubts as to whether, among the employees in employment, there are members of the trade union that have informed him in writing about the start of its operation.

842. The dispute is solved by an arbitrator agreed upon by the parties to the dispute; if the parties to the dispute do not agree on the person of the arbitrator, at the request of any of the parties to the dispute, he will be appointed by the Ministry of Labour from the list of arbitrators, if the arbitrator agrees to accept the resolution of the dispute regarding the operation of the trade union at the employer. The arbitrator informs the parties to the dispute and the employer, if the employer is not a party to the dispute, about the acceptance of the settlement of the dispute regarding the operation of the trade union at the employer. The employer is obliged to provide the arbitrator with a list of employees in an employment relationship within the period specified by him, and the trade union organization is obliged to provide the arbitrator with a list of employees in an employment relationship with the employer who are its members and to prove their membership in the trade union organization. The parties to the dispute are obliged to provide the arbitrator with further necessary cooperation; failure to provide cooperation is the responsibility of the party to the dispute who did not provide it.

843. The arbitrator is obliged to notify the parties of the dispute and the employer, if he is not a party of the dispute, whether there are members of the trade union among the employees in the employment relationship within thirty days of receiving the resolution of the dispute about the operation of the trade union at the employer.

844. Twelve months from the date the arbitrator announced that there are no trade union members among the employees in the employment relationship, that trade union is not considered a trade union operating at that employer. A trade union that, according to the arbitrator's notification, does not have members among its employees in an employment relationship may once, during twelve months from the date of this announcement, request an arbitrator from the list of arbitrators maintained by the Ministry of Labour, social affairs and family, for a reassessment of whether it has members among its employees in an employment relationship.

845. The arbitrator shall be entitled to a remuneration agreed upon by the parties to the dispute for resolving the dispute over the operation of the trade union at the employer; if the parties to the dispute do not agree on the remuneration, the arbitrator is entitled to a remuneration of EUR 500 for the resolution of the dispute regarding the operation of the trade union at the employer. The arbitrator's fee is paid by the employer or trade union that raised the doubt. If the arbitrator informs the parties to the dispute that there are no members of a trade union among the employees in the employment relationship, the employer or the trade union that expressed the doubt has the right to reimbursement of the remuneration paid to the arbitrator by this trade union. In case of reassessment within twelve months from the previous assessment, the arbitrator is entitled to a reward of EUR 1,000 for the assessment; the trade union pays the remuneration.

§2. Dispute Over the Distribution of Work Leave Provided by the Employer for the Performance of the Function of Employee Representatives

846. The employer shall provide a member of a trade union body for the activities of a trade union organization, a member of the works council for the work of a works council, or an employee confidant for his activities with work leave with compensation for the time agreed between the employer and the trade union or the employer and the works council or the employee confidant. If an agreement is not reached, the employer will provide the members of the trade union body for the activities of the trade union organization and the members of the works council for the work of the works council or the employee confidant for his work with work leave with compensation of wages per month in total to the extent determined as the product of the average number of employees working for the employer during the previous calendar year and a period of fifteen minutes. When several employee representatives act simultaneously, they must agree on the division of work leave and notify the employer of the division; in the event of a disagreement on the division of work leave, the arbitrator they appoint will decide.

847. In this dispute, the arbitrator decides on the distribution of work leave between several employee representatives. The Labour Code does not indicate the method of determining the person of the arbitrator; it only assumes that the individual forms of employee representation at the workplace are agreed upon in his person. It is not clear from the wording of the Labour Code whether any natural person can be an arbitrator in a specific case or whether it must be an arbitrator entered in the list of collective bargaining mediators and arbitrators under the Act on Collective Bargaining. Theoretically, the disputing parties can agree to proceed analogously according to section 13 of the Act on Collective Bargaining. However, the Act does not contradict a different procedure when any natural person is designated arbitrator. In contrast, the disputing parties have assessed the quality of this person in the agreement itself. The Labour Code does not regulate the arbitrator's remuneration in any way.

§3. Dispute on the Submission of an Application for the Provision of Support During Short-Time Work

848. In connection with the adoption of legislation on support during short-time work, employers are entitled to apply for support during short-time work through the relevant Offices of Labour, Social Affairs and Family. Short-time work is when, due to an external factor, employers cannot assign work to at least one-third of the employees or part of the employer to the extent of at least 10% of the established weekly working time. One of the conditions for applying is that the employer has concluded an agreement with employee representatives or with the employees themselves (if the employer does not have employee representatives) that the employer will request the provision of support. The condition is, therefore, that the employees agree to such a procedure. The amount of the employer's supplement is also part of the agreement since the state support does not cover the total wage expenses. If no agreement is reached, an arbitrator can decide on the matter.

849. The arbitrator shall notify the parties to the dispute within ten days of accepting the resolution of the dispute regarding the submission of an application for the provision of support during the period of reduced work, whether he agrees to the submission of the application for the provision of support during the period of reduced work, and in the event of a dispute between the employer and the employee, only to the employer, whether he agrees to by applying the provision of support during short-time work to individual employees.

850. In such a case, the arbitrator's consent will replace the agreement between the employer and the employees' representatives (or with individual employees) necessary for the application to support reduced work during short-time work.

851. For resolving the dispute, the arbitrator is entitled to a fee paid by the employer; the amount of the reward depends on the agreement between the employer and the arbitrator; if the employer and the arbitrator do not agree on the amount of the reward, the arbitrator is entitled to a reward of EUR 600.

§4. Dispute Over the Determination of a Trade Union Authorized to Conclude a Collective Agreement in the Case of a Plurality of Trade Unions Operating at the Employer

852. The Act on Collective Bargaining assumes that if several trade unions operate side by side at the employer when concluding a collective agreement on behalf of the collective of employees, the relevant trade union bodies operating at the employer may act and act with legal consequences for all employees only together and in mutual agreement unless they agree otherwise. When the trade unions do not agree on the procedure according to the first sentence, the employer is entitled to conclude a collective agreement with the trade union with the largest number of members at the employer or with other trade unions whose sum of members at the employer is greater than the number of members of the largest trade union. An analogous provision also solves the plurality of trade unions when concluding collective agreements at a higher level.

853. The law provides two options for the trade union solution of plurality at the employer when concluding a collective agreement – trade unions act together and in mutual agreement, or trade unions do not act together and in mutual agreement; subsequently, the solution to the representativeness of trade unions will be applied through the so-called majority principle and the collective agreement with the employer will be concluded by the one or those that have a larger number of members than the others.

854. On the assumption that there is no agreement on the common procedure and action in mutual agreement between the trade unions and the trade unions not agreeing on another way, two solutions come into consideration. As long as there is no doubt as to which trade union or trade unions together have a greater number of members (they are more representative), the employer may enter into a collective agreement with this/these authorized entities. If this procedure (i.e., the employer's decision on a representative trade union organization – for example, the employer has doubts about which trade union organization is representative) is not applied, a dispute arises regarding the determination of the trade union organization entitled to conclude a collective agreement.

855. The arbitrator issues a document that authorizes the relevant trade union or trade unions to negotiate and conclude a collective agreement. The law does not regulate the more detailed conditions of the arbitrator's procedure, such as the deadline for issuing a decision, the details of the decision, the facts the arbitrator must consider when making a decision, or remedies.

§5. COLLECTIVE DISPUTES

I. Dispute Over the Conclusion of a Collective Agreement

856. From the point of view of counting time, it is impossible to determine, not even by the time horizon, when a dispute over the conclusion of a collective agreement arises. In order to determine whether it is a dispute over the conclusion of a collective agreement, the agreement of both contracting parties is not necessary. At the same time, there is a minimal assumption that the parties will reach an agreement that there is a dispute over the conclusion of a collective agreement, especially when they do not agree on the text of the collective agreement itself. For the unequivocal determination of the existence of a dispute and the possibility of using legal means to resolve a collective dispute, the existence of the dispute must be established in writing in the record from the meeting (collective bargaining). A dispute is also considered if one of the contracting parties refuses to respond to a written proposal to conclude a collective agreement.

II. Dispute Over the Fulfilment of the Obligations of the Collective Agreement

857. In this case, it must be a type of commitment that does not give rise to claims for individual employees. The first prerequisite for such a dispute is the existence of a validly concluded collective agreement; the second prerequisite, which must be fulfilled simultaneously, is the non-fulfilment of an obligation agreed in the collective agreement, which, however, does not have an individual character.

III. Settlement of Collective Disputes

858. As a procedural norm, the Act on Collective Bargaining regulates special procedural procedures for resolving collective disputes. If a collective agreement is not concluded, or if a dispute arises regarding the fulfilment of collective agreement obligations, the law allows these disputes to be resolved through mediators and arbitrators, whose list is kept by the Ministry of Labour, Social Affairs and Family. The Ministry selects mediators and arbitrators based on the request of a citizen of the Slovak Republic or the proposal of state bodies, scientific institutions, universities, employers and representatives of trade unions. A mediator or arbitrator can be a citizen who:

(a) has the capacity to perform legal acts in its entirety;
(b) has a permanent residence in the territory of the Slovak Republic;
(c) is blameless;
(d) has completed university education;
(e) is professionally qualified.

859. The Ministry verifies the professional competence of mediators and arbitrators every three years. Verification of the professional competence of mediators and arbitrators is carried out by a selection committee appointed and dismissed by the Minister of Labour, Social Affairs and Family of the Slovak Republic. The members of the selection committee are representatives of the state, a representative of employees and a representative of employers.

860. The Ministry shall enter the mediator in the list of mediators, and the arbitrator in the list of arbitrators for three years shall issue a written confirmation to the mediator and arbitrator on the execution of the registration, which authorizes them to resolve collective disputes.

A. *Proceedings Before the Mediator*

861. The first stage of resolving a dispute over the conclusion of a collective agreement is the so-called proceeding before a mediator.

1. Designation of a Mediator

862. According to section 11 of the Act on Collective Bargaining, the contracting parties may agree on a mediator to resolve this collective dispute. Proceedings before the mediator begin on the day the request for dispute resolution is received by the mediator. If the contracting parties do not agree on the person of the mediator, he will be appointed by the Ministry from the list of mediators at the request of any of the contracting parties. With the delivery of the decision on the appointment of a mediator, the proceedings before the mediator began. In a dispute over the conclusion of a collective agreement, the request may be submitted no earlier than sixty days after submitting a written proposal for the conclusion of this agreement. This request must contain a precise definition of the subject of the dispute supported by written materials.

2. Proposal for Resolution of the Dispute

863. The mediator shall draw up a written record of the proposal for dispute resolution before the mediator within fifteen days from the date of receipt of the request for dispute resolution by the mediator or from the date of delivery of the decision to appoint a mediator, which, after verification of correctness, the contracting parties are entitled to sign without undue delay, unless otherwise agreed with the contracting parties. The mediator will hand over the record to the contracting parties and the Ministry. This written record includes:

(a) designation of the contracting parties;
(b) facts on which the contracting parties did not agree;
(c) dispute resolution proposal and its justification;

(d) date of creation of the record;
(e) name and surname of the intermediary and his signature.

864. Each contracting party pays one-half of the costs of the proceedings before the mediator. Part of the intermediary's costs is mainly his remuneration and travel allowances. When the contracting parties do not agree with the mediator on the remuneration, he is entitled to the remuneration according to the Decree of the Ministry of Labour, Social Affairs and Family of the Slovak Republic no. 315/2009 Coll. on the amount of remuneration to the mediator and the arbitrator and the amount and method of payment of the costs of proceedings before the arbitrator.

3. Ending of Proceedings Before the Mediator

865. If the contracting parties agree to the proposal to resolve the dispute, they can enter into a collective agreement based on its intentions. In this case, the dispute over the conclusion of a collective agreement ends.

866. If a collective agreement is not concluded after proceedings before a mediator, another method of collective dispute resolution is considered: proceedings before an arbitrator. However, if the contracting parties do not request an arbitrator to resolve the dispute, a strike or lockout can be declared as a last resort over the conclusion of a collective agreement already at this stage.

B. Proceedings Before an Arbitrator

1. Designation of Arbitrator

867. Therefore, if the proceedings before the mediator were unsuccessful, based on section 13 of the Act on Collective Bargaining, we distinguish between two options for appointing an arbitrator (he must not be a person who was a mediator in the same dispute) – optional or mandatory procedure.

868. Optional procedure, i.e., agreement on the person of the arbitrator – the contracting parties may, after agreement, ask the arbitrator for a decision in the dispute. Proceedings before the arbitrator are started on the day the request for dispute resolution is received by the arbitrator. The arbitrator and the parties to the contract will write a record of the arbitrator's acceptance of the request for dispute resolution. The arbitrator will hand over the record to the contracting parties and the Ministry.

869. The mandatory procedure, i.e., appointment of an arbitrator – if the contracting parties do not agree, or if it is a dispute over the conclusion of a collective agreement that arose at a workplace where striking is prohibited, or a dispute over the fulfilment of obligations from a collective agreement, the Ministry will appoint an arbitrator at the request of any of the contracting parties. Delivering the decision to the arbitrator initiates proceedings before the arbitrator. The Ministry cannot appoint an arbitrator from one of the contracting parties in dispute.

870. The dispute settlement request before the arbitrator contains a precise definition of the subject of the dispute supported by written materials, which are handed over to the arbitrator in two copies and the opinion of the other contracting party.

871. Unlike the mediator, the costs of proceedings before the arbitrator, including his remuneration and travel allowances, are covered by the Ministry of Labour, Social Affairs and Family.

2. Resolution of the Dispute

872. The arbitrator must notify the contracting parties in writing of his decision within fifteen days from the start of the proceedings. This decision must include:

(a) designation of the contracting parties;
(b) facts on which the contracting parties did not agree;
(c) the arbitrator's statement and its justification;
(d) date of issue of the decision;
(e) name and surname of the arbitrator and his signature.

873. The arbitrator's decision in the dispute about the conclusion of a collective agreement is final, and upon its delivery to the contracting parties, this agreement is concluded.

3. Review of the Decision on the Fulfilment of Obligations from the Collective Agreement

874. Unlike a dispute over the conclusion of a collective agreement, the arbitrator's decision on the fulfilment of obligations from a collective agreement can be reviewed by a court. According to section 14 of the Act on Collective Bargaining, the court shall cancel the arbitrator's decision on fulfilling obligations from the collective agreement at the contractual party's proposal if it conflicts with legal regulations or collective agreements.

875. The contracting party can submit a motion to cancel the decision within fifteen days of its delivery. Jurisdiction is the district court in which district the contractual party is domiciled, against whom this proposal is directed. The court proceeds according to the Code of Contentious Civil Procedure when deciding. No appeal or reopening of the proceedings is admissible against the decision in the matter.

876. If the court cancels the arbitrator's decision, the same arbitrator will decide the dispute; if at least one of the contracting parties does not agree, or if it is not possible for other reasons, the Ministry of Labour, Social Affairs and Family will appoint a new arbitrator. When making a new decision, the arbitrator is bound by the court's legal opinion.

877. If a motion to cancel the arbitrator's decision on the fulfilment of obligations from the collective agreement was not submitted to the court within the mentioned period of fifteen days, or if the court did not comply with such a motion, the arbitrator's decision on the fulfilment of obligations from the collective agreement is enforceable.

Chapter 6. Strikes, Lockouts and Other Legal Forms of Industrial Action

§1. Constitutional Strike

878. The right to strike is enshrined in the Constitution of the Slovak Republic. It is included in the second chapter of the fifth section as one of the economic, social and cultural rights. Citing the constitutional enshrinement, we can state that Article 37(4) guarantees the right to strike. The conditions shall be established by law. Judges, prosecutors, members of the armed forces, and members and employees of the fire and rescue services do not have this right.

879. The Constitution of the Slovak Republic, therefore, recognizes and guarantees the right to strike, which belongs to everyone to the same extent, except for special work categories. The Constitution entrusts the determination of specific conditions for exercising this right to the legislator.

880. Since no law has been adopted to date that would regulate strikes in general, it follows from the valid legal status de lege lata, regulated in the collective bargaining law, that the only law regulating strikes is a strike in a dispute over the conclusion of a collective agreement. It raises the question of how to perceive the legality of strikes other than strikes covered by the Collective Bargaining Act.

881. In this context, applying a constitutionally compliant interpretation supported by jurisprudence is necessary to define the right to strike. The decision of the Supreme Court of the Slovak Republic 1 Co 10/98, in which the court concluded that 'other strikes, even if not regulated by the Collective Bargaining Act or other legislation, are not prohibited by our legal system. Otherwise, it would lead to an impermissible restriction or denial of the right to strike, guaranteed by Article 37(1) of the Constitution of the Slovak Republic. The right to strike is then the subjective right of the trade union, which is authorized to use this right for the entire time since the strike was declared'. The Supreme Court justified this statement by saying that the right to strike is one of the fundamental rights and freedoms. Thus, it is also covered by Article 12(4) of the Constitution, according to which no one should be harmed because he exercises his fundamental rights and freedoms. According to the court, this constitutional right must also be interpreted under the constitutional principle stated in Article 2(3) of the Constitution, according to which everyone can act in that is not prohibited by law, and no one can be forced to do something that is not required by law. Article 37(4) of the Constitution guarantees the right to strike because the conditions are established by law. At the same time, the court claims that the absence of such a law cannot lead to questioning the constitutional right to strike and the right to exercise it. The Supreme Court further stated that no law in the legal order of the Slovak Republic would limit or prohibit the right to strike (except the Act on Collective Bargaining), and thus that it does not follow from any legal regulation and cannot be deduced even from the interpretation of Article 37(4) of the Constitution, that any strikes other than those regulated by the executive regulation are prohibited. Article 51 of the Constitution of the Slovak Republic does not allow such an interpretation. The Supreme Court claims that this article cannot be taken out of the context of the Constitution and must be interpreted and applied also in connection with Article 7(5) of the Constitution. Therefore, it is necessary to apply the International Covenant on Economic, Social and Cultural Rights, which in Article 8(1)(d) stipulates that the states party to the Covenant undertake to ensure the right to strike, provided that it is exercised under the laws of the respective country. Based on those mentioned above, the Supreme Court of the Slovak Republic concluded that the Constitution of the Slovak Republic in Article 51 guarantees that laws establishing the conditions for the exercise of the rights mentioned in this article will be adopted. He claimed, however, that it is impossible to derive the opinion unequivocally from it that the right to strike can only be claimed within the limits of a particular law. According to the Supreme Court, the rights regulated in Article 51 (including the right to strike) would thus be relegated to the level of the so-called quasi-constitutional rights (i.e., those that are formally established in the Constitution but in reality would only be introduced by law, i.e., by a regulation of lower legal force).

§2. Strike under the Collective Bargaining Act

882. We find special legal regulation in the Act on Collective Bargaining. This strike is the only strike in a dispute over the conclusion of a collective agreement, which the Act on Collective Bargaining allows only as a last resort if the conclusion of a collective agreement does not take place even after proceedings before a mediator and the parties to the contract do not request an arbitrator to resolve the dispute.

883. According to section 16 of the Act on Collective Bargaining, a strike is an employee's partial or complete interruption of work. A strike in support of the demands of striking employees in a dispute over the conclusion of another collective agreement is called a solidarity strike in the sense of the law. An employee who agreed to the strike is considered a participant for the entire duration, while an employee who joined the strike is considered a participant from the day of joining the strike. Generally, an employee may not be prevented from participating in a strike or forced to participate.

I. Declaration of Strike

884. The Act defines special conditions for declaring a strike in a dispute over the conclusion of an enterprise collective agreement and in a dispute over the conclusion of a higher-level collective agreement. A strike in a dispute over the conclusion of a company collective agreement:

(a) announces and decides on its initiation by the relevant trade union body;
(b) it must be agreed to by the majority of the employer's employees participating in the strike vote, to whom this collective agreement is to apply;

(c) at least a majority of the employees counted from all employees must participate in the vote.

885. A strike in a dispute over the conclusion of a collective agreement of a higher level:

(a) the relevant higher union body declares it;
(b) the relevant trade union body decides its initiation;
(c) it must be agreed to by the majority of the employer's employees participating in the vote on the strike, to whom the higher-level collective agreement is to apply;
(d) at least a majority of employees counted from all employees must participate in the voting.

886. Details of the preparation and course of voting on a strike can be adjusted by the relevant trade union body in the strike regulations.

II. Obligations Related to the Declaration of a Strike

887. In the event of a declaration, the relevant trade union body is obliged to:

(a) notify the employer in writing at least three working days before the start of the strike:
  (i) the day the strike starts;
  (ii) reasons and goals of the strike;
  (iii) a list of names of representatives of the relevant trade union body who are authorized to represent the participants in the strike.
(b) provide the employer in writing, at least two working days before the start of the strike, with information related to the strike that is known to the employer and that will help the employer establish work schedules to ensure necessary activities and necessary services during the strike;
(c) obliged to provide the employer with the necessary cooperation for the entire duration of the strike in ensuring the protection of equipment against damage, loss, destruction or abuse and in ensuring the necessary activity and operation of equipment where their nature or purpose requires this concerning safety and health protection or the possibility the occurrence of damage to these devices;
(d) representatives of the relevant trade union body, who are authorized to represent participants in the strike, must allow adequate and safe access to the employer's workplace and not prevent employees who want to work from accessing and leaving this workplace or threatening them with any harm.

III. Illegal Strike Within the Meaning of the Collective Bargaining Act

888. Section 20 of the Collective Bargaining Act exhaustively establishes the reasons for the illegality of a strike. A strike is illegal in these cases:

(a) the strike was not preceded by proceedings before a mediator; this does not apply in the case of a solidarity strike;
(b) the strike was declared or continues after the initiation of proceedings before an arbitrator or after the conclusion of a collective agreement;
(c) the strike has not been announced or has not started under the conditions established in section 17 (*see* previous subsection);
(d) a strike is announced or initiated for reasons other than in a dispute over the conclusion of a collective agreement;
(e) solidarity strike, as long as the employer of the participants of this strike, especially concerning economic continuity, cannot influence the course or outcome of the strike of the employees, in support of whose demands the solidarity strike is declared;
(f) strike in the time of state military alert and at the time of extraordinary measures;
(g) strike of employees of medical facilities or social service facilities if their participation in the strike would endanger the life or health of citizens;
(h) strike of employees operating nuclear power plant equipment, equipment with fissile material and oil or gas pipeline equipment;
(i) strike of judges, prosecutors, members of the armed forces, members and employees of fire brigades and rescue teams and employees in the management and provision of air traffic;
(j) strike of employees providing telecommunications operations and employees serving and operating public water supply systems if their participation in the strike would endanger the life or health of citizens;
(k) strike of employees who work in areas affected by natural disasters in which the relevant state authorities have declared emergency measures, civil servants appointed as superiors and civil servants who perform duties directly to protect life and health if their participation in the strike would endanger the life or health of the population.

889. In addition to regulating illegal strikes in the Act on Collective Bargaining, we also find legal restrictions on the right to strike in other legislation. An example is Constitutional Act no. 227/2002 Coll. on the security of the state in time of war, state of war, state of emergency and state of emergency, as amended, which in special provisions directly or indirectly affects the limitation of the right to strike.

890. The employer, employers' organizations, or the prosecutor may submit a proposal to determine the illegality of the strike to the court in whose district the relevant trade union body against which this proposal is directed is based; the proposal does not have a suspensory effect. The court decides according to the Code of Contentious Civil Procedure provisions governing proceedings in the first instance.

IV. Labour Rights in the Event of a Strike

891. According to section 22 of the Act on Collective Bargaining, although participation in a strike before the legality of a court decision on the illegality of a strike is considered to be an excused absence from work, during the period of participation in the strike, the participant in the strike is not entitled to wages or compensation. This provision is significant from the point of view of mandatory social and health insurance contributions. Participation in a strike after the legality of a court decision on the illegality of a strike is considered an unexcused absence from work.

892. During the strike, the employer may not hire other citizens to replace the participants.

893. The employer will allow employees who are not participating in the strike to perform their work. If, as a result of a strike, these employees cannot perform work or activities, their wage claims are subject to special provisions of the Labour Code on obstacles to work on the employer's part.

V. Liability for Damage

894. Even though a strike is an extraordinary institution of collective labour law, Act on the Act on Collective Bargaining stipulates that the strike participant is liable to the employer or the employer to the strike participant under the Civil Code for damage caused by an event that occurred during the strike. The only exception is when there is damage during the provision of activities under section 19 when the participants in the strike are liable according to the Labour Code.

895. However, the strike participant is not liable to the employer, and the employer is not liable to the strike participant for damage caused solely by the interruption of work due to a strike.

896. According to special regulations, the trade union whose body decided to start the strike is liable to the employer for the damage caused by the failure to provide the necessary cooperation according to the Act on Collective Bargaining. If the court decided that the strike was illegal, the trade union, whose body declared the strike, is liable to the employer for the damage caused by such a strike.

VI. Ending the Strike

897. The strike is ended if the trade union body that declared the strike or decided to start it decided to do so. The competent trade union body must notify the employer in writing of the end of the strike without undue delay.

§3. Lockout in a Dispute Over the Conclusion of a Collective Agreement

898. In order to maintain balance in collective bargaining, in disputes about the conclusion of a collective agreement, the employer (or employers) is given the right to use lockout. Like a strike, a lockout is one of the ways to resolve collective disputes. According to the Act on Collective Bargaining, it belongs to the optional phase of dispute resolution, in which the parties can ask an arbitrator to resolve the dispute or resolve the dispute through a strike, in the given case, a lockout. According to Article 10 of the Basic Principles of the Labour Code, employees and employers have the right to collective bargaining, and in the event of a conflict of interests, employees have the right to strike, and employers have the right to lockout.

899. Under the term lockout, under section 27 of the Act on Collective Bargaining, we understand a partial or complete stoppage of work by the employer. It is the ultimate means of resolving a dispute about the conclusion of a collective agreement declared only by the employer.

I. Declaration of Lockout

900. When a collective agreement is not concluded even after proceedings before a mediator and the contracting parties do not request an arbitrator to resolve the dispute, exclusion may be declared as a last resort to resolve the dispute over the conclusion of the collective agreement. The employer must notify the relevant trade union body in writing at least three working days in advance of the beginning of the lockout, including its scope, reasons, goals, and the list of employees against whom the lockout is applied. Within the same period, the employer must notify the employees against whom it is applied.

II. Illegality of Lockout

901. According to section 28 of the Act on Collective Bargaining, the same grounds of illegality as for a strike apply to a lockout. The illegality of the lockout is decided by the court in whose district the relevant employer, against whom the motion to determine the illegality of the lockout is directed, has its seat. This proposal can be submitted by the relevant trade union body or the prosecutor, while the submission of this proposal does not have a suspensory effect. The court decides according to the Code of Contentious Civil Procedure provisions governing proceedings in the first instance.

III. Labour Law Claims in Case of a Lockout

902. If the employee cannot perform work because an exclusion was applied to him, this is an obstacle to work on the part of the employer. If it is not an illegal lockout, the employee is only entitled to compensation of half of the average earnings. If the court decides the lockout was illegal, the employer would be obliged to compensate the employees up to the average earnings.

IV. Liability for Damage

903. Similar to a strike, also in the case of a lockout, the employee against whom the lockout was applied to the employer and the employer to the employee against whom the lockout was applied according to the Civil Code are liable for damage caused by an event that occurred during the lockout. The employee, against whom the lockout was applied, is not liable to the employer and the employer to the employee, against whom the lockout was applied, for damage caused solely by the interruption of work due to lockout.

V. Ending of Lockout

904. The lockout is over if the employer who announced the lockout has decided to do so while notifying the relevant trade union body of the termination of the lockout without undue delay in writing, as well as to employees against whom the lockout was applied.

Selected Bibliography

Legislation

Act no. 40/1964 Coll. Civil Code, as amended.
Act no. 2/1991 Coll. on Collective Bargaining, as amended.
Act no. 513/1991 Coll. Commercial Code, as amended.
Constitutional Act no. 460/1992 Coll. Constitution of the Slovak Republic, as amended.
Act no. 311/2001 Coll. Labour Code, as amended.
Act no. 435/2001 Coll. on Patents, Supplementary protection certificates (the Patent Act), as amended.
Act no. 283/2002 Coll. on Travel Allowances, as amended.
Act no. 461/2003 Coll. on Social Insurance, as amended.
Act no. 462/2003 Coll. on Wage Compensation during Temporary Incapacity to Work, as amended.
Act no. 552/2003 Coll. on the Performance of Work in the Public Interest, as amended.
Act no. 553/2003 Coll. remuneration of certain employees for the performance of work in the public interest and on the amendment of certain laws as amended by later legal regulations, as amended.
Act no. 5/2004 Coll. on Employment Services and amendments to certain laws, as amended.
Act no. 265/2004 Coll. on Equal Treatment in Certain Areas and on Protection Against Discrimination and on the amendment of certain laws (Anti-discrimination Act), as amended.
Act no. 82/2005 Coll. on Illegal Work and Illegal Employment, as amended.
Act no. 124/2006 Coll. on Occupational Safety and Health Protection at Work, as amended.
Act no. 125/2006 Coll. on Work Inspection, as amended.
Act no. 103/2007 Coll. on Trilateral Consultations at the National Level (Tripartite Act), as amended.
Act no. 355/2007 Coll. on Protection, Support and Development of Public Health, as amended.
Act no. 160/2015 Coll. Code of Contentious Civil Procedure, as amended.
Act no. 55/2017 Coll. on Civil Service and on amendments to certain laws, as amended.

Selected Bibliography

Act no. 54/2019 Coll. on the protection of whistleblowers of anti-social activity and on the amendment of certain laws, as amended.

Monographs, Books (in Slovak)

Barancová, H. et al. *Zákonník práce: komentár.* 3. ed. Bratislava: C.H. Beck, 2022. 1624 p., ISBN 978-80-8232-024-7.

Barancová, H. – Lacko, M. – Križan, V. *Medzigeneračná solidarita a zákaz diskriminácie podľa veku.* Plzeň: Vydavatelství a nakladatelství Aleš Čeněk, 2012. 368 p., ISBN 978-80-7380-393-3.

Barancová, H. – Olšovská, A. – Hamuľák, J. – Dolobáč, M. *Slovenské pracovné právo.* Bratislava: Sprint 2, 2019. 664 p., ISBN 978-80-89710-48-5.

Dolobáč, M. et al. Zákonník práce: Veľký komentár. 1. ed. Žilina: Eurokódex, 2023. 917 p., ISBN 978-80-8155-118-5.

Lacko, M. *Materská a rodičovská dovolenka.* 1. ed. Praha: Nakladatelství Leges, 2016. 160 p., ISBN 978-80-7502-191-5.

Lacko, M. *Dočasná pracovná neschopnosť zamestnanca.* 1. ed. Praha: Nakladatelství Leges, 2019. 110 p., ISBN 978-80-7502-366-7.

Nováková, M. et al. *Pracovné právo 1.* 1. ed. Bratislava: Wolters Kluwer SR s. r. o., 2024, 236 p., ISBN 978-80-571-0676-0.

Olšovská, A. *Jednostranné právne úkony v pracovnom práve.* Bratislava: Veda, vydavateľstvo Slovenskej akadémie vied, 2010. 122 p., ISBN 978-80-224-1145-5.

Olšovská, A. *Skončenie pracovného pomeru.* 1. ed. Praha: Wolters Kluwer ČR, 2015. 199 p., ISBN 978-80-7552-001-2.

Olšovská, A. *Pracovný pomer.* 1. ed. Praha: Wolters Kluwer ČR, 2017. 200 p., ISBN 978-80-7552-946-6.

Olšovská, A. – Divékyová, K. – Mészáros, M. *Okamžité skončenie pracovného pomeru.* 1. ed. Praha: Wolters Kluwer. Wolters Kluwer ČR, 2019. 104 p., ISBN 978-80-7598-668-9.

Olšovská, A. – Divékyová, K. – Mészáros, M. Organizačné zmeny zamestnávateľa a skončenie pracovného pomeru. 1. ed. Bratislava: Wolters Kluwer SR, 2023. 164 p., ISBN 978-80-571-0596-1.

Olšovská, A. et al. *Agentúrne zamestnávanie.* Bratislava: Wolters Kluwer, 2015. 384 p., ISBN 978-80-8168-289-6.

Olšovská, A. et al. *Kolektívne pracovné právo s príkladmi.* Bratislava: Friedrich Ebert Stiftung, zastúpenie v Slovenskej republike, 2017. 305 p., ISBN 978-80-89149-55-1.

Olšovská, A. – Švec, M. *Zástupcovia zamestnancov a ich kompetencie pracovný čas, dovolenka, bezpečnosť a ochrana zdravia pri práci.* 1. ed. Praha: Nakladatelství Leges, 2018. 168 p., ISBN 978-80-7502-283-7.

Švec, M. – Olšovská, A. *Kurzarbeit a iné prekážky v práci na strane zamestnávateľa.* 1. ed. Bratislava: Wolters Kluwer, 2022. 192 p., ISBN 978-80-571-0450-6.

Švec, M. – Toman, J. – Olšovská, A. – Žuľová, J. – Dušeková Schuszteková, S. *Zákonník práce: zákon o kolektívnom vyjednávaní: komentár.* 2. ed. Bratislava: Wolters Kluwer. Wolters Kluwer SR, 2023, 2776 p., ISBN 978-80-571-0584-8.

Švec, M. – Žul'ová, J. Zákon o podpore v čase skrátenej práce: komentár. 1. ed. Bratislava: Wolters Kluwer SR, 2022. 136 p., ISBN 978-80-571-0477-3.

Toman, J. *Individuálne pracovné právo – Všeobecné ustanovenia a pracovná zmluva*. Bratislava: Friedrich Ebert Stiftung, zastúpenie v SR, 2014. 391 p., ISBN 978-80-89149-41-4.

Chapters in Monographs and Anthologies (in English)

Dolobáč, M.: Slovakia: Traditions and New Challenges of Labour Law. in jakab, N. (ed.).

Fundamentals of Labor Law in Central Europe. Miskolc–Budapest: Central European Academic Publishing. pp. 37–56.

Križan, V. Obstacles to work due to childcare In: *Festschrift für Otto Kaufmann Armağanı*. Istanbul: Legal yayincilik san. ve tic. ltd. şti., 2021, pp. 351–361. ISBN 978-605-315-920-9.

Chapters in Monographs and Anthologies (in Slovak)

Barancová, H. Formy diskriminácie a právna ochrana pred diskrimináciou. In: *Diskriminácia v zmluvnom práve*. Trnava: Trnavská univerzita v Trnave. Typi Universitatis Tyrnaviensis, spoločné pracovisko Trnavskej univerzity v Trnave a Vedy, vydavateľstva Slovenskej akadémie vied, 2015. pp. 89–109. ISBN 978-80-8082-835-6.

Dolobáč, M. Metamorfózy definície závislej práce In: *Opus laudat artificem: pocta prof. JUDr. Helene Barancovej, DrSc.* Trnava: Trnavská univerzita v Trnave. Typi Universitatis Tyrnaviensis, spoločné pracovisko Trnavskej univerzity v Trnave a Vedy, vydavateľstva Slovenskej akadémie vied, 2019. pp. 78–89. ISBN 978-80-568-0353-0.

Dolobáč, M. Aktuálne otázky sociálneho práva z ohľadu slovenskej legislatívy a právnej praxe. In: *Pracovní právo a sociální ochrana v. nejisté době.* Praha: Univerzita Karlova v Praze, 2022. pp. 150–159. ISBN 978-80-7630-025-5.

Dolobáč, M. Výpovedný dôvod pre dosiahnutie dôchodkového veku. Domnelá či skutočná diskriminácia? In: *Diverzné a inkluzívne pracoviská – legislatívne východiská: zborník abstraktov z vedeckej konferencie.* Košice: Univerzita Pavla Jozefa Šafárika v Košiciach, 2023. pp. 10–13. ISBN 978-80-574-0245-9.

Hamuľák, J. – RAK, P. Osoby so zdravotným postihnutím z hľadiska pracovného práva. In: *Sociálna ochrana osôb so zdravotným postihnutím v pracovnom práve a práve sociálneho zabezpečenia.* Bratislava: Univerzita Komenského v Bratislave. Právnická fakulta UK, 2022, pp. 7–50. ISBN 978-80-7160-659-8.

Križan, V. Nástroje na podporu uplatnenia osoby so zdravotným postihnutím na trhu práce In: *Osoby so zdravotným postihnutím v práve Slovenskej republiky a Českej republiky.* Plzeň: Vydavatelství a nakladatelství Aleš Čeněk, 2014, pp. 176–204. ISBN 978-80-7380-497-8.

Križan, V. Obsahové náležitosti pracovnej zmluvy. In: *Zmluvná autonómia v súkromnom/ pracovnom práve*. Bratislava: Wolters Kluwer. Wolters Kluwer SR, 2020, pp. 32–44. ISBN 978-80-571-0308-0.

Križan, V. Pracovné podmienky žien a mužov starajúcich sa o deti. In: *Slaďování soukromého a pracovního života.* Praha: Wolters Kluwer. Wolters Kluwer ČR, 2023. pp. 155–165. ISBN 978-80-7676-418-7.

Selected Bibliography

Križan, V. Transpozícia smernice 2019/1158 o rovnováhe medzi pracovným a súkromným životom rodičov a osôb s opatrovateľskými povinnosťami do slovenského pracovného práva. In: *Pracovní právo a sociální ochrana v nejisté době.* Praha: Univerzita Karlova v Praze, 2022. pp. 28–38. ISBN 978-80-7630-025-5.

Križan, V. Aplikačné problémy kolektívneho vyjednávania v Slovenskej republike In: *Zákoník práce a sociální zabezpečení 2023 aneb tempora mutantur – leges semper moventur.* Praha: Univerzita Karlova v Praze. Právnická fakulta, 2023. pp. 88–105. ISBN 978-80-7630-039-2.

Lacko, M. Právna úprava dohôd o prácach vykonávaných mimo pracovného pomeru. In: Barancová, H. (ed.) *Možnosti a hranice liberalizácie pracovných vzťahov.* Bratislava: Sprint dva, 2011. ISBN 978-80-89393-50-3.

Lacko, M. Dohody o prácach vykonávaných mimo pracovného pomeru a ich opodstatnenosť. In: *Prieniky pracovného práva do iných odvetví súkromného práva (a vice versa): reformy v práve, justícii a verejnej správe: zborník príspevkov z medzinárodnej vedeckej konferencie.* Trnava: Trnavská univerzita v Trnave. Typi Universitatis Tyrnaviensis, spoločné pracovisko Trnavskej univerzity v Trnave a Vedy, vydavateľstva Slovenskej akadémie vied, 2022. pp. 113–130. ISBN 978-80-568-0546.

Lacko, M. Opatrenia na podporu starostlivosti zamestnanca o rodinného príslušníka v Slovenskej republike. In: *Slaďování soukromého a pracovního života.* Praha: Wolters Kluwer. Wolters Kluwer ČR, 2023. pp. 185–210. ISBN 978-80-7676-881-9.

Olšovská, A. – Švec, M. Pluralita podnikových kolektívnych zmlúv u zamestnávateľa. In: *Pocta Milanu Galvasovi k 70. narozeninám.* Brno: Masarykova univerzita, 2019. pp. 70–83. ISBN 978-80-210-9303-4.

Olšovská, A. – Švec, M. Reintegrácia zamestnankyne do pracovného prostredia po návrate z materskej a rodičovskej dovolenky a vhodná úprava pracovného času. In: *Budúcnosť práva – právo budúcnosti 2.* Bratislava: Paneurópska vysoká škola. Fakulta práva, 2022. pp. 361–381. ISBN 978-80-8275-000-6.

Rak, P. Zodpovednosť odborovej organizácie pri štrajku. In: *Ochrana, prevencia a zodpovednosť v právnych vzťahoch: recenzovaný zborník príspevkov z vedeckej konferencie.* Košice: Univerzita Pavla Jozefa Šafárika v Košiciach, 2020, pp. 414–423. ISBN 978-80-8152-871-2.

Švec, M. – Olšovská, A. Suspenzia pracovných povinností počas výkonu funkcie v odborovom orgáne a/alebo počas činnosti pre odborovú organizáciu. In: *Sine amicitia vitam est nullam: pro memoria prof. Zdeňky Gregorovej.* Praha: Nakladatelství Leges, 2019. pp. 49–64. ISBN 978-80-7502-394-0.

Journals (in English)

Giedrewicz-Niewińska, A. – Križan, V. – Komendová, J. The obligations of the employer in the implementation of remote work: The examples of Slovakia, the Czech republic and Poland. DOI 10.15290/bsp.2024.29.02.07. In: *Białostockie studia prawnicze.* Białystok: Uniwersytet w Białymstoku. Faculty of Law, 2024, Year 29, no. 2, pp. 83–97. ISSN 2719-9452.

Križan, V. Working time of employees posted on a business trip. In: *Juridical Tribune – Tribuna Juridica*. Bukurešť: The Bucharest University of Economic Studies, 2016, Year 6, no. Special Issue, October, pp. 118–127. ISSN (online) 2248-0382.

Križan, V. Good manners and the prohibition on the abuse of rights in Slovak labor law. DOI 10.15290/bsp.2021.26.02.06. In: *Białostockie studia prawnicze*. Białystok: Uniwersytet w Białymstoku. Faculty of Law, 2021, Year 26, no. 2, pp. 95–106. ISSN 2719-9452.

Laclavíková, M. – Olšovská, A. The employment contract as a central institute of labour law – past vs. Present. In: *Societas et Iurisprudentia: medzinárodný internetový vedecký časopis*. Trnava: Trnavská univerzita v Trnave. Právnická fakulta, 2015, Year 3, no. 1, pp. 109–132. ISSN 1339-5467.

Olšovská, A. – Laclavíková, M. Termination of employment under the Slovak legislation. In: *Societas et Iurisprudentia: medzinárodný internetový vedecký časopis*. Trnava: Trnavská univerzita v Trnave. Právnická fakulta, 2015, Year 3, no. 3, pp. 21–40. ISSN 1339-5467.

Olšovská, A. – Švec, M. The admissibility of arbitration proceedings in labour law disputes in Slovak Republic In: *E-Journal of International and Comparative Labour Studies*. [s.l.]: ADAPT University Press, 2017, Year 6, no. 3, pp. 112–123. ISSN 2280-4056.

Journals (in Slovak)

Barancová, H. Ochrana slabšej strany v pracovnom práve. In: *Societas et Iurisprudentia: medzinárodný internetový vedecký časopis*. Trnava: Trnavská univerzita v Trnave. Právnická fakulta, 2019, Year 7, no. 1, pp. 19–46. ISSN 1339-5467.

Barancová, H. COVID-19 a renesancia domáckej práce. In: *Právny obzor: teoretický časopis pre otázky štátu a práva*. Bratislava: Slovenská akadémia vied. Pracoviská SAV. Ústav štátu a práva SAV, 2020, Year 103, no. 4, pp. 243–257 ISSN 2729-9228.

Barancová, H. Nová právna úprava domáckej práce a telepráce. DOI 10.31577/pravnyobzor.2022.1.01. In: *Právny obzor: teoretický časopis pre otázky štátu a práva*. Bratislava: Slovenská akadémia vied. Pracoviská SAV. Ústav štátu a práva SAV, 2022, Year 105, no. 1, pp. 3–18. ISSN 2729-9228.

Barancová, H. Zodpovednosť zamestnanca v pracovnom práve Slovenskej republiky a príprava nového Občianskeho zákonníka. DOI 10.31577/pravnyobzor.2022.4.01. In: *Právny obzor: teoretický časopis pre otázky štátu a práva*. Bratislava: Slovenská akadémia vied. Pracoviská SAV. Ústav štátu a práva SAV, 2022, Year 105, no. 4, pp. 271–284. ISSN 2729-9228.

Barancová, H. Statusové otázky platformovej práce [elektronický dokument]. DOI 10.31262/1339-5467/2023/11/3/34-55. In: *Societas et Iurisprudentia: medzinárodný internetový vedecký časopis*. Trnava: Trnavská univerzita v Trnave. Právnická fakulta, 2023, Year 11, no. 3, pp. 34–55. ISSN 1339-5467.

Križan, V. Postavenie účastníkov dočasného vyslania v novej úprave Slovenskej republiky [elektronický dokument] In: *Acta Iuridica Olomucensia: vědecký časopis právnický: Journal for Legal Research*. Olomouc: Univerzita Palackého v Olomouci. Právnická fakulta, 2017, Year 12, no. 2, pp. 60–75. ISSN 1805-9554.

Lacko, M. Právo na štrajk. In: *Studia Iuridica Cassoviensia.* Košice: Univerzita Pavla Jozefa Šafárika v Košiciach. Právnická fakulta, 2014, Year 2, no. 2, pp. 12–25. ISSN 1339-3995.

Lacko, M. Materská dovolenka a materské. In: *Forum Iuris Europaeum: recenzovaný časopis pre právnu vedu: journal for legal science: Zeitschrift für die Rechtswissenschaft.* Trnava: Trnavská univerzita v Trnave. Právnická fakulta, 2017, Year 5, no. 1, pp. 41–66. ISSN 1339-4401.

Lacko, M. Vyjadrenie závislej práce v poisťovacom systéme SR. DOI 10.14712/23366478.2019.4. In: *Acta Universitatis Carolinae: Iuridica.* Praha: Univerzita Karlova v Praze. Právnická fakulta, 2019, Year 65, no. 1, pp. 33–54. ISSN 0323-0619.

Lacko, M. Sociálnoprávne inštitúty podpory starostlivosti zamestnaného rodiča o dieťa. DOI 10.31262/1339-5467/2022/10/3/96-124. In: *Societas et Iurisprudentia: medzinárodný internetový vedecký časopis.* Trnava: Trnavská univerzita v Trnave. Právnická fakulta, 2022, Year 10, no. 3, pp. 96–124. ISSN 1339-5467.

Olšovská, A. Súdne rozhodnutia a oznamovanie protispoločenskej činnosti In: *Acta Iuridica Olomucensia: vědecký časopis právnický: Journal for Legal Research.* Olomouc: Univerzita Palackého v Olomouci. Právnická fakulta, 2017, Year 12, no. 3, pp. 32–48. ISSN 1801-0288.

Olšovská, A. – Švec, M. Pluralita zástupcov zamestnancov u zamestnávateľa – kto je partnerom v kolektívnych pracovnoprávnych vzťahoch?. In: *Forum Iuris Europaeum: recenzovaný časopis pre právnu vedu: journal for legal science: Zeitschrift für die Rechtswissenschaft.* Trnava: Trnavská univerzita v Trnave. Právnická fakulta, 2017, Year 5, no. 2, pp. 55–68. ISSN 2644-4364.

Olšovská, A. – Švec, M. – Drobný, M. Konto pracovného času – aplikačné problémy. In: *Justičná revue: časopis pre právnu teóriu a prax.* Bratislava: Ministerstvo spravodlivosti Slovenskej republiky, 2015, Year 67, no. 12, pp. 1431–1446. ISSN 2730-0471.

Švec, M. – Olšovská, A. Spolupôsobenie odborových organizácií v individuálnych pracovnoprávnych vzťahoch In: *Studia Iuridica Cassoviensia.* Košice: Univerzita Pavla Jozefa Šafárika v Košiciach. Právnická fakulta, 2018, Year 6, no. 1, pp. 99–110. ISSN 1339-3995.

Žuľová, J. Prestávky na dojčenie z pohľadu pracovnej legislatívy a diverzity managementu. In: *Štát a právo: vedecko-teoretický časopis pre otázky vedy o štáte a práve v Slovenskej republike.* Banská Bystrica: Univerzita Mateja Bela v Banskej Bystrici. Vydavateľstvo Univerzity Mateja Bela v Banskej Bystrici – Belianum, 2024, Year 11, n. 1, pp. 61–70. ISSN (online) 2644-643X.

Index

The numbers here refer to paragraph numbers.

Index

Index

www.ingramcontent.com/pod-product-compliance
Lightning Source LLC
Chambersburg PA
CBHW070245030525
26096CB00033B/1270